A HISTORY

OF

SAVINGS BANKS

IN THE

UNITED STATES

FROM THEIR INCEPTION IN 1816 DOWN TO 1874.

WITH DISCUSSIONS OF THEIR THEORY, PRACTICAL WORKINGS AND INCIDENTS, PRESENT CONDITION AND PROSPECTIVE DEVELOPMENT.

BY

EMERSON W. KEYES,
LATE DEPUTY SUPERINTENDENT OF THE BANKING DEPARTMENT OF THE STATE OF NEW YORK.

IN TWO VOLUMES.

Vol. I.

NEW YORK:
PUBLISHED BY BRADFORD RHODES.
1876.

WEED, PARSONS & COMPANY,
PRINTERS AND STEREOTYPERS.
ALBANY, N. Y.

PREFACE.

The relation sustained by the writer for a number of years to the Savings Banks of the State of New York is set forth with sufficient detail in the progress of these volumes. That relation and its incidents were considerations in his favor in undertaking the preparation of a History of Savings Banks. It is unfortunate, however, that his claims to special fitness for such a work should not extend beyond the foregoing; that the favorable conditions mentioned could not be supplemented in him by literary culture, by the genius or the habit of authorship, nor yet by that release from engrossing pursuits, which, faithfully employed, might serve to atone for the deficiencies herein acknowledged.

That a record of the origin, growth and achievements of an interest which in its present development ranks among the first in magnitude and importance in our country, is desirable, it is believed will not be questioned; that it is desirable now, before much pertaining to its inception and early progress shall pass beyond our reach, receding into the obscurity of the buried past, is scarcely more open to question. It is in this conviction that the author has entered upon the preparation of these volumes. He bespeaks for their faults no tenderness of criticism, for upon these he has none himself to bestow. His ideal of such a record is as high as that of any one can be, and no one can know better than he how far short of that ideal is what is here offered for acceptance. Still, he cannot resist the conviction that, despite its defects, the work has a certain value that justifies its submission to the public.

Dropping the stiffness of the impersonal form, — I can assert with truth, that into the preparation of these volumes I have put my conscience most thoroughly. Upon many of the elaborate tables in the second volume, I have spent as much time, and have been as careful and painstaking in the processes for reaching approximate accuracy, where perfect accuracy was unattainable, as though the result would affect the balance of some poor depositor's account. Of course such care and pains make no record of themselves, for even very considerable errors would pass wholly unnoticed and would not appreciably affect the grand aggregates into which they must enter. Haste, carelessness and indifference might have been indulged with impunity, for no one could challenge the substantial accuracy of estimates and calculations for whose results the only claim asserted is, that of a rational approximation from which the elimination of all errors is simply impossible.

In further justice to myself upon another point, I may mention that, had I known when I set out, how voluminous would be the material which I could command, or which would be required for such an exposition of the subject as would satisfy my own sense of completeness in its treatment, I should have rejected some and condensed more in the earlier portion of the work. Besides, had the idea of two volumes presented itself at the inception of the work, I should have aimed to make a more natural division of the subject matter between the two volumes, than was possible under the circumstances as they occurred.

I desire herein to acknowledge my obligation to the New York State Library, at Albany, for important, indeed indispensable, material, in the preparation of this work, and not elsewhere attainable. Under an intelligent administration, not always seconded by corresponding liberality in legislative appropriations, this library has become, probably, more thoroughly furnished with the early laws, documents and official transactions of the several States than any other in the country, not excepting that of Congress, at Washington. Not the least of the many pleasing features which distinguish the management of this valuable library, are the courteous attention and cheerful aid rendered by those in charge to students or others seeking information.

I am likewise indebted for many courtesies to the Librarian, of the Vermont State Library, and to the Secretary of State, and the Auditor of State, in Rhode Island.

BROOKLYN, N. Y., *May*, 1876.

CONTENTS OF VOLUME I.

FIRST SECTION.

INTRODUCTORY.

SECOND SECTION.

SAVINGS BANKS IN THE STATE OF MASSACHUSETTS.

THIRD SECTION.

SAVINGS BANKS IN THE STATE OF CONNECTICUT.

FOURTH SECTION.

SAVINGS BANKS IN THE STATE OF RHODE ISLAND.

FIFTH SECTION.

SAVINGS BANKS IN THE STATE OF NEW HAMPSHIRE.

SIXTH SECTION.

SAVINGS BANKS IN THE STATE OF MAINE.

SEVENTH SECTION.

SAVINGS BANKS IN THE STATE OF VERMONT.

EIGHTH SECTION.

SAVINGS BANKS IN THE STATE OF NEW YORK.

PART I.

INCEPTION OF THE IDEA AND INCORPORATION OF THE BANK FOR SAVINGS.

PART II.

GENERAL COURSE OF LEGISLATION AND OF OFFICIAL DISCUSSION CONCERNING SAVINGS BANKS.

Conclusion of Part II, in Volume II.

HISTORY OF SAVINGS BANKS.

FIRST SECTION;

INTRODUCTORY.

CHAPTER I.

THEORY OF SAVINGS BANKS.

It has been truly remarked that among a free people laws grow rather than are made. The enactment of statutes by legislatures and the enunciation of decisions by courts are but embodied forms of public sentiment, of the people's will, which is the law. But public sentiment is a thing of growth and change, and hence the laws, which are its emanation and expression in form, must likewise change and grow.

Human institutions are a form of law, they are an embodied public sentiment concerning some condition or want of the social state. They may be purely voluntary in their organization, methods and appliances, or they may have the support and countenance of statutes, acts of incorporation and judgments of courts, but in so far as they reflect the popular will or popular acquiescence, in their plans, purposes and methods, they are a form of law, and grow with the growth and strengthen with the strength of the social condition or necessity which called them into being. If the condition to which any institution is called to minister is evanescent and passes away, so, too, the institution will pass away with the necessity that made occasion for it, or it will put on a new form of being and action, adapted to some new necessity that superseded the old. Or, if an institution is found not adapted to the purpose to which it is applied, it is changed, modified, re-created, until it will serve the purpose designed, or is abandoned for other and more effective forms of organization. The institution that lives, succeeds and accomplishes results; which grows, expands and adapts itself to the varying phases of the social necessity which it was ordained to minister unto, is an embodied law of the social fabric; it is an organic function of society itself, and is to be watched, guarded and cared for with the solicitude with which men watch and protect their vital organs.

It is not presumed that the reader will be startled by the novelty or profundity of these observations. They are neither new nor profound. On the contrary, they are in fact, if not in form and expression, both familiar and common place. And so may have been the text of last Sunday's sermon, and neither text nor sermon in the least the worse for it. The sermon was the expanded or amplified idea embodied in or suggested by the text; so the history of Savings Banks is an amplified illustration of the truth embodied in the foregoing observations. They are correlative. Savings Banks, as an independent, isolated fact, are only so many columns of figures; but Savings Banks, as an organic element in the social state — as an essential, vital force in human society — as part of the social machinery adapted to accomplish a great purpose, and doing it thoroughly and well, and, in doing it, ever broadening and deepening the range of its power and influence — in short, Savings Banks, as an expression and embodiment of public sentiment, as a law of the social state, not only declarative of, but *enforcing*, public order, temperance, virtue, sobriety, industry, thrift and prosperity, as well as promotive of public credit, public faith and financial stability, demand a broader and more comprehensive treatment than their consideration as a mere incident or fortunate accident in human experience would justify.

Had Savings Banks been superimposed upon, instead of being an outgrowth from the social structure — had their relation to, and mission in, the social state been forced and unnatural — they would have no history to record, at least none worth reading, though it should engage the pen of a Macaulay or a Motley. But being in fact an outgrowth from certain social conditions, called into being by exigencies in the social state to which it was believed such an institution could acceptably minister, and more than justifying the hopes of its founders in its adaptation to the purpose for which it was designed, the institution has, during the first half century of its operations in our country, made for itself and for humanity a record so wonderful in its aggregate of results, and so thrilling in its individual incidents, that no faults nor follies of the historian can render wholly worthless the story of its achievements. There is comfort for both writer and reader in that!

And what is the great underlying fact in human experience, this all-pervading, ever-present condition or need in the social state, to minister unto which, Savings Banks were conceived and ordained, and in behalf of which they have successfully and triumphantly wrought during the last sixty years?

In one word, it is POVERTY! Out of the condition in society expressed or defined by that word and its incidents, and as its exponent and representative, there has been evolved in this country during the last half century, an imposing financial system, firmly and indissolubly inwrought in the very fabric and framework of the social structure, an INSTITUTION which first and last has wrought for not less than 7,000,000 of our people, and has concerned itself with the care of more than $4,200,000,000.

Paradoxical as this appears, such is the legend, to be inscribed on POVERTY'S MONUMENT in this country to-day.

I believe we may safely challenge any other financial institution to show a corresponding aggregate.

Could any other scheme have been devised that should parallel this in the magnitude and grandeur of its success? How feeble, how absolutely insignificant, in comparison, must have been the results of any merely charitable organization. Not alone in the amount of money contributed, but in the work wrought by it, in the latent energies of body and mind stimulated and utilized, in the self-respect created, in the character built up, in the courage inspired, in the hopes kept alive, in the despair kept at bay.

The one is an emollient to soothe and assuage a present distress; the other a tonic that invigorates the system and imparts to it strength to repel the malady by removing its predisposing cause.

In treating of the relations of poverty to the institution of Savings Banks, we must exercise care lest misconception of our meaning be entertained, and the subject come to be regarded from a wrong stand-point. To prevent this let us elaborate this unpleasant theme somewhat, in its relations to the present discussion.

And first, there are of course degrees of poverty. We do not mean by it mendicity, destitution, pauperism, though it embraces these. These are the extremes of poverty. But he who with steady, patient industry can from day to day, earn barely the necessaries of life for himself and family, is surely *poor*, though he may thus keep absolute want from his door. Even if he may do a little, and barely little, better than this; if he may from his scant wages save a pittance for the day when labor cannot, perchance, be found, or when sickness of himself or some member of his household adds to the expense or diminishes the income, even then he is poor. There is no defining with rule and line the boundary where poverty ceases and wealth or affluence begins. As well define the hour or day when boyhood ends and the youth comes upon the stage. But, in general, the poor are those who gain their living by their own labor of hand or brain, with no accumulated capital yielding an assured income.

But again, poverty is to be considered under its two aspects, as an existing practical fact, and as a result of certain conditions in the social economy. As a practical fact, in its extreme degrees, it demands relief; it is a present, urgent call that cannot, must not be denied or deferred. To this condition of affairs *Charity* must minister by gratuities from its bounty.

But while thus ministering, a wise, sagacious Charity will busy itself with a study of the causes which have wrought these sad results in human experience. Here will be found food for reflection. Side by side with the imbecile, whose poverty is the result of causes over which he could have no control, will be found the strong man, able and willing to work, but finding nowhere a market for his labor. On questioning the latter it may be found that so long as he could find employment he was above want. He will doubtless freely confess that, could he but get employment now at *half* wages, or, what is equivalent, could he but get employment at former wages for half the time, he could keep himself and family beyond the need of charity. Of course there would be privation; the food must needs be common, the clothing poor and coarse, the shelter rude, fuel must be very economically provided and used; but for all that, with even such moderate provision as half pay or half time employment would give, affairs would be tided over until more prosperous days.

It could not fail to strike the thoughtful observer, that the ranks of pauperism are largely recruited from this class. That congenital pauperism, so to speak, is comparatively rare, and if only those become Charity's charge who became so through bodily infirmity, incapacitating them for labor, the burden of society in this direction would be greatly lessened, and could be borne with comparative ease.

The question presented relates then to the condition of these objects of charity, who became such through the mutations in the demand for and supply of labor. The observer sees at once, that if he could assure constant employment, at fair wages, to all who are able and willing to labor, one great cause of destitution and suffering would be removed. It was some such thought that suggested the enactment, hereinafter noted, to establish public workshops. But it would quickly be found, as it was found, that the relations of capital and labor are too subtle and recondite to be thus controlled by legislation, or by any voluntary scheme or device, for assuring to labor at all times abundant employment. But our thoughtful, suppositious observer will have had his attention aroused by the confession of our candid indigent, that if he could *now*, in his extremity, have even *half* wages, he could in some sort maintain his family above want. It will occur to him, that the seasons or periods that assure to labor constant employment, bestow upon it also rewards more than commensurate with the absolute necessities of living. This will be proved to him, not only by the words of the unfortunate, but by his knowledge of the ways of life. Wages are seldom doled out in exact proportion to the needs of actual subsistence. When there is a demand for labor, it can command wages that afford a small but fair margin beyond the necessities of the laborer. Such is the law of supply and demand. If it were otherwise, the wages that would barely suffice the family of four would be insufficient for the family of six, and want and suffering must ensue. But we find that two laborers, earning the same wages, support respectively their families of four and six, while another, with the same or even less wages, supports his family of eight or ten — one or more of these, perchance, an invalid, requiring more costly attention and provision than the others. The feather that broke the camel's back has never been found outside of allegory, and the precise amount that would barely suffice to feed, clothe, shelter and warm a given household, with not a dime over at the end of the twelvemonth, has never yet been determined, or made the basis of wages in the transactions between capital and labor. Doubtless the necessities of the laborer in the matter of a support for his family, are an element entering into the question of wages in a general way; but I mean to say, that the precise measure of these necessities, the absolute limit, is never fixed and determined, and made the rule and measure of wages. The necessities and the wages may approximate very nearly, may leave a very narrow margin, may insensibly blend together for a season in dull times, and in duller times the margin may pass to the other side; but when this is the case, it comes in the form not so much of less wages as of less work, until it passes to the final extreme of no work and no pay. But all this does not affect our theory, that when labor is in demand the rewards or wages of labor will, and uniformly do, exceed the mere absolute necessities of the laborer.

It is said of the duke of Wellington, that, when applied to to favor a proposal for regimental Savings Banks, for the benefit of British soldiers, he replied, "Has a soldier more pay than he requires? If he has, it should be lowered to those enlisted hereafter." But the spirit that prompted that answer, fortunately does not control the relations of capital and labor. These are governed by immutable laws, which it is vain for avarice, selfishness, or even heartlessness and indifference to human welfare, to contend against. These laws are not inscribed upon our statute books, they are not promulgated from the judicial bench, but they have their origin in the nature of man, *as* man, demanding recognition as such, which is something more than to be fed, warmed and clothed. For man as an animal, these would suffice; but for man as an intelligent, responsible and immortal being, he has cravings above and beyond these, cravings which will not be denied. These latent possibilities of his nature, unfolding day by day, suggest and inspire new and varied needs to which yesterday he was a stranger. To supply these, as they come in the form of domestic affection, the love of home, the desire of possession, a thirst for knowledge, a refinement of taste, or any of the myriad ways in which *human* life is enriched and beautified, the wages that will serve barely to keep soul and body together are wholly inadequate. But society is only an aggregation of *human beings*, whose aggregated needs, desires and aspirations determine or *become* the *law* of the social state which they form. The great demand of man's nature is for *opportunity* to attain something higher than a merely animal existence. To insure this, he must needs receive, in return for the faithful employment of his energies of body or mind, more than will serve the necessities of his animal nature; and thus out of the nature of man, is evolved the law of labor and its rewards, whereby the latter are measured and adapted to the needs of the laborer as a *man* and not as a brute.

It will, of course, be understood that I am discussing conditions of the social structure in a state of freedom, for we know there may be brought to bear upon society a repressive *force* that shall prevent the development of man's manhood, and hold him in thrall to a power stronger for the time than his own will. Where such a condition prevails, the law of the social state is not evolved from the nature of man, but is arbitrarily imposed at the will of an external force called despotism.

We are conscious, too, that even in free society there will be exceptional conditions which seem to be, and in fact are, at variance with the laws of labor and wages as we have propounded them. We recognize as such the condition of poor sewing women and girls, whose scanty pittance as wages scarcely serves as a provision for their merely animal wants. But these exceptional conditions do not invalidate the general law. Any single department of labor may be over supplied for a time, which brings into operation other laws of the social state, the effect of which is to reduce wages in that department. But our larger law, still operative in its sphere, soon corrects the evil by withdrawing laborers from the overburdened department, and employing them elsewhere, and thus the equilibrium *and the wages* are again restored.

We think, then, that it must be conceded, that in any natural state of society the wages of the laboring classes in seasons of prosperity will ever be such as to enable them, *if they will*, to reserve a portion for future need. The neglect to do this, or the want of opportunity to do this, must ever be a fruitful source of poverty, indigence, pauperism, *crime.*

Here, then, is the inviting field for the efforts of Philanthropy. Here is the idea which it is to elaborate into a scheme of practical and beneficent activity. Discarding as chimerical the suggestion of measures to insure employment for labor under any and all circumstances, it directs its attention to the means whereby the possible surplus earned during the period of active employment, may be saved and applied toward independent support during the periods of stagnation in the labor market.

In this direction is the blow to be struck, at the very root of the evils of indigent poverty. It aims at a removal of the cause of a large part of the destitution and suffering of humanity. It preserves from *falling into destitution* that large class of the poor who are ever hovering upon the brink of pauperism, ready, upon the first adverse condition in the labor market, to recruit its ranks. Dry up the springs, and the river will never be full.

Such is the philosophy of Savings Banks. They offer to this large class from which the indigent are liable to be and are recruited, the opportunity of putting safely aside the surplus earnings of prosperous years, to be called for when the day of adversity comes. They appeal to the manliness of man, to his love of independence, to his scorn of dependence, to his domestic affections, to his pride, to his instinct of accumulation, in short, to his better nature. They tender him no gratuitous charity, beyond the exercise of supervision over the fund accumulated by his industry. They say to him, "you were created self-helpful, endowed with powers to gain for yourself and family a decent and comfortable subsistence. With life and health preserved, the constitution of the social state is such as will *average* to demand your service long enough and at sufficient wages to give you a decent maintenance according to your station. But it will be an average only. For the law is not the less immutable, that there will come periods of depression, when you will seek employment in vain. But by careful and provident saving of the assured surplus of prosperous seasons, you may hold in reserve the means that shall carry you safely through the season of adversity."

Such is the nature of the appeal. I have said it is an appeal to man's higher and better nature, to his pride, to his dignity, to his love of independence, to his self-respect.

It says, be industrious, be frugal, be temperate; or, suggestively, be not idle when work is to be done, be not wasteful or extravagant, be not intemperate. It says, live *within* your income, lay aside the surplus saved, for future need, and draw not upon it until the need shall come.

We know too well, that all men will not be influenced by appeals to their higher nature. We know that with some, the love of idleness and ease is greater than the love of conscious independence which steady industry assures. With some, the instinct and passion is to spend rather than to save, is to self-indulgence rather than self-denial. With some, the instinct is to vice and crime and all vicious indulgence, rather than to virtue, honesty, and a reputable career.

It is not to be presumed therefore, that this appeal will revolutionize human nature. It will not make the slothful vigilant; the wasteful frugal; the vicious virtuous. It cannot, in the nature of things, banish poverty from the earth, not even the poverty that comes as the result of one's own follies.

Savings Banks were founded upon no such misconception of human nature. Their theory was simple, modest and well founded. It was only that *some*, *many*, perhaps a majority of mankind, would prefer honest independence, the result of industry, to beggarly dependence, the consequence of idleness; that they would be frugal rather than wasteful, if the savings of frugality could be carefully garnered for the time of need; that they would guard against vicious indulgence rather than steep themselves in drink, if there was the incentive of accumulation held out as the sure reward of self-denial.

Such is the simple theory of Savings Banks. The

purpose of this work is to show how far this theory has been proved true, during the first half century of its experiment in our country. It will also be in our way to note how this instrumentality has been found serviceable to larger uses than those to which it was originally applied, and, expanding the area of its operations, has enriched the country through its benign ministration.

CHAPTER II.

INCEPTION OF THE IDEA IN EUROPE.

Before entering upon this field of investigation, it seems pertinent to give a brief resume of the early inception of Savings Banks in Europe, before the system was transferred to these shores.

In this resume we shall be brief, as we employ it only as a natural and proper introduction to the work in hand. We do not purpose advancing any thing new, any thing not entirely familiar to those who have investigated the subject, but merely to note a few facts of the origin and progress of the principle, of which the exemplification in our country is but a branch.

Concerning the origin of Savings Banks, I quote largely from memoranda furnished me by Andrew Warner, Esq., secretary of the Institution for Savings of Merchants' Clerks in the city of New York, who, with an intelligence and zeal rarely equaled and not exceeded, has made the subject of Savings Banks a matter of thorough and careful study.

Mr. Warner says: "The first Savings Bank is claimed to have been founded at Hamburg so early as 1778, though it had generally been believed that the first institution of the kind was formed at Berne, in Switzerland, in 1787."

Concerning this claim, Mr. Lewins, in his "History of Banks for Savings in Great Britain and Ireland," remarks, "That, from the best investigation he has been able to make, the institutions in question were something very different from Savings Banks as English people understand them, dealing, as they did, in business more like the sale of deferred annuities. The institution at Hamburg simply took the spare cash of domestic servants and handicraftsmen, and granted annuities on the members arriving at a certain age. No withdrawal of money was allowed."

I again quote from the memoranda of Mr. Warner. "The credit of introducing Savings Banks into Great Britain is claimed in behalf of several different persons, but doubtless there may be earlier unrecorded instances of arrangements having been made to receive small savings from the poor, and to return them on demand with interest.

In 1798,* a "Friendly Society for the benefit of women and children" was established at Tottenham High Cross, under the superintendence of Mrs. Priscilla Wakefield, and before 1801 there had been combined with its main design (which appears to have been the granting of annuities to members after a certain age, or an allowance weekly in case of sickness, and a sum for burial at decease), two other objects, viz., a fund for loans and a '*bank for savings.*' In 1804 this Bank for Savings was regularly organized and trustees were appointed.

A prior claim is raised, however, in behalf of the Rev. Joseph Smith, of Wendover, who, in 1799,† cir-

---

* Lewins says, 1799.

† 1798, according to Lewins.

culated in his parish, proposals to receive any sums in deposit during the summer, and to return the amount at Christmas with the addition of one-third to the whole, as a bounty upon the depositor's economy."

Which of these claims is entitled to priority, "will," as Mr. Lewins very justly remarks, "be determined, according to the judgment of the reader, as to which of these two original schemes best deserves the name Savings Bank, or whether either of them is entitled to that honor." "In the mind of each of these estimable persons," he continues, "we think the question of becoming bankers for the poor around them was at first only a subordinate measure, and quite auxiliary to other matters deemed of greater importance."

I deem it quite sufficient to set forth what was undertaken and accomplished by those persons respectively, and leave the *name* by which their effort shall be characterized out of the discussion. That each, in his own way, instituted a scheme to encourage industry, frugality and virtue, whereby the poor should *help themselves* and receive the reward of their industry and self-denial, which was or became the germ of what are now known as Savings Banks, is quite sufficient for our purpose, and entitles each to recognition as one of the founders of this beneficent agency, without regard to the priority by a day or a year in the introduction of the Savings Bank principle, pure and simple.

Citing again the memoranda of Mr. Warner, he proceeds to say: "The first publication in England of the idea of a Savings Bank is also attributed to the celebrated Jeremy Bentham, in whose well-known schemes for the management of paupers (1797), was included a system of frugality banks, as he called them. His suggestions, however, were never acted upon."

Malthus in his "Essay on Population," 1803, favors the establishment of county banks to facilitate the saving of small sums, and to encourage young laborers to economize their earnings, where the smallest sums might be received, and a fair interest granted for them.

"The next society formed," continues Mr. Warner, "of which we have any account, was opened in 1808, at Bath (chiefly through the instrumentality of ladies), for receiving deposits from female servants."

But it appears from Mr. Warner's notes that, prior to this, in 1806, the Provident Institution of London was established, to which a Savings Bank was at first attached, but this was shortly after discontinued.

"In 1810," continues Mr. Warner, "the first Savings Bank in Scotland was formed by the Rev. Henry Duncan, minister at Ruthwell, Dumfrieshire. Various papers were published by him on the subject of forming banks for savings in the different parishes of the country, and the regular and simple organization of his 'Parish Bank' served as a model for other institutions. He communicated the rules of this bank to the Edinburgh Society for the suppression of mendicity, and the result was the establishment, in 1814, of the Edinburgh Savings Bank. Under the same inspiration similar institutions were commenced about the same time in Kelso and Hawick."

The name of Rev. Henry Duncan, in association with the establishment of Savings Banks, deserves more than merely incidental mention. Lewins devotes several pages of his history to a consideration of the labors of Dr. Duncan in behalf of these institutions. That he first conceived the idea is not claimed, but he probably did more than any other man, perhaps more than all others, to reduce the idea to practical form, and to impart to it success.

And yet in a sense, he is claimed as their *founder*, in that he "originated and organized the first self-sustaining bank, and succeeded in so arranging his scheme as to make it applicable not to one locality only, but to the country generally." The amount of travel, correspondence and public speaking performed by Dr. Duncan in connection with, and for the establishment of these institutions was, for that period, immense. It is but just to say that but for such efforts as he put forth, and upon some basis or plan as well considered and practicable as his, Savings Banks would not have been organized to any considerable extent at so early a period, or, if organized, would not, for want of practical plans of operation, have been successful.

The notes of Mr. Warner, however, bring to view an earlier claimant for the honor of the first *public* announcement of a practicable *scheme* for the organization of Savings Banks. This is no other than Patrick Colquhoun, a local magistrate in London, of whom we shall have more to say in connection with the origin of Savings Banks in the State of New York. Mr. Warner says: "It will be perceived by the following extract from a letter of Patrick Colquhoun, of London, to Thomas Eddy, of New York, dated London, 20th February, 1818, that Mr. C. claims that the idea of Provident Banks originated with him. 'You will observe,' he says, 'that so far back as in the year 1806, I recommended Provident Banks (in my treatise on indigence), upon a national plan. The idea of such institutions originated with me; but the public mind was not then prepared for them, and I much fear they will not be rendered permanent under the present system. Had my plan been adopted in 1806, I am certain that not less than seven millions sterling of the property of the laboring classes would now have been yielding interest. The institutions, however, as now constituted, have become popular, and they *are* spreading fast all over the country.'" "Again, in June, 1818, he writes to the same, 'You will see, by referring to my treatise on indigence, which I sent you, that I was the first to suggest the establishment of Savings Banks so far back as 1806. Happy would it have been for this country if this and my various other suggestions for the amelioration of society, had been attended to at the time they were brought forward. But the public mind in this country, and particularly the Parliament, do not see good objects quickly. The proposition was made when a leading member brought in a bill for amending the Poor Laws, in 1806, which did not pass the lower house. Three years ago, the establishment of local banks for savings originated in Scotland, and their utility being (as I had predicted), rendered manifest, they got a footing in this country. They have recently been recognized by government, and there are now about two hundred establishments in different parts of Great Britain and Ireland; but as the superintendence is gratuitous, and the organization of a nature not to secure permanency (which was the main feature of my plan), I doubt their success on the present footing.' "

The claim of Mr. Colquhoun to having originated the idea of Savings Banks relates, I presume, to their organization on a general and systematic plan, under the protection, control and encouragement of the government; for the idea, as a voluntary and local effort of charity, had, as we have seen, already been put in operation as early as 1798–9. And we have seen also that Malthus, as early as 1803, had suggested the idea of county banks for the benefit of the laboring classes. Whether he proposed these as purely voluntary organizations, or that they be under the protection of the government, does not appear.

Mr. C. is evidently in error as to the date of the first organization of Savings Banks in Scotland, which he makes out to be 1815, whereas, the first was organized, as we have seen, in 1810, and at least one other as early as 1814.

If the bill for amending the Poor Laws, to which he refers as being introduced in 1806, was the bill of Mr. Whitbread, as I have good reason to believe, he is in error as to the date of its introduction by one year. The bill introduced by Mr. Whitbread in 1807, and which failed to pass the lower house, is remarkable for having proposed measures for the establishment of government Savings Banks, which, though rejected then as being in advance of the public sentiment of the period, were recognized and incorporated into legislation nearly half a century later. If these measures were, as it would seem, the suggestion of Mr. Colquhoun, he is entitled to greater credit for far sighted wisdom upon this subject than he has received from any writer whose work I have seen. Lewins in his history on Savings Banks, gives an interesting account of the effort made by Mr. Whitbread to secure governmental recognition in the establishment of Savings Banks, and of the opposition encountered by him, and also gives an abstract of the provisions of his bill. But he makes no mention of Mr. Colquhoun in connection with the measure, probably for the sufficient reason that he was not publicly known in connection with it. But this letter plainly points to such connection, and, as it would seem, a very intimate connection, indeed no less than the progenitor of the plan of which Mr. Whitbread was in fact only sponsor. It is not the less creditable to the latter gentleman that he should entertain, and strive in his official and responsible relation to promote a project so far in advance of the time, and should enforce the proposition by arguments so clear, logical and cogent, which the practical experience of half a century later has amply verified and confirmed.

I have dwelt at some length upon this phase in the history of Savings Banks in Great Britain, because it seemed an act of justice toward one whose claims to recognition in this relation have been overlooked, for the reason that they were unknown, and because we shall see hereafter, that however little or much Patrick

Colquhoun may have in fact suggested or achieved in behalf of English Savings Banks, he certainly, by his letters, suggestions and advice, did much to give embodiment and direction to the sentiment in their favor in the State of New York.

It was not until 1817 that Savings Banks in Great Britain were recognized at all by the government. Prior to this they were merely voluntary associations, of gentlemen or ladies in various localities who sought in this way to assist the poor in their immediate neighborhoods. They were necessarily limited in their operation, and depended for their success upon the confidence reposed in the character of their projectors, and the degree to which that confidence was justified. It is a pleasure to record that the trust thus voluntarily assumed was rarely if ever abused.

But as they extended the range of their operations and influence, the necessity for their recognition and protection by law became apparent. This was secured by an act of Parliament, passed August, 1817; but, owing to radical defects in the plan or details of organization approved by Parliament, they became subject to frauds and abuses such as had never characterized them under the voluntary system. The most astounding frauds were perpetrated by officers of Savings Banks, amongst whom were clergymen, and all of whom previous to these disclosures, had been men of the highest respectability, enjoying the confidence of the trustees and of the community in an unlimited degree. Indeed it was this overweening confidence, this perfect trust in the integrity of reputable men that gave opportunity for and incited the terrible disasters that followed. In this blind confidence no thorough examination and comparison of the books was made, and the returns of the institution to the government office, as prepared by the officer in charge, were accepted and sworn to by the trustees without question or suspicion. After various fruitless efforts to satisfactorily amend the system on its original basis, it was in 1861 superseded by the post-office Savings Banks, a brief account of which will be found elsewhere.

But it is not my purpose to trace further the history of Savings Banks in Great Britain. It is foreign to the plan of the present work, which is only to indicate in outline the leading features of the movement of public sentiment in this direction, until it culminated in legislative recognition and protection as among the authorized institutions of society.

Their history in detail prior to this period, as well as subsequently, has been admirably written, and to the work already cited the reader interested in the subject is referred.

CHAPTER III.

ANTECEDENT EFFORTS OF PHILANTHROPY.

The conditions of society in our country antecedent to and cotemporaneous with the institution of Savings Banks as a means to the amelioration of the evils of and sufferings from indigence; and the rise and progress of the spirit of philanthropy, which after many years of experiment in other directions, at length found expression and embodiment in this agency, may now properly engage our attention.

The war which resulted in securing the independence of the United States, left them in a feeble and impoverished condition. Trade, industry and finance had all become demoralized by the seven years' struggle. The accumulations of scarcely more than a century of rugged experiences, by no means peaceful, had been nearly exhausted. The country was yet new. It was rich in undeveloped resources only. It was full of possibilities for the future, but was crowded with urgent necessities as well, demanding instant relief. Until something could be organized out of this social chaos, to bring relief through the operation of the natural laws of industry and trade, extraneous and adventitious methods must be and were resorted to. That these in the haste with which they were conceived and applied to a pressing and instant emergency, were not always the wisest, may well be believed.

Among the earliest of these efforts was an act passed by the legislature of New York, in March, 1778, and during the progress of the war, entitled "An Act to regulate the wages of Mechanics."

But it was found after very brief experience, that it is inexpedient, if not impossible, to change the operation of natural laws concerning labor and wages, by legislation. The operation of the law was accordingly suspended at the June session following, and at the October session in the same year was repealed.

But the act is significant, as showing the prevalent and urgent need of relief for the industry of the people, and of the effort to meet the want and apply the remedy. It was the first groping step in the darkness toward the light subsequently revealed. That it was a step in the wrong direction and had to be retraced deprives it of none of its value as an historical illustration of the needs of the people, and of the efforts to afford relief. Such is the nature of all early efforts toward progress and reform. The mistakes of yesterday are corrected to-day. The failure of to-day opens our eyes to the means of success to-morrow.

Our attention is next directed to a general act for the relief and settlement of the poor, considered by the legislature in 1779, but not passed. At this period it must be remembered, all the energies of that State in common with other States, were being taxed to the utmost in maintaining the war for independence. It was doubtless, the superior urgency of measures to this end that prevented the consummation of the act in question. But its introduction and reference to the committee of the whole, is evidence of the ever present and overpowering necessity for relief from the evils of poverty, which forced itself upon the attention of the representatives of the people. In 1780 an act was introduced and passed for a general limitation of prices, which only further illustrates the urgent needs of a people, when such abortive efforts to secure relief could engage the attention of any legislature. It was not to take effect, however, until certain other States should pass similar laws, which they never did, so that the act never became operative.

At various times, subsequently, the legislature, as will be seen by consulting its journals, was concerned with measures for the relief of the poor. These efforts culminated in 1824 in an elaborate and exhaustive report upon the whole subject of the care and settlement of the poor, founded upon statistics from the various counties of the State, and suggestions and recommendations from officers charged with the management of poor-houses and other pauper or charitable institutions. This report reviewed the whole subject, and showed the defects in our system, derived from that in England, which tended rather to promote than allay the evil which it was instituted to relieve. But it is not our purpose to trace minutely the efforts of legislation, instituted upon its own motion, induced by the prevalence of poverty and want observable upon every hand, to apply means of relief. It is sufficient to say, that the State papers of the period, in other States as well as in New York, messages of governors, addresses of the houses of the legislature, reports of State officers and of standing and select committees, are full of the subject, and of suggestions to mitigate the evils of poverty. It was out of this condition that lotteries for charitable and public purposes became, for a time, a recognized and legally authorized institution in many of the States.

Though want and suffering are by no means unknown in our day, nor will they ever be strangers to us, it is significant how much less prominent is the discussion of these as an overshadowing evil, than in the later years of the last, and the earlier years of the present century.

In this is the evidence that it is certainly less prevalent, less a universal condition than formerly, and that some means or agency has been devised, whereby this evil has been diminished, at least relatively to the general growth and prosperity of the country.

But, as a further illustration of the prevalence of destitution, and of the efforts toward its amelioration during the period anterior to the institution of Savings Banks, let us glance at the efforts of philanthropy outside of the legislature, looking in the direction of relief.

As the conditions were similar in all the States at that time, it will sufficiently serve our purpose to cite some of the more notable of these efforts in the State of New York.

The course of these efforts was commonly through voluntary association for special or general charitable purposes, seeking from the legislature only such corporate powers as would give greater permanence and efficiency to their organization.

Singularly enough, among the earliest, if not the earliest, of these distinctively charitable institutions, incorporated by the legislature of New York, is one which still exists, and which holds an honored and prominent place among the institutions of New York city. This is The Society of Mechanics and Tradesmen of the city of New York, incorporated in 1792.

As illustrating the direction and scope of charitable effort at that period, it is not inapt to insert here the preamble to the enactment, as follows:

"Whereas, Robert Boyd and others, Mechanics and Tradesmen of the city of New York, associated as a society under the style of 'The General Society of the Mechanics and Tradesmen of the city of New York,' for the laudable purposes of protecting and supporting such of their brethren as by sickness or accident may stand in need of assistance, and for the relief of the widows and orphans of those who may die leaving little or no property for their support, have prayed to be incorporated to enable them more beneficially to carry into effect their charitable intention; therefore, be it enacted, etc."

This institution has neither outgrown its usefulness, nor altogether grown away from its original charitable purpose, though the latter is hardly now its central idea. It has become more a social, educational and literary, than a charitable, organization, maintaining a large and well selected library and reading room, a school for the instruction of young mechanics, and other appliances designed for the benefit of the class to whose improvement, rather than to whose necessities, it acceptably ministers.

In 1801 a similar society, under the name of the

Society of Mechanics in Albany, was incorporated, having similar objects and purposes in view, and which maintained a library and a school for many years, the latter being one of its distinguishing features, until superseded by the public school system. It did not become wholly disorganized until a few years since.

Also in this year, 1801, a general act for the settlement and relief of the poor was passed, which was variously amended in subsequent years.

In 1803 the legislature considered at some length the petition of Edward Livingston, Samuel Osgood and others, of New York, praying for incorporation with power to erect workshops and purchase materials for the employment of the poor, etc.

I extract from the report of the committee in the assembly to whom it was referred the following: "That the object of the petitioners is the prevention of vice and the removal of poverty by the establishment of a house of industry in which indigent persons may at all times find employment," etc. The subject was, however, dismissed, because of the advanced period in the session at which it was introduced.

But our purpose is only to briefly indicate the course and direction of philanthropic effort during this early period, and not to trace the history of the several organizations that illustrate it, nearly all of which have passed away, superseded by new methods and institutions. We only cite them as illustrations of the growth and development of the spirit of philanthropy, at this period, working toward a practical solution of the great problem of human want, and its appropriate relief.

The names of a few of these benevolent institutions, and the date of their incorporation will suffice for our purpose.

Marine Society, New York.................. 1786
The New York Dispensary.................. 1795
The New York Lying-in Hospital......... ... 1796
Society of Mechanics, Albany................ 1801
Society for the Relief of Poor Widows, New York, 1802
Lottery for public improvements and charitable purposes.. 1803
Act for relief of indigent women and children.. 1804
German Society for Charitable Purposes....... 1804
Columbian Friendly Union, Albany............ 1804
Provident Society, Mutual Relief Society, Benevolent Society, and Albion Benefit Society, all of New York, and Social Society, of Schenectady 1805
New York Free School Society............... 1805

I quote the following extract from the preamble:

"WHEREAS, De Witt Clinton and others have associated themselves for the laudable purpose of establishing a free school in the city of New York, for the education of the children of persons in indigent circumstances, etc."

Society of Tammany, or Columbian Order in the City of New York.......................... 1805

As it may be new to many that this organization, which is now only known as the most powerfully organized political institution in the country, was originally incorporated as a charitable institution, I here quote the preamble to the charter:

"WHEREAS, William Mooney and others, inhabitants of the city of New York, have presented a petition to the legislature, setting forth that they, since the year one thousand seven hundred and eighty-nine, have associated themselves under the name and description of 'The Society of Tammany, or Columbian Order,' *for the purpose of affording relief to the indigent and distressed members of the said association*, their widows and orphans, and others who may be found proper objects of their charity, they therefore solicit that the legislature will be pleased to incorporate the said society *for the purposes aforesaid*, etc.; therefore be it enacted, etc."

It is said that the association was originally formed as a burlesque upon the various friendly societies then springing up in the country upon the model of similar institutions in Great Britain; the object being to ridicule the growing practice of importing our institutions from the country from which we had so recently declared and established our independence.

But we proceed with our list as follows:

Orphan Asylum, New York	1807
St. Andrew's Society, Schenectady	1808
Mutual Benefit Society of Cordwainers, N. Y.	1808
Thistle Society, New York	1808
Mutual Relief Society, New York	1808
General Society of Mechanics, Poughkeepsie	1808
Albany Humane Society	1808
Mechanics' Humane Society, Troy	1808
Harlem Friendly Society	1809
Manhattan Provident Society	1809

Assistance Society, New York............... 1810
New York African Society..... 1810
Geneva Friendly Society.................... 1810
Society for Relief of Poor Widows and Small Children.................. 1810
Society of Teachers, New York (for charitable and literary purposes)................. .. 1811
Wilberforce Philanthropic Association, N. Y... 1812
Female Association for Charitable purposes, N. Y. 1812
Poughkeepsie Humane Society............... 1812
Humane Society, New York.................. 1814
An act for the exemption of certain property loaned to indigent widows and females from sale on execution 1814

This act was passed at the solicitation of certain charitable societies in the city of New York, among whose measures of relief was one of loaning to indigent females spinning wheels and other domestic machinery, to aid in making more effective their labor. The same principle is recognized in our statutes to-day in the general exemption from sale on execution of similar articles and of sewing machines.

Butchers' Benevolent Society, New York....... 1815
Widows' Fund Society, under the auspices of the Reformed Dutch Church.................. 1815
Society for the relief of Indigent and Aged Females, New York........ 1815
Ancient Britons' Benefit Society, New York.... 1815
Pilots' Charitable Society, New York.......... 1817
Female Assistance Society, New York 1817

Roman Catholic Benevolent Society........... 1817
New York Typographical Society............. 1817
New York Benevolent Society............... 1817

Though some of the foregoing, doubtless, were organized for the purpose, in part, of social enjoyment and improvement, the act of incorporation always recognized the charitable purpose of the organization as predominant.

We have thus sufficiently indicated the course and direction of public philanthropy, and its methods, through legislation and otherwise, to meet and overcome the overshadowing evils of poverty during the early years of the history of the country. These are introductory and preparatory to the organization of Savings Banks, which had their origin in the same causes, and their purpose the amelioration of the same conditions, that gave rise to the institutions which we have been considering. These, though doubtless useful in a limited degree, were too narrow and circumscribed in their operation, were directed too much to effects and too little toward causes, to sensibly affect the great masses of society.

The condition of the country was ripe for the more intelligent and more practical measures whose introduction and progress we are now prepared to sketch.

CHAPTER IV.

ORDER AND PLAN OF THE WORK.

There are certain disadvantages under which one labors in giving or in attempting to give order and coherency to his treatment of the subject-matter of this history. These arise from the necessity of tracing the origin, growth and progress of Savings Banks in this country, not as one connected system, incited, directed and controlled by a central source of authority and power, but as a series or multiple of systems, each regulated by its own special source of authority, a State Legislature. A History of Savings Banks in the United States is, therefore, a collection of histories of the origin and progress of Savings Banks in each of the several States. It is impossible to avoid in such a work, the recurrence of the same topics for record and for discussion, as these have arisen in the legislation and public administration of these institutions in the different States.

Thus it will be seen that the subject of Savings Bank investments, as well as others that will be noticed in the progress of the work, is one, pervading the course of legislation in all of the States, where Savings Banks have attained such prominence and distinctness in the body politic, as to constitute a system.

It will be found, however, that there is sufficient unity of purpose in their organization, and of method in the plans for the accomplishment of that purpose; and sufficient consonance or identity in the character of the work performed and of the results accomplished, to justify, indeed to demand, a comprehensive grouping of these elements and incidents into a summary and general exposition of this great interest, as it has found its practical development in the country at large.

These conditions and considerations have impressed upon the writer a task of no inconsiderable magnitude in determining the form or plan of the work, which should thus preserve the individual characteristics of development in the several States, and at the same time give opportunity to note and record the more general and comprehensive aspects of the development, of which these individual cases are but sections or parts.

These considerations have controlled in the mechanical plan or form of this work. The subdivision into sections was a form imposed by the necessity of giving to the record of each State an individuality of its own. It could not be done under the title of chapters, without, in most instances, protracting these to great length and embracing under one general head, topics incongruous or irrelevant. The term "section" has been employed in preference to the more common designation of "part," for the reason that "part" as commonly used, hardly defines the nature of the subdivision here employed. In making reference from one portion of the work to another, it seems to be more fitting and appropriate to refer to sections than to parts; thus, reference to the New York section or Massachusetts section, seems more distinctive and suitable, than would be similar reference to New York part, etc.

The order in which the States should be introduced in the work, was also a subject of considerable reflection. A strict chronological order, founded upon the date of the incorporation or organization of Savings Banks, would be attended by many inconveniences. We should thus have to begin with Pennsylvania, follow with Massachusetts, continuing with Maryland, after which would come New York, to be followed by other New England States, between which would be sandwiched New Jersey, winding up with Vermont.

It was deemed preferable to start with the first recognized legislation upon Savings Banks, and thereafter let the chronological order be subordinate to geographical position; or rather to follow the chronological order within geographical limitations. Hence after Massachusetts we follow with the other New England States, then New York, New Jersey, Pennsylvania, Maryland, etc.

Outside of these States which have been mentioned, Savings Banks, as voluntary associations of persons acting in the interest of depositors, with no personal or pecuniary interests of their own to serve, are almost, if not quite, wholly unknown. But the institutions known and recognized as Savings Banks in the newer States, in so far as information could be gained of them, are given a place in this history, as forms into which this interest has developed itself under different auspices from those which attended its inception in the earlier years of the century; and their arrangement has been controlled largely by considerations of convenience.

SECOND SECTION.

SAVINGS BANKS IN THE STATE OF MASSACHUSETTS.

CHAPTER V.

INCEPTION AND GROWTH, 1816-1833.

To Massachusetts belongs the honor of being the first State to give legislative sanction to the Institution of Savings Banks. The plans and address of the London Institution for savings, fell accidentally into the hands of the Hon. James Savage, of Boston, in the year 1816. Impressed with the importance and efficacy of this means of contributing to the welfare of the working classes, he early concerted measures for the establishment of such an institution in Boston. The first public announcement of the purpose, so far as I can learn, was in The *Christian Disciple*, for December, 1816, a small religious monthly, published in Boston. It is in the following words:

"*Saving Banks.*"

"Under this novel title, it is proposed to form an institution in Boston, *for the security and improvement of the savings of persons in humble life*, until required by their wants and desires. A meeting of gentlemen has been called, and a large and respectable committee appointed to apply to the legislature (now in session) for an act of incorporation, and to digest suitable rules and by-laws, to be proposed to an adjourned meeting. Similar institutions exist in England and Scotland; in the former place under the appellation of 'Provident Institutions for Savings,' and in the latter of 'Savings Banks.' The *Edinburgh Review*, No. 49, and the *Pamphleteer*, No. 14, contain essays on the subject, explaining their objects and principles, and narrating their beneficent effects. In Philadelphia it is proposed to establish one of these societies. We agree in the following sentiment, and wish every success to the laudable schemes contemplated: 'It is not by the alms of the wealthy, that the good of the lower class can be generally promoted. By such donations, encouragement is far oftener given to idleness and hypocrisy, than aid to suffering worth. He is the most effective benefactor to the poor, who encourages them in habits of industry, sobriety and *frugality*.'"

It is very probable that notices of the movement appeared in other public journals of the day. At the time of the publication of this notice, the plans of the projectors of the enterprise must have been very far matured, for the act to incorporate the Provident Institution for Savings, in the town of Boston, was approved on the 13th of December, 1816. With characteristic modesty becoming a genuine philanthropist, the name of James Savage appears as the last in a list of forty-eight trustees or directors of the Society thus formed.

So far as I can ascertain, this was the first public act of legislation in the world, which recognized the beneficent character of Savings banks, and invested them with the sanction and protection of the law. Even in England, where they had their inception as detailed in a previous chapter, they were at this time purely voluntary associations, the first act of Parliament to give protection to such institutions having passed in 1817. The act incorporating the Provident Institution for Savings in Boston, will be found in full in the appendix, where we have inserted the original or first Savings Bank charters of the several States.

It is evident that the measure encountered in the General Court of Massachusetts none of the hostility which subsequently defeated a similar effort in the legislature of the State of New York, as is hereinafter narrated. How far this may be owing to the exclusion of the word "Bank" from the act of incorporation, and the substitution of the more innocent title of "provident institution," we have not evidence sufficient to form an opinion. It only appears that the project was favorably considered, and a conclusion satisfactory to the promoters of the enterprise was speedily reached. The population of Boston at this time, probably, was between 35,000 and 36,000.

The institution was organized and commenced business in the following spring, promising to divide to depositors one per cent quarterly, and more if practicable. The first dividend was declared in July following according to the terms of the promise made. Thereafter, one and one-fourth per cent quarterly, equal to five per cent annually, was declared until January, 1822. At this time the total deposits in the institution amounted to over $600,000, and the surplus was

$6,200, or about one per cent. It was then proposed to reduce the regular dividend to the original amount of one per cent quarterly, and that once in five years there be made an extra dividend to all depositors existing at such time, and corresponding to the term of their deposits in the institution. This policy was adopted, and the first dividend of reserved surplus, made in July following, amounted to $8,000. It was divided on the principle that a deposit of five years should receive five times as much as a deposit of one year. In 1827, the termination of the second period, the reserved profits for an extra dividend were $34,000, on a total deposit of $793,000. In 1832, the reserved profits were $60,500; total deposits, $1,442,000. In 1834, the deposits were $2,058,000, and the reserved surplus for an extra dividend $99,300. During the next five years the institution suffered losses on its investments in bank stocks and loans to banks, and on bank stock collaterals, amounting to over $275,000. These losses, spread over the period of five years, absorbed the earnings in excess of four per cent, so that in 1839 no extra dividend was declared.

The Institution for Savings in the town of Salem was next incorporated, January 29, 1818, and the others in order, to 1834, will be found below. These charters were in their form, and in the character of their provisions, substantially like that of the Boston institution. Such also appears to have been the usual form in the incorporation of all savings institutions in the State of Massachusetts down to 1834, with a single exception to be hereafter noted.

The features in which these charters are worthy of special notice, as corresponding with or differing from the legislation in other States, are the following:

The charters were perpetual, and the number of trustees or managers was, it would seem, fixed by the promoters of the institution, according to their judgment of the expedient number to be inserted in the bill. As will be seen from the charter of the Boston institution, authority was given to the managers to increase their number at discretion. There is no prohibition against the trustees or managers receiving compensation for their services and charging the same to account of expenses, neither is there any prohibition against the trustees being themselves borrowers from the institution. It will also be observed that the discretion of the trustees in the matter of investments was almost absolutely unlimited. It is presumed that the well-known character of the corporators for integrity and worth, and their reputation for business sagacity and discernment, were regarded by the legislature as a sufficient guaranty that the trust reposed would be wisely and unselfishly administered.

In 1833 power was granted to the Boston Provident Institution to purchase real estate to an amount not exceeding $30,000. At the same session of the General Court the Savings Bank for Seamen in the city of Boston was incorporated, with this provision concerning investments: "All deposits may be invested in any public stocks, created under and by virtue of any law of the United States, or of this commonwealth, or loaned on promissory notes secured by pledge of such stocks, at no more than ninety per centum of their par value; and *no part of the deposits shall be invested in any other manner, or loaned upon any other securities than those herein mentioned.*"

This was the last act of incorporation prior to the passage of a general law to be presently noted, and we will here enumerate the institutions incorporated prior to that act, in the order in which the charters were granted.

Provident Institution for Savings in the town of Boston, December 13, 1816.

Institution for Savings in the town of Salem and vicinity, January 29, 1818.

Institution for Savings in the town of Portland and vicinity, June 11, 1819; not organized.

Institution for Savings in Newburyport and vicinity, January 31, 1820.

Provident Institution for Savings in the town of Hallowell and vicinity, February 21, 1820; not organized.

Institution for Savings in the town of Roxbury (since became a part of Boston) and vicinity, February 22, 1825.

New Bedford Institution for Savings, June 16, 1825.

Lynn Institution for Savings, June 20, 1826.

Provident Institution for Savings, in the town of Taunton and vicinity, February 26, 1827.

Springfield Institution for Savings, June 16, 1827; original charter limited the term of the corporation to thirty years.

Institution for Savings in the town of Haverhill and vicinity, February 8, 1828.

Worcester County Institution for Savings, February 8, 1828.

Provident Institution for Savings in the towns of Salisbury and Amesbury, February 20, 1828

Fall River Institution for Savings, March 11, 1828.

Plymouth Institution for Savings, June 11, 1828.

Lowell Institution for Savings, February 20, 1829; originally limited to thirty years.

Warren Institution for Savings in the town of Charlestown, February 21, 1829.

Institution for Savings in the town of Barnstable, January 29, 1831.

Provident Institution for Savings in the town of Gloucester and vicinity, February 3, 1831.

Dedham Institution for Savings, March 19, 1831.

Institution for Savings in the town of Newton, June 17, 1831.

Institution for Savings in the town of Fairhaven, February 10, 1832.

Weymouth and Braintree Institution for Savings, February 16, 1833.

Savings Bank for Seamen, in the city of Boston, March 7, 1833; name afterward changed to Suffolk Savings Bank.

Thus, prior to 1834, twenty-four Savings Institutions were incorporated, all but two of which organized and commenced business.

Two of these, Taunton, chartered 1827, and Gloucester, chartered 1831, subsequently failed.

The remainder appear to be still in operation, with an aggregate of deposits amounting to nearly $74,000,000. See table, *post*, p. 111.

It is significant that the word "Bank" is employed in but one, and that in the last of the above titles.

CHAPTER VI.

GENERAL SAVINGS BANK LAW, 1834.

Until 1834, no supervision appears to have been exercised over these institutions, not even to the extent of requiring from them any public statement of their transactions or condition. The reason is to be found, probably, in the fact of their generally safe and satisfactory management, giving rise to no complaint, and the comparatively moderate amount of accumulation; the deposits in 1834 being less than three and a-half millions ($3,407,773), distributed among twenty-two institutions and 24,256 depositors.

It is probable that the increasing frequency of applications for charters for Savings Banks impressed the subject somewhat forcibly upon the attention of the legislature, and suggested the idea of the growing importance of this interest, and the propriety, by proper safe-guards, of placing about it some measure of restraint. Accordingly, in this year (1834), an act was passed, quite comprehensive in its scope, and of such important bearing upon the interest concerned, and of so marked a character in defining the general policy of the State regarding these institutions, that its insertion in full seems to be demanded as a necessary incident in this history.

AN ACT TO REGULATE INSTITUTIONS FOR SAVINGS.

PASSED April 2, 1834.

SECTION 1. *Be it enacted by the Senate and House of Representatives in general court assembled, and by the authority of the same:* That all Savings Banks or institutions for savings which now do or may hereafter exist, by virtue of any statute of this Commonwealth, shall be corporations possessed of the powers and functions conferred by law upon corporations generally, and shall be governed by the rules, and subject to the duties, restrictions, liabilities and other provisions contained in this act.

SEC. 2. *Be it further enacted,* That the officers of every such corporation shall consist of a president and treasurer, and such number of trustees or managers as the corporation shall agree upon, together with such other officers as may be found needful for the orderly management of the affairs of such corporation.

SEC. 3. *Be it further enacted,* That the officers aforesaid shall be chosen at regular annual meetings of such corporations, to be holden at such times as the by-laws thereof may direct, except the treasurer, who shall be appointed by the managers or trustees, and hold his office during their pleasure; and except, also, that in case of any office becoming vacant during the year, the managers or trustees may appoint a person or persons to fill the same until the same be regularly filled at the next annual meeting. And all the officers shall be duly sworn or affirmed to the faithful discharge of their respective duties, and shall hold their several offices until others are chosen or qualified in their stead; and the treasurer shall also give a bond to the satisfaction of the managers or trustees for the faithful discharge of his duties as treasurer.

SEC. 4. *Be it further enacted,* That in addition to the regular annual meetings of such corporations, special meetings thereof may be holden at any time, on due notice by order of the trustees or managers thereof;

and it shall be the duty of the treasurer to notify a special meeting, at the requisition in writing of any ten members of the corporation; notice of all such meetings to be given by public advertisement in some newspaper of the town or county where the corporation is established, or if there be no newspaper in such town or county, then in some newspaper of the city of Boston.

SEC. 5. *Be it further enacted*, That every such corporation shall have power, at meetings legally holden, to elect by ballot any citizen of this Commonwealth to be a member thereof; and any member may withdraw from and cease to be a member of such corporation by filing a written notice of such intent with the treasurer of the corporation three months at least before the regular annual meeting; and every member shall cease to be such on removing out of the Commonwealth.

SEC. 6. *Be it further enacted*, That every such corporation may receive on deposit all sums of money offered for that purpose; *provided*, that it shall not hold at the same time more than one thousand dollars from any one depositor, other than a religious or charitable corporation; said sums to be invested, used and improved for the benefit of said depositors.

SEC. 7. *Be it further enacted*, That all deposits may be invested in the stock of any bank incorporated by a law of this Commonwealth or of the United States; *provided*, that the whole amount of investment or security in any one bank shall not exceed one-half the capital stock of said bank; or said deposits may be deposited in any such bank on time and interest; or said deposits may be invested in bonds or notes with collateral security of any such bank stock at not more than ninety per centum of its par value; or they may be invested in mortgages of real estate, not exceeding in the aggregate three-quarters of the whole amount of moneys held on deposit by said corporation; or in the public funds of this Commonwealth, or of the United States, whether by direct investment or by conveyance of the property in such funds as collateral security for a loan at their par value; or in loans to any county, city or town in this Commonwealth.

Sec. 8. *Be it further enacted*, That if the moneys held on deposit by any such corporation cannot be conveniently invested in any or all of the modes of investment hereinbefore prescribed, then it shall be lawful to loan, not exceeding one-fourth part of the amount thereof, on bonds or other personal security, with at least one principal and two surety promisors, *provided*, that all such parties shall be citizens of this Commonwealth.

Sec. 9. *Be it further enacted*, That no officers or committee of such corporation, specially charged with the duty of investing the deposits, shall borrow any portion thereof, or use the same, except in payment of the expenses of the corporation.

Sec. 10. *Be it further enacted*, That the income or profit of all deposits shall be divided among the depositors, their executors, administrators, assigns or other legal representatives, in just proportion, with deduction of all reasonable expenses incurred in the management thereof; and the principal deposits may be withdrawn at such time, or in such form, as the corporation shall in its by-laws direct and appoint.

Sec. 11. *Be it further enacted*, That the treasurer of every such corporation shall, in every year, make a return of the state thereof, as it was at two o'clock in the afternoon of the last Saturday of some preceding month, to be prescribed by the Governor, which return shall be made to the Secretary of the Commonwealth within fifteen days after an order to that effect; and said return shall specify the following particulars, namely:

Number of depositors; total amount of deposits; amount invested in bank stock; amount deposited in banks on interest; amount secured by bank stock; amount invested in public funds; loans on mortgages of real estate; loans to county, city or town; loans on personal securities; amount of cash on hand; total dividends for the year; annual expenses of the institution.

All which shall be certified and sworn to or affirmed by the treasurer; and five or more of the trustees or managers of such corporation shall also certify and make oath or affirmation that the same is correct, according to their best knowledge and belief. And blank forms of such return shall be furnished said corporation by the Secretary of the Commonwealth, who shall prepare suitable yearly abstracts thereof, to be laid by the Governor before the general court.

SEC. 12. *Be it further enacted*, That the general court may at any time make other or further regulations for the government of such corporations, or determine and take away their corporate powers; and all such corporations and their officers shall be subject to examination by a committee of the general court, in like manner, and under all the liabilities and penalties, provided in the seventeenth section of the "Act to regulate banks and banking."

The purpose of the act was to reduce to uniformity the powers and duties of these corporations, thus simplifying the law concerning their administration, imposing restraints in those directions in which experience had shown a tendency to laxity or abuse, and making all alike amenable to a single and simple code of procedure. The effect of this law in creating limitations not prescribed in the charters of institutions previously incorporated, was questioned by some of them, but in the main the provisions of the act may be regarded as the policy of the State thereafter, except as modified by subsequent general legislation.

The object of reducing to a uniform system the

operations of those institutions, whereby they should find in this general law their powers and duties fully defined, was steadfastly adhered to in subsequent legislation by the adoption of a charter for all institutions thereafter incorporated in the following form :

Be it enacted, etc., That , their associates and successors, are hereby incorporated by the name of , and shall be entitled to all the powers and privileges, and be subject to all the duties, liabilities and requirements, contained in the statute of one thousand eight hundred and thirty-four, entitled " An act to regulate institutions for savings."

It must be conceded that this is a great improvement over the system, or want of system, so long prevalent in New York and other States, where each charter embraces provisions unknown to any other, and commonly more or less in conflict with the general legislation concerning these institutions.

Though the general law inserted above is sufficiently clear in itself, it may not be out of place to call attention, somewhat in detail, to its leading provisions or features.

The power to increase the number of trustees or managers indefinitely, was conferred upon the corporation; but no quorum was named in the act, as had been done in previous charters.

Deposits were limited to $1,000 from any individual, but might be received in any amount from religious or charitable corporations.

Officers, and members of any committee charged with the duty of making investments, were prohibited from borrowing or using the funds of the corporation; but the prohibition was not extended to trustees generally.

The authorized investments were: 1. Stock of any bank incorporated by the Commonwealth or the United States; but not to exceed one-half the capital stock of any one bank. 2. Deposits on time and on interest in any such bank were allowed. 3. Bonds or notes of private individuals, secured by such stock at not exceeding ninety per cent of its par value. 4. Bonds and mortgages to an amount not exceeding three-fourths of the total deposits. No limit as to the location of the real estate thus accepted as security, nor concerning the relative value of the property to the loan, was named, these matters being left to the discretion of the managers. 5. Public funds (bonds) of the Commonwealth of Massachusetts, or of the United States. 6. Loans to any county, city or town in the Commonwealth. It would seem as though this range of investment was sufficiently broad and diversified; but lest it should prove otherwise, it was further provided: 7. That not exceeding one-fourth part of the deposits might be loaned to citizens of the Commonwealth only, upon personal security, with one principal and two surety promisors.

The usual provisions for a division of the entire income among the depositors, after deducting reasonable expenses for management, are embraced in the act. No accumulation of surplus to meet losses or depreciation in the value of securities was provided for.

The requirement to make a return to the Secretary of the Commonwealth, of the financial condition of each institution, upon a day to be designated by the Governor, was, I believe, the earliest effort of general legislation in this country to make public record of the condition of this interest, unless we regard the requirement in most of the earlier charters of Savings Banks in New York, to report annually to the legislature, as an exception.

Though made subject to visitation and examination at the discretion of the General Court, this power seems not to have been exercised until, by a subsequent act in 1838, the appointment of bank commissioners was provided for, upon whom this duty was imposed.

The subject-matter of the returns to be made by Savings Banks is set forth in the act, and fails to embrace many items of desirable information which have since been included in these reports, and which are essential to a really complete history of the growth and progress of these institutions. The object appears to have been simply to call for such facts as would indicate existing financial conditions, from which the status of solvency or insolvency could be derived. The current transactions of the year, from which a knowledge of the practical work wrought by Savings Banks could be gained, were not included in the items to be furnished, until seven years later. Hence the grand total accomplished by this agency is nowhere made a matter of record, and my efforts to supplement the reports of the last few years, with information derived from the institutions themselves, as will be seen hereafter, have not been attended with very gratifying success.

Nothing further of interest or importance affecting Savings Banks, marked the course of legislation until 1838. The features of this, as well as of subsequent legislation, we will reserve for the next chapter.

CHAPTER VII.

COURSE OF LEGISLATION; SUPERVISION AND REPORTS, 1838-1860.

In 1838 an act was passed providing for the appointment of three bank commissioners, upon whom was devolved the duty to visit at least once in twelve months every bank and Provident Institution for Savings in the Commonwealth. They were to have free access to the vaults, books and papers, and to thoroughly examine all the affairs of said corporations, and make any and all such inquiries as might be necessary to ascertain their condition, their ability to fulfill all the engagements made by them, and whether they had complied with the provisions of law applicable to their transactions. It was further provided, that whenever upon the examination of any institution a majority of the commissioners were of opinion that the same was insolvent, or its further operations hazardous to the public or to depositors, or had exceeded its powers, or failed to comply with the law, the commissioners were empowered to apply to the Supreme Court for an injunction restraining the institution from further operations, etc. The commissioners were to report to the Governor, who would transmit the same to the Legislature.

The first report of Commissioners Waldo Flint, Julius Rockwell and Jonathan Shore, made December 31, 1838, embraces forty-five pages, of which forty-three are devoted to banks, and two to Savings Institutions.

As illustrating the character of the system at that time, we extract the substance of that report, as follows:

FIRST SAVINGS BANK REPORT, 1838.

"The attention of the commissioners, in their examination of Savings Institutions, has been directed especially to the investments, and the system of accountability as provided for in the by-laws, and as carried out in practice. An examination of the individual accounts would be a work of great labor and of little advantage. The investments, with very few exceptions, have all been made in some of the modes provided for by law, but there has been found a great difference of opinion as to the best mode of investment within the rules prescribed by the statute. Some have loaned almost wholly on collateral securities, and as far as convenient, on mortgages of real estate; while others have loaned on mortgages only as a last resort, and have gone to the extreme limits of the law in their loans on personal security. Some have preferred bank stocks, while others have regarded all other modes of investment as preferable to that in bank stock. In several instances the opinion has been given to the commissioners that the law ought to be so far altered as to allow a larger amount to be invested on personal security. But the fact that some of the best institutions prefer all other investments to that in personal securities, furnishes a pretty strong presumption that the law is, after all, right as it stands. Some of them have recently sustained losses upon their bank stocks, but not to an extent at all calculated to impair their usefulness, or seriously to affect the interests of depositors."

No schedules of the results of these examinations are given, probably for the reason that the annual statements were relied upon to furnish all the information deemed necessary.

As part of the history of that period, pertinent to the foregoing, we subjoin here a statement of the various classes of securities, constituting the assets of these institutions on the last Saturday of October, 1838.

Bank stock..............................	$1,426,188
Deposits in bank.......................	568,787
Loans on bank stock....................	536,931
Public funds...........................	70,000
Loaned on public funds................	10,000
Mortgages of real estate..............	1,121,300
County and town loans.................	465,247
Loans on personal security............	672,117
Cash on hand...........................	144,162
	$5,014,732

INVESTMENTS, 1841.

In 1841, the power of investment by the managers of Savings Banks was enlarged by the adoption of the following provision:

"All Saving Banks and Institutions for Savings may make loans upon bonds or notes, with the pledge of the stock of any railroad company incorporated under the authority of this Commonwealth, the whole amount of whose capital is actually paid in, such loan not to exceed eighty-five per centum of the par value of such stock; *provided*, that no such loan shall be made upon the stock of any company whose road or franchise is subject to any mortgage or pledge; and *provided further*, that no loan shall be made on any railroad stocks, which stocks shall not, at the time said loan is made, command at least their par value in the market; and no such bank or institution shall so loan more than fifty per cent of the amount of their deposits."

It must be conceded, that if railroad stocks are to be regarded as a proper security for Savings Bank loans, their admission could hardly be more carefully guarded than in the foregoing.

REPORTS, 1846.

In 1843 the office of Bank Commissioners was abolished, and of course the examination of Savings Banks was discontinued, though statements of their condition were still made annually to the Secretary of State. An effort was made to revive this office in 1846, but without success. In this year, however, the number of items in the annual statements of these institutions was increased, embracing the rate as well as the amount of dividends declared for the previous year, and also the average annual dividend during the five preceding years, and the name and location of the institution. They were also required to specify the amount of each of the different stocks or bonds held for investment or as collateral.

From 1834 till 1847, the abstracts of returns made by Savings Banks were transmitted by the Secretary of the Commonwealth to one or the other of the two houses of the legislature (General Court), and were published among the documents of the house by which they were received. In the latter year, however, instead of being published as formerly, these abstracts were referred to the Committee on Banks and Banking, with instructions to report whether these corporations had or had not complied with the laws of the Commonwealth during the previous year. The report of the committee is chiefly occupied with the discussion of technical, and apparently immaterial violations of the law concerning investments; as concerning the stocks of other States and of cities in other States, also concerning stocks and bonds of railroad and manufacturing companies as collateral for loans. Here is brought to view the controversy concerning the application of the act of 1834, to those institutions previously incorporated, with less restricted powers in their charters than those of the general law. The question was litigated by the Provident Institution for Savings, but was decided adversely to the claims of that institution. In the opinion of the court, although the bank was chartered in 1816, it was, nevertheless, subject to the general laws of the Commonwealth passed since that time, relating to investments of deposits by Savings Banks and Institutions for Savings.

This decision is important, as it establishes a precedent concerning the power of the legislature over these institutions, which would doubtless be regarded as authoritative by the courts of other States, if the question were ever to be brought to a test. Of course it concerns only the power of the legislature to regulate the affairs of these institutions in respect to the mode of conducting their business and their relation to depositors generally; but cannot, by implication or otherwise, be stretched to the extent of justifying the legislature itself, upon any pretext, in confiscating these deposits to the use of the State. That involves other and different and graver considerations, which we shall have occasion hereafter to consider.

In 1849, the Senate Committee on Banks and Banking reported a bill to revive the office of Bank Commissioners, with power to visit and examine Savings Banks, substantially as under the act of 1838. In their report upon this bill, the committee refer to the valuable work accomplished by former commissioners.

The bill did not pass, however. In this year, also, treasurers of Savings Banks were required to make returns to the assessors of the names of borrowers from Savings Banks, and of the securities deposited by them as collateral, the object being, of course, to reach these for purposes of taxation.

TAXATION OF SAVINGS BANKS.

In 1850, the question of taxing the *deposits* of Savings Banks themselves was agitated, and a petition was presented to the House of Representatives, asking for a law requiring treasurers of Savings Banks to report the names of depositors to the assessors for the purpose of taxation. The Committee on Banks and Banking, to whom the petition and subject were referred, reported adversely thereon. The policy of taxing Savings Bank deposits involves questions of grave importance to these institutions, and we shall probably have occasion to consider the subject more or less in subsequent chapters of this history. With a view to an intelligent apprehension of the light in which the matter was regarded by those especially charged with its examination, and to a better understanding of the subject generally, I subjoin extracts from the committee's report. The committee say:

"That it has been the settled policy of enlightened governments to foster and encourage such institutions, by avoiding all legislation which would be likely to interfere with or retard their prosperity and usefulness. They are of opinion that these depositors should be dealt with, protected, encouraged and vigilantly watched, as a means by which a great public good is conferred upon the community, by increasing the common stock of industry, frugality and thrift, by husbanding the earnings of the laborer and returning to him in safety, with use, in the day of his need, the fruits of his toil, and by increasing the feeling of the importance of public peace and of the perpetual stability of good order and good government, and by impressing it upon the great mass of the community with that strong conviction which individual interest never fails to inspire."

The committee then refer to the fostering care exercised over these institutions by the Government of Great Britain, which not only refrains from taxing these deposits, but pays a larger interest upon the public fund in which these deposits are invested, than upon any other part of its consolidated debt.

In conclusion, the committee are of opinion that the act petitioned for

"Would deter people from depositing in Savings Banks, and would weaken the stimulants and inducements to industry and frugality among the people of the Commonwealth, and increase the number of the poor, the poor-rates and the taxes upon property already subject to taxation, thus injuring many and benefiting none." *

In 1851, the Bank Commissioners were again invested with substantially the same powers of visitation

* For further argument upon the subject of taxing Savings Bank deposits, see Vol. II.

and examination of Savings Banks as those conferred by the act of 1838.

DIVISION OF PROFITS.

In 1852, an attempt was made to secure legislation to promote a more just and equitable distribution of the profits of Savings Institutions, but the Committee on Banks in the Senate reported adversely upon the measure, as uncalled for, and cited the policy of the Provident Savings Institution of Boston, referred to *ante*, p. 41, as evidence that no legislation of the kind sought was required.

In this year, the apprehension lest depositors in Savings Banks were not contributing their full quota to the support of the government, through taxation, culminated in the passage of an act requiring the treasurers of Savings Banks, upon application, to report to the overseers of the poor the names of depositors asked for, and to the assessors, all those whose deposits exceeded $100. Of course, the former was for the purpose of ascertaining how many paupers had bank accounts! and the latter, to subject to taxation all deposits over $100. This seems to have been an amendment of an act of the previous year of similar import, but which only required the return of depositors whose deposits were $500 or more.

In 1854, the Provident Institution of Boston was authorized to hold real estate to the value of $100,000, but only for the purpose of a building for banking purposes.

GROWTH OF THE SAVINGS BANK SYSTEM.

In the five years, from 1849 to 1855, the number of Savings Banks had nearly doubled, and twenty institutions had been organized within the two years previous. This rapid increase gave rise to discussion concerning the expediency of incorporating so many institutions, and forms a topic for consideration in the report of the Committee on Banks, in the Senate. The committee say:

"That they have endeavored to discriminate properly, and to grant no charters where strong cases were not made out. The committee believe institutions of this kind, placed in proper hands, and located where a reasonable amount of deposits may be expected, are beneficial to the poorer classes, and also may furnish loans to the worthy mechanic, who would otherwise be unable to procure them; and thereby the small savings of the poor, not only benefit themselves, but furnish a capital for enterprising mechanics to help to build up and enrich our cities and villages."

DEPOSITS OF MINORS.

In this year (1855) an act was passed limiting the amount that might be invested in the stock of any corporation by any Savings Bank to ten per cent of its deposits, or $100,000. Also an act securing the deposits of minors to their exclusive use. This principle of protection was recognized in the State of New York as early as 1820, as will be found recorded in that part of the work which treats of the growth of the system in that State. The principle was also recognized in the first legislation concerning Savings Banks in England, in 1817.

SAVINGS BANKS AND BANKS OF DISCOUNT.

The report of the Bank Commissioners for 1858 shows that the same questions concerning the general policy in the management and direction of these institutions arose in Massachusetts, as in New York and other States. This arises naturally enough from the fact that the conditions to be served, and the conditions under which the service was to be rendered, were so nearly alike in the different States. Among the subjects of discussion in this report, are the control of the affairs of Savings Banks by banks of discount through their officers, and the exercise by Savings Banks of the business and functions of ordinary banks, as in discounting business paper. Both practices are earnestly condemned by the commissioners.

The former practice had its origin, naturally enough, in the fact, that in small neighborhoods, where it was thought a Savings Bank might be of service to the manufacturing classes, it would be found that the patronage secured would hardly be sufficient to warrant the expense of an independent establishment. Economy would therefore be promoted, by transacting the business of the Savings Bank in the office, and through the officers of an ordinary bank. A small addition to the salary of such officers would compensate them for the service rendered, and the bank would be at no additional expense, and the slight inconvenience suffered by the accommodation thus afforded would be compensated by the balance of Savings Bank funds left with it for deposit and use. But the tendency of such connection was to make the affairs of the Savings Bank subordin ate to those of the bank of discount. Whenever the affairs of the Savings Bank became prosperous, and its business profitable, these would be made to inure to the benefit of the stock corporation. A larger proportion of salaries would be apportioned from Savings Bank profits, rent for the accommodation furnished would be charged and allowed, and the heaviest possible line of deposits from the Savings Bank would be carried or held by the bank of discount. In short, the interests of the bank of discount would be in conflict with the interests of depositors in the Savings Bank, and in this conflict of interests, with the power of control all in the hands of one of the parties, it was plain enough to see which party would fare worst in the strife. Human nature is much the same in boards of Saving Bank managers as elsewhere, and the temptation to make the most of such a connection, without dishonesty, would be hard to resist. In short, it would be found, quite generally, that where this connection existed between two institutions of such diverse purposes, the expense of sustaining it was greater than would be the maintenance of a separate establishment for the transaction of Savings Bank business. Such, at least, was the line of argument suggested.

The other practice complained of arose from the wide discretion granted to trustees under the form of charters originally adopted, and, indeed, under the general law. As we have seen, the disposition that should be made of the moneys deposited was scarcely subject to restraint at all, and as discounting the notes of responsible parties was the common business of banks, and

9

of moneyed men and moneyed institutions generally, and afforded the readiest means of making the deposits received produce immediate profits, it is not strange that the practice should have gained currency in Savings Banks. But it is not the less true, that such use and employment of the funds of Savings Banks is not in accordance with Savings Bank principles. There is a hazard concerning the best personal security, from which bonds and mortgages and public stocks are exempt, and the only true theory concerning the administration of Savings Banks is, that so far as possible, every element of hazard shall be eliminated from its transactions. Every thing for safety, and nothing for profit that is incompatible with safety, should be the rule and guide of these institutions.

Besides, the invasion of what is distinctively the province of ordinary banks, and of what distinctively is not the province of Savings Banks, tends naturally to incite jealousies and competitions on the part of the former institutions, which find themselves thus supplemented in their proper sphere of operations.

The commissioners further note and comment upon the attitude of some of the older Savings Banks, which claimed the right to exercise the full powers granted by their charters, without regard to the restrictions imposed by the general act for the regulation of Savings Banks, passed in 1834.

The result of this conflict of opinion is given elsewhere. *Ante*, p. 59.

LEGISLATION IN 1858.

The act prohibiting any officer, or member of a committee, charged with the duty of making investments, from borrowing the funds of the institution, was in this year amended so as to prohibit them from being sureties for any borrower; for the purpose, doubtless, of preventing these parties from obtaining moneys from the institutions which they controlled, under cover of lending to third parties, for whom they would become sureties.

SUGGESTIONS AND LEGISLATION IN 1859-60.

In 1859, attention is directed by the commissioners, to a practice then gaining currency, which has its parallels in other States, of declaring an agreed rate of interest or dividend, without reference to the earnings or profits of the institution declaring the same. Legislation is recommended to correct the abuse arising from this practice.

The commissioners further recommend, that investments be authorized in the stocks of the New England States and of the State of New York, also in the bonds or securities of the cities of New York, Albany and Brooklyn, and the cities of New England generally.

The practice, by Savings Banks, of discounting paper is again fully discussed, and it would seem with more force and fervor than the occasion demanded, in view of the fact that the practice was falling rapidly into disuse, through the voluntary action of the institutions themselves.

The recommendation of the commissioners concerning dividends, appears to have been favorably considered by the legislature, in the passage of an act requiring the managers to cause an examination to be made, prior to declaring any dividend, and prohibiting them from making any except out of profits accrued at the time; and treasurers were prohibited from paying a dividend to any depositor until authorized by a vote of the trustees. Both wise and salutary provisions.

MULTIPLYING SAVINGS BANKS.

In the report of the Bank Commissioners, made in 1860, the discussion of the topics of the previous report, to which reference has been made, was continued. The commissioners also refer to and discountenance the policy of the legislature, which there, as in other States, was rapidly gaining ground, of incorporating Savings Banks to be located near each other, thus introducing competitions and jealousies, increasing the aggregate expense of sustaining the system, substituting conditions of weakness for conditions of strength, and all without any compensating advantage in the way of promoting the convenience of depositors.

The report for the following year marks an era in this department of information, so distinctive as to justify a chapter for its exposition.

CHAPTER VIII.

BANK COMMISSIONERS' REPORT, 1861.

The report of the Bank Commissioners, made in 1861, was by far the most valuable contribution to the subject, ever made to the legislature of Massachusetts. It was a thorough and complete review of the theory, policy, condition and workings of these institutions.

The commissioners were George Walker, J. F. Marsh and W. D. Forbes, and they seem to have entered upon the duties assigned to them with an earnest conviction of the importance of the interest which they were called to serve, and with a very clear and intelligent apprehension of the nature of the work which they were engaged to perform.

I believe I can render no more acceptable service than to introduce copious extracts from this valuable report. As will be seen, it gives an admirable summary of the condition of the Savings Bank interest, not only in Massachusetts, but elsewhere in New England, in the State of New York, and in Great Britain, and valuable comparisons are drawn concerning the growth and progress of the system in these different localities.

Extracts from the Report of 1861, *of the Condition and Operation of Savings Banks for* 1860.

The savings of the industrial classes are a fair index of the prosperity, and indeed of the moral condition of any people. The periodical valuation of estates shows the increase of realized wealth among those who control the capital, and direct the business energies of the Commonwealth, and in great measure support the burden of its taxes; but it gives no token of the condition of the poor. It has been claimed to be the tendency of modern civilization to make the rich richer and the poor poorer. However true this may be in countries governed on a different system from our own, it does not seem to be the character of our material development. Whatever of wealth and of the comfort and even luxury which wealth brings, and is enjoyed by our people in the aggregate, is shared to a degree which is unknown elsewhere, by all classes of the population. * * * * * * *

It will be observed that the number of Savings Banks has increased from twenty-two in 1834, to eighty-nine in 1860, or more than fourfold; the number of depositors from 24,256 to 230,068, or 858 per cent; the deposits from $3,407,774 to $45,054,236, or 1,222 per cent; the average to each depositor from $140.49 to $195.83, or 39½ per cent: the average of the deposits to each person of the population from $5.58 to $36.59, or 555 per cent; the percentage of the population who are depositors from 4 per cent, or one person in 25, to 18⅗ per cent, or one person in 5$\frac{4}{10}$. The average expense of management for six years from 1834 to 1839, was ⅓ of one per cent on the deposits; while for six years from 1855 to 1860 it was only $\frac{28}{100}$ of one per cent. In 1860 it had fallen to ¼. The average of dividends for the five years from 1840 to 1844, inclusive, was about 5¼ per cent. In the six years, from 1855 to 1860, inclusive, it was a little less than 6¾ per cent.

Taking the ten years from 1850 to 1860, the deposits increased from $13,660,024 to $45,054,235, or 231 per cent. In the same period the population of the Commonwealth increased from 994,512 to 1,231,065, or about 24 per cent; the valuation from $597,936,992 to $897,795,326, or about 50 per cent; and the bank capital (the means required to carry on the business of the Commonwealth), from $36,925,050 to $64,519,200, or nearly 75 per cent. This comparison shows how greatly the accumulation of industrial savings has exceeded the other ratios of development in the State.

Let us now examine the progress of Savings Banks in Great Britain and Ireland (the United Kingdom). As we have not all the items necessary to a full comparison down to 1860, we will take the period from 1831 to 1857, inclusive, which covers the same number of years as that embraced in the Massachusetts returns. From 1831 to 1857 the deposits in the whole United Kingdom increased from £14,575,165 to £37,090,558, or 154 per cent; the depositors from 436,670 to 1,366,560, or 213 per cent, while the average to each depositor declined from £33 7s., or about $161.47, to £27 1s. 6d., or about $131.05. The population of the United Kingdom in 1831 was 24,419,429, and in 1857 it is estimated to have been nearly 29,000,000; an increase of about 18 per cent. The wealth of that country is not so easily ascertained, there being no valuation of all property, real and personal, for taxation. The total value of British property can only, therefore, be estimated by a complicated process, and we have not seen any such estimate for 1831. Prof. Levi, in his recent and valuable treatise on taxation, estimates it in 1841 at £4,000,000,000 and in 1858 at £6,000,000,000, an increase of 50 per cent in seventeen years. The proportion of the population who were depositors in 1857 was $4\frac{7}{10}$, or one person in 21, and the average of deposits about £1 5s., or $6.25 to each person of the population. Mr. Scratchley estimates that in England and Wales alone the proportion in 1858 was about £1 12s., or $8 to each person of the population, and that one person in 16 was a depositor. We learn from the same author, that at the same date, the depositors in Savings Banks stood in the following proportion to the population in other countries: In France, one in 37; in Belgium, one in 8½; in Germany, one in 42. The expense of management in Great Britain averages a little more than ⅓ of one per cent, while in France it rather exceeds that fraction.

In New York the first general return of Savings Banks was made January 1, 1858, in pursuance of statute 1857, chapter 136. The increase in the several items from that date to the last return, 1861, was as follows: The number of institutions increased from 54 to 71; the depositors from 203,804 to 300,693, or 47½ per cent; the deposits from $41,472,672 to $67,-440,397, or 62½ per cent; the average to each depositor from $203.24 to $224.28; the percentage of the population who are depositors from 5.88, or one in 17, to 7.16, or one in 14; and the average of deposits to each person of the population from $12.66 to $15.79. Besides the amount specifically due to depositors, the institutions of New York hold a considerable surplus to cover depreciation of assets. We shall speak of this surplus fund in another connection. In 1861 it amounted to $2,949,260, or 4⅜ per cent on the whole deposits. * * * * * * *

Having now stated the condition and progress of the savings institutions of our own State, and also of those of Great Britain and New York, separately, let us for a moment, place the results side by side, and state the conclusions to which they lead. We have selected the two States named for illustration, because they may be taken as the best types, the one of European, and the other (if we except our own State), of American advancement; yet a comparison will show, that the savings of the poorer classes, as represented by deposits in Savings Banks, have grown to a greater volume, relatively, in our own State than in either of the others. While in Massachusetts one person in a little more than five of the population is a depositor, in Great Britain the proportion is not more than one in 20. In the most favored part of that kingdom, England and Wales, it is one in 16; in New York it is one in 14. Again, the average deposit to each person of the population is in Massachusetts $36.59, while in Great Britain it is only $6.25, in England and Wales alone, $8, and in New York, $15.75. Looking again at the rapidity of accumulation, we find that while in Massachusetts the increase in deposits in a period of twenty-seven years was 1,222 per cent, in Great Britain in a like period it was only 154 per cent. It is but just to mention that the increase of deposits in New York has been more rapid in the four years covered by its returns, than in our own State. This is partly due to a more rapid increase in the number of depositors, but it is also measurably attributable to the compounding of the interest upon a greater capital, the *ratio* of growth increasing, year by year, with the magnitude of the principal upon which the interest is cast.

We may be justly proud of this comparison. It shows a superior and an improving condition of the laboring classes, and it reflects the highest honor upon that educational system, which, while it involves a heavy annual outlay to the State, brings back to it a far richer return, in the intelligence, the virtue, and the material condition of her people.

But there are other lessons yet to be learned from the study of these figures. They are an "annual register" of the business condition of the country. Their periods of rapid growth, or of stagnation or decline, indicate a corresponding prosperity or depression in commercial affairs affecting the whole people. Let us examine some of these periods. The most rapid increase in deposits took place in the years 1852 to 1853, 1858 to 1859, and 1859 to 1860. In the first of these years it was $4,968,794; in the second, $5,509,-448, and in the third, $5,629,817. The greatest actual amount of money deposited was doubtless in 1852–3, since in the later years the accumulation from compound interest has largely swelled the aggregates. To illustrate this proposition: The total deposits in 1852 were $18,401,307. If we may suppose the whole of this to remain undrawn and productive for a year, the interest upon it at six per cent would be $1,004,078; while upon the deposits of 1858, $33,914,791, the interest would be $2,034,888, and on $39,424,418, the deposits of 1859, it would be $2,365,465. Deducting these sums severally from the increase stated for the years in question, and the net increase from money deposited, would be $3,964,716 in 1853; $3,474,560 in 1859; and $3,264,352 in 1860. Such are the fluctuations which always attend a general tide of progress. The waves of the sea do not encroach upon the shore with equal footsteps, and the irregular circles in the oak's trunk, indicate a growth, now rapid, now slow, as it has been stimulated or retarded by external influences.

We have noticed the periods of progress; those of depression are no less remarkable. Thus, if we go back to the disastrous year 1837, we find that the increase of deposits to 1838 was only $87,966, and of depositors 499, while from 1836 to 1837 the increase of deposits was $406,847, and of depositors, 2,778, and from 1838 to 1839 the increase of deposits was $738,766, and of depositors 3,623. Still more striking is the following contrast: From 1842 to 1843, the increase of deposits was only $35,095, and of depositors only 630; while from 1843 to 1844 was witnessed the hitherto unparalleled addition of $1,325,798 to the deposits, and 6,482 to the depositors.

Equally noticeable is the fluctuation in the average amount held by each depositor. A decline in the ratio of increase shows a general depression of the industry of the State, which stops accumulation; a decline in the average deposit shows how far this depression has compelled those who have already begun to husband their earnings, to fall back upon these reserves for subsistence. While in Great Britain we have seen a steady decline in the average, between 1831 and 1857, from $161 to $131, or $30, in Massachusetts, in a like period, we witness the gratifying increase from $140 to $195, or $55. This upward progress has, however, been marked by occasional pauses, and even retrogressions. The largest average was in 1853, when it reached $199.05, having increased nearly $20 in two years, but in the following year, 1854, the decline was equally rapid, for the average fell to $189.88. At no time (until the present exceptional year) has there been an actual decline, either in the deposits or number of depositors. In Great Britain and Ireland the fact has been far otherwise. In Ireland, famine and emigration wrought such a change in the aggregate resources of the poor, that between 1846 and 1849, the deposits had declined from £2,924,910 to £1,223,851, and the depositors from 96,650 to 45,839. The decline had indeed brought the industrial savings to a lower point than where they had stood sixteen years before, the figures having stood in 1833 — deposits, £1,327,122, depositors, 49,170. A similar, though less marked decline, occurred in Great Britain. In England, between 1846 and 1848, the deposits fell from £26,759,817 to £24,985,730, and the depositors from 900,933 to 899,606. In Scotland, the decline was from £1,383,866 to £1,081,110, and in the number of depositors from 90,301 to 86,056. In Wales, the decline in amount was slight, while the number of depositors experienced a slight increase. In the whole United Kingdom, the deposits declined, between 1846 and 1848, from £33,694,642 to £30,117,771, and it was not till 1852, after an interval of six years, that they recovered their former volume.

The history of the withdrawal of deposits in Great Britain is also valuable, as illustrating the important service which Savings Banks render to the laboring classes in periods of idleness or distress. In the seventeen years from 1841 to 1857 inclusive, the amount withdrawn by depositors exceeded the amount deposited by £3,114,136; yet, in spite of this, by the cumulative power of compound interest, the aggregate deposits increased, in the same period, £10,718,751. In nine out of the seventeen years, the withdrawals exceeded the deposits, and in the years 1847 and 1848, which were marked by great commercial distress in England, the excess of withdrawals over deposits was more than five millions of pounds sterling. These figures show how much more frequently in great Britain than in our own State, the annual earnings of the poor prove inadequate to their subsistence, and how much oftener they are forced to rely on their accumulated savings. Our own returns do not state the amount of withdrawals, but there is no doubt that with us even, they sometimes exceed the deposits. This was probably the case in 1857, when the yearly gain was only $899,215, a sum considerably less than the interest upon the deposits of 1856. Nearly a million of dollars must have been withdrawn more than was deposited, in that disastrous year. In New York, the excess of withdrawals was more than $1,700,000.

It is to be regretted that the annual withdrawals, as well as deposits, have not hitherto been stated in our Savings Bank returns. They are given both in England and New York, and we recommend that hereafter these returns be required to specify the amounts deposited and withdrawn during the year. * * * *

The investment of Savings Bank funds is a subject of some embarrassment, and complaints are frequently made by managers, that they cannot always find a use for their money in the investments authorized by law. As we have shown by reference to bank capital, the funds have accumulated faster than the channels for their employment, and the difficulty has hitherto seemed of a serious and growing character. The course of legislation has been, in some respects to enlarge, and in others to restrain the liberty of investment. The public stocks of the New England States, other than Massachusetts, have recently been added to the list of authorized securities, and we see no reason why this list may not, with equal safety and advantage, be enlarged by adding the public debt of the cities of Portland, Hartford, Providence, New York, Albany, and Brooklyn. All these cities possess an ample municipal property, and enjoy a high credit. The unhappy events which have plunged our country in a civil war may, however, furnish the Savings Banks with abundant securities of a high order, without opening to them a wider choice than now exists by law. It is not probable that deposits will increase rapidly during the pendency of this struggle,* but as the industry of the State returns to its wonted channels, or finds new ones opened to it, as is now rapidly being done, the accumulations will again commence, and Savings Banks will be in the receipt of moneys both from deposits, and interest, and the payment of loans. It is to be hoped, that, both from motives of patriotism and of pecuniary advantage, large investments will be made in the debt of our own and the neighboring States, which have, with such alacrity, come forward, in the time of their country's peril, to pledge the wealth and the creative energies of their people to sustain our national existence. These debts are based upon an ample property, upon a State credit which has never been tarnished, and upon the promises and faith of a people whose productive capacity, and habits of economy, could not be more forcibly illustrated than in the history of those very institutions whose aid they will now invoke. In urgently commending these State stocks to the attention of Savings Bank trustees, we do not by any means, exclude from their favorable regard the public stocks of the United States, of which we have elsewhere spoken. The pledge of the nation's faith and resources comprehends those of each and all the States, but in the creation of great local debts in every State, it will be necessary hereafter, more than ever before, to find a market for them among their own citizens, and the institutions which garner up the savings

* A reference to the tabular statement of the growth of Savings Banks during the period covered by the war, will show how far astray were the commissioners in their judgment.

of those who individually possess too little to invest it for themselves.

We would also recommend, as has been done in a former report, that Savings Banks be authorized to loan directly to the Commonwealth, as well as to invest in its public securities.

Notwithstanding the present and prospective prominence of public stock, other investments will absorb a considerable portion of the funds of these institutions, and the character of each of those authorized by law, demands from us a passing notice. It is to be borne in mind, in the first place, that *safety* and not *profit* is the consideration mainly to be regarded in the investment of trust funds. There must be no ambition to make large dividends; no alluring of depositors by promise of extraordinary interest; no trenching on the ground reserved for banks of discount; and above all, no rivalry between Savings Banks themselves. All have not equal advantages of locality or association, and some will necessarily be more profitable than others. The location of a Savings Bank is not selected with reference to the opportunities for investment, but solely with a view to facilitate and encourage the saving of those earnings, which might otherwise be wasted. A great diversity does, and must, on this account, exist, in the kinds of investment most favored by trustees in different parts of the Commonwealth.

Next to safety, *convertibility* is of the highest consequence. The funds of depositors are subject to withdrawal on short notice, and a considerable part of them must be so invested as to be readily turned into cash at any moment. It is not deemed wise to keep a large amount of cash on hand, and to obviate the necessity of it, deposits on interest in banks of discount are authorized by law. Formerly, the amount of these deposits was not restricted, but it is now limited to seven per cent of the total deposits in the savings institution. We think the limit might safely be extended to ten per cent, provided the whole deposit should not exceed a certain amount. In New York the limit for such deposits is twenty per cent, and not exceeding $100,000 in any one bank.

The public stocks of which we have spoken, possess the element of convertibility in the highest degree. Next to these stand bank stocks. In ordinary times these can be readily sold, and without any considerable sacrifice on their fair value. This is especially true of the stocks of Boston banks, for which the daily sales at the brokers' board, and the weekly sales by auction, afford a constant market. Country bank stocks are only less convertible, because the circuit within which their value is known is more limited, and contains fewer buyers, but they seldom fail to bring a fair price, when required to be parted with. The present depression of bank stocks will probably lead Savings Banks to invest more guardedly in them in future, but as the causes of this depression are altogether temporary and exceptional, and the extent of their depreciation in value is greatly overestimated in the popular mind, we believe that they will speedily regain their place in public favor.

Loans on stock collaterals stand next in order. If the securities are judiciously selected, and taken with a sufficient margin, such loans can usually be realized in a very short time; but it is, unfortunately, too often true, that borrowers expect the greatest indulgence in the time of payment, so long as the security remains good, and managers are slow to press them, or to force the sale of their collaterals.

Loans upon the credit of individual names will, perhaps, be regarded as next in the rank of convertibility. This class of investments is somewhat peculiar to our State. In New York it is prohibited altogether, and in England and France it is not included in the authorized classes, and even in our own Commonwealth it is permitted to be resorted to only when the deposits "*cannot be conveniently invested in any or all the modes*" otherwise specified. The language of the statute indicates that the legislature preferred other modes of investment, and permitted this to be availed of only when those previously enumerated should prove inadequate conveniently to absorb the accumulating funds. There have, no doubt, been periods when other investments could be less conveniently found than at present, and certain localities where it was not deemed prudent to lend on mortgage of a generally declining property, but we think that in the increasing abundance of public stocks, there will be less inducement hereafter than heretofore to invest on merely personal security, and that the limit, now fixed at fifty per cent of the total deposits, might with propriety be restricted within narrower limits. Such would seem to be the prevailing sentiment in the Commonwealth, the average of personal loans in the whole State being less than 20 per cent of the whole deposits. While there are many personal loans of a very high character, and upon which there is very small risk of loss, and also great readiness of convertibility, there are many others which are very slow and practically inconvertible. We think it highly desirable that such loans should be made upon a definite time, when they should be required to be paid; but we do not, in making this suggestion, wish to be understood as sanctioning a considerable class of loans upon personal security, which have obtained favor in certain localities, and which, if within the letter of the statute, are certainly foreign to its intention. We refer to loans upon what is essentially business paper. The form of these loans is according to the statute, the notes being signed by three parties, and they are usually written on a time which would fall within the limits of ordinary bank accommodation; but the makers are sometimes all partners of one house, and exposed to the same business risks; and to show that they themselves regard such notes as single name paper, they pledge their regular business paper for its security. We have observed often, that the class of paper so pledged is of an inferior character, being either too long, too remote, or too little known to meet with favor at the discount banks. We recall an instance last summer, when exchange in western cities ruled at ten per cent and upwards, where all the collaterals held by a certain Savings Bank near Boston, for the notes of a respectable mercantile house, were payable in Illinois, Wisconsin and other western States, of which not a single piece could then have been discounted at a bank in State street. It is true that they were taken at a margin, and this is usually the case; but they ought not to have been taken by a Savings Bank at all.

The operation of such loans is precisely this, that a merchant, having culled out of his "bills receivable" all such notes as he can get discounted at bank, carries the balance, which are either too long, or too poor, to be negotiated in the regular way, to a Savings Bank, where he gets a considerable loan upon them. He is enabled, by this process, not only to expand his own credit to an unwarrantable degree, but also to indulge his customers in longer credits than it is either well for them to have, or for him to give. The injury to the public and to the mercantile system is great and immediate. Long credits have done more than any other instrumentality (unless it be an unsound currency) to injure American trade. There is a growing conviction of this truth, and the spirit of legislation should promote, rather than impede, the introduction of a better system. We see no more simple method of preventing such a misuse of Savings Bank funds as we have pointed out, than by further restricting the amount which may be loaned on personal security.

Loans to cities, counties, and towns have not the element of convertibility, but they are usually a very safe kind of investment. We cannot but think, however, that the facility with which loans have been of late years procured by municipal corporations, both from Savings Banks and the free banks (which are allowed to deposit such securities with the Auditor as a basis for their circulation), has tempted them to increase their indebtedness to an unwise degree. There is great laxity in the manner of taking municipal loans, and legal questions have already arisen as to the authority of a town treasurer to bind the corporation he represented. The strictest formality should be required by the lender, both as to the manner of authorizing the loan, and as to the execution of that authority. Authority to make a specific loan, of a specified institution, is altogether preferable to a general authority to borrow not exceeding a certain sum; and when notes are given by a treasurer, some other authority should certify upon them, that they are duly given, and a certified copy of any vote authorizing the loan should invariably be required, and should be kept on file with the note. We desire to impress this caution earnestly upon bank managers, because we have had frequent occasion to object to the manner in which loans of this character have been authenticated.

The only investments remaining to be considered, are loans on mortgage. These in the form usually adopted — with a power of sale — are securities of the highest order. They are, however, among the slowest and least convertible of investments, and they need, therefore, to be selected with great caution, and with an eye to future contingencies. It is not prudent to loan on real estate which is declining in value, unproductive, or slow of sale as compared with other property. Property which yields an income is always safest, because it provides for the interest for which it is pledged. We highly approve the plan adopted by some institutions, which requires a certain percentage of the loan to be paid annually. Although it adds somewhat to the labors of the officers of the bank, it is a great safeguard against depreciation in the security, and it encourages thrift and economy in the borrower; and if the property is not of a kind to emancipate itself gradually from debt, it is not such as a Savings Bank ought to loan upon. There are now localities within the Commonwealth, where, from a general depreciation in the value of real estate, the mortgages held by the local Savings Banks cannot be made to pay the debts for which they are held. The statute limit for mortgage investments is seventy-five per cent of the deposits. We think it will be rarely found expedient, in practice, to approach this limit. The president of the largest Savings Bank in this country, after an experience of more than a quarter of a century, in a communication to a member of this Board, expresses the opinion, that "real estate securities may be safely taken to the extent of about one-third of the entire deposits."

The propriety of keeping a surplus fund to cover depreciation, has been discussed in former reports. We have seen that such a fund is maintained by the Savings Banks of the State of New York. It now amounts to nearly five per cent on the total deposits. The statute (Act of May 6, 1839, section 3) authorizes it to be reserved to the extent of ten per cent. We think such a measure extremely judicious, and would recommend the adoption of a law in this Commonwealth permitting, and perhaps requiring, such a reserve.

The present condition of the industry of the country will not encourage petitions for the incorporation of new Savings Banks, nor, in our opinion, would it justify the legislature in granting such petitions if presented. The facilities for depositing savings are already everywhere ample, and the number of small and languishing institutions is quite too large. * * * * * * *

The separation of Savings Banks from banks of discount, which has been frequently advocated by our predecessors, needs to be again urged. There are at present twenty-seven such institutions, which are located in the same rooms with banks of discount, and managed by the same officers. The evils resulting from this practice are manifold. There is danger of relations growing up between the two institutions more intimate than the law allows, and it is almost certain that the interests of one or the other will be, sooner or later, neglected. The experienced manager whose opinions we have already once quoted, lays it down as an axiom, that Savings Bank officers "should be free from entanglements with other moneyed institutions." In our examinations we have often found the books of a Savings Bank sadly in arrear, because the treasurer had been too much occupied with his duties as cashier to keep them written up. Nothing is of more dangerous tendency than a neglect to keep the transactions of a moneyed corporation properly entered and posted.

* * * * * * * * * *

CHAPTER IX.

COURSE OF LEGISLATION, 1862-1873.

In 1862, Savings Banks were required to report how often extra dividends were declared, and the average for a series of years. In this year also a tax was for the first time placed upon the deposits of Savings Banks, of one-half of one per cent, which was increased the following year to three-fourths of one per cent, and in 1865 reduced to one-half per cent, but raised to three-fourths per cent again in 1868.

In 1863 Savings Banks were authorized to invest in "the public funds of the State of New York, in bonds or notes of the cities of the New England States, first mortgage bonds of any railroad company incorporated under the authority of this State, which is in possession of and operating its own road, and which has earned and paid regular dividends for two years next preceding such investment, or in the bonds of any such railroad unincumbered by mortgage, or on the notes of any citizen of this State with a pledge as collateral of any of the aforesaid securities, or with a pledge as collateral of the stock of any of said railroad companies at not over 80 per cent of the market value, and at not over 90 per cent of the par value of such stock. Horse railroads excluded from the foregoing provisions."

The Board of Bank Commissioners was abolished in 1865 by an act to take effect on the 1st of January, 1866, but the legislature in that year created the office of Commissioner of Savings Banks, with substantially the powers and duties of the previous board, and requiring the reports of Savings Banks to be made to him, instead of to the Secretary of State as before. In addition to the items previously reported, Savings Banks were also for the first time required to return the number and amount of deposits received, the number exceeding $300 at one time, the number and amount of withdrawals, number of accounts opened and closed, and the amount of surplus on hand.

No further legislation of importance is found until 1870, when Savings Banks were authorized to hold real estate to an amount not exceeding ten per cent of their deposits, but only for a site and the erection of a banking house, all the income to be devoted to the interests of the corporation; but no Savings Bank to invest in this way more than $200,000.

In 1871 we find the first legislation relating to dormant, commonly called unclaimed deposits, which, however, did not take the absurd and unreasonable form of confiscating these to the State, but was limited to a measure designed simply to apprise depositors or their representatives of the status of their deposits with reference to dividends. The act was to the effect that depositors were to be notified when the amount of their deposits exceeded the sum upon which interest was allowed, and once in five years the treasurer of each Savings Bank was required to publish a list with the last known residence of the depositors respectively, of the amounts which for two years previously had, for the reason above stated, been entitled to no interest.

The purpose of putting the depositor in possession of the facts concerning his deposit, which it might be for his advantage to know, and of which there was a fair presumption that he was unaware, is just and salutary, though whether this might not be effected in some less objectionable way than by publication in the above form, may be seriously questioned. The general subject receives full consideration hereafter in our discussion of the methods which have been at various times proposed in dealing with these deposits in the State of New York.

The legislation in 1872 would seem to indicate that abuses in the form of favoritism in making loans, and in the form of charges or commissions by officers for effecting the same, had crept into the management of some of the Savings Banks. The mode of meeting the evil, whether real or imaginary, will best be seen from the following extracts from the act of that year:

CHAPTER 293.

SECTION 1. No Savings Bank, or any person on its behalf * * * * shall negotiate, take or receive any fee, commission or brokerage, for or on account of any loan made by or in behalf of any such bank * * either to his own use or to the use of said bank, other than shall appear on the face of the note or contract in which the loan shall be made, except expense of examining titles, etc.

§ 2. No officer, etc., shall refuse to consider an application for a loan, because presented by, or coming directly from the borrower; and if such application is rejected when there is sufficient money in the treasury to meet it, and the security offered is ample, and the same is afterward considered on application through a broker or third party, the officer so violating the provisions of this act shall be deemed ineligible to fill any position of honor or trust in any Savings Bank.

§ 3. All applications for loans shall be made in writing, through the secretary, or in his absence through the treasurer of the bank; record to be kept of applications showing date, name of applicant, amount asked for and security offered; and same to be presented to board of investment. Only one of active officers, as president, secretary or treasurer, to be at same time member of board of investment.

§ 4. Savings Bank Commissioner to see that foregoing provisions are not violated.

§ 5. Penalty not less than twice the amount illegally taken and received.

This concludes all that is material pertaining to the course of legislation concerning Savings Banks in the State of Massachusetts. It will be seen that since 1834 these institutions have been subject to the operation of a general statute, no provisions conflicting with the general law on the subject ever being introduced into acts of incorporation, which have all been of uniform tenor, as shown on p. 51, *ante.*

The system of supervision established under the direction of an officer having no other duties to engage his attention, and who was required to examine each Savings Bank annually, would seem to afford every guaranty possible of thoroughness and efficiency. Of course it is possible for the best devised system to fail, by committing its administration to unworthy hands; but no such misfortune has befallen this great interest in the State of Massachusetts.

The policy concerning investments which has prevailed in Massachusetts, in the admission of personal securities, bank stocks, and the like, is one that would not be deemed safe in New York; but we shall see that bad or corrupt management has in the latter State sometimes defeated conservative legislation, while the air of more liberal Massachusetts is free from the taint of fraud in the administration of her Savings Banks.

CHAPTER X.

STATISTICS OF GROWTH AND PROGRESS.

Inasmuch as the reports of Savings Banks in Massachusetts did not, until quite recently, embrace a statement of the amount deposited, and the amount withdrawn in each year, it was of course impossible from these to arrive at any conclusion concerning what is a most interesting subject of inquiry, the aggregate work performed by these institutions for the public since their institution in that State in 1816. It would be gratifying to be able to trace the growth and progress of each institution from year to to year, through all their vicissitudes. But this is rendered impossible as stated. I had hoped, however, by application to the institutions themselves, to obtain from them the aggregates of their deposits and accounts, as these would give a comprehensive summary of the work they had accomplished of great interest to the statistician and philanthropist. The ill success which attended that effort will be seen in the statistics which follow. With details of individual Savings Banks as here given, I have connected a statement of such items as seem to be of general interest.

STATISTICS FURNISHED BY SAVINGS BANKS.

Salem Savings Bank.

This was the second chartered institution in the State, and its progress has been gradual, but constant, as will be seen from the statistical statement below. I am informed by the treasurer of the institution, Chas. L. Symonds, Esq., that the bank has never lost a dollar by any investment made. The late president, Joseph S. Cabot, who died during the last summer, had been connected with the institution as trustee, vice-president and president, for fifty-two years. From the following statement it appears that its growth from organization to as late as 1834, a period of sixteen years, was quite slow. The first deposit was received April 15, 1818.

Statistical Statement, 1834.

Open accounts	2, 205
Amount on deposit	$360, 852

January 1, 1874.

Number of accounts opened since organization	54, 100
Number of accounts closed	38, 300
Number of open accounts, January 1	15, 800
Amount deposited including interest	$19, 709, 337
Amount withdrawn	14, 109, 337
Amount on deposit, January 1	5, 600, 000
Interest credited	4, 702, 887

The foregoing does not correspond exactly with the figures in the tabular statement, for the reason that the latter is made up for October 25, 1873, while the above is furnished by the treasurer as an approximation for January following.

New Bedford Institution for Savings.

Incorporated June, 1825; first deposit received August 15, 1825.

The following table compiled by the treasurer, Chas. H. Peirce, exhibits in detail the growth and progress of this institution. The table as furnished was even more full and complete than the following, but I was compelled to omit three columns of statistics to adapt the table to these pages. The column of deposits does not include dividends, which must be added to the former to produce a correct result. The columns of cents are omitted, but were used in finding the totals.

Memorandum of Progress of the New Bedford Institution for Savings.

Year.	No. of open acc'ts.	Deposited during the year.	Withdrawn during the year.	Dividends credited.	Total am't of deposits.
1825......	145	$13,051	....	....	$13,051
1826......	276	22,414	$2,524	$501	32,941
1827......	430	55,476	7,436	1,500	80,981
1828......	602	39,955	16,942	3,623	103,993
1829......	748	48,392	22,956	4,765	134,195
1830......	973	77,795	25,185	6,313	193,120
1831......	1,160	71,149	41,530	8,799	231,538
1832......	......	59,185	64,863	14,270	240,130
1833......	......	50,146	58,943	11,612	242,945
1834......	......	26,070	69,529	7,871	207,358
1835......	......	67,710	50,808	6,467	230,727
1836......	......	63,788	72,717	10,243	232,042
1837......	......	31,627	65,604	10,741	208,805
1838......	......	51,862	43,834	9,230	226,063
1839......	......	55,325	53,733	10,887	238,543
1840......	......	55,555	47,322	11,807	258,582
1841......	......	67,133	64,154	12,507	274,070
1842......	......	55,235	66,768	13,151	275,688
1843......	......	73,182	73,123	11,634	287,382
1844......	......	133,561	79,542	13,435	354,836
1845......	2,102	157,415	91,343	16,468	437,376
1846......	2,286	113,019	134,067	18,129	434,457
1847......	2,332	163,321	120,022	18,920	496,676
1848......	2,493	109,963	150,257	19,699	476,081
1849......	3,132	204,362	159,354	40,667	561,758
1850......	3,402	430,140	175,991	29,122	845,030
1851......	4,572	577,901	359,218	43,655	1,107,369
1852......	5,113	432,533	397,496	52,944	1,195,351
1853......	5,463	480,200	410,271	54,716	1,319,996
1854......	5,978	444,738	512,901	147,543	1,399,376
1855......	6,171	532,265	485,900	81,408	1,527,149
1856......	6,638	475,034	508,015	88,260	1,582,429

Year.	No. of open acc'ts.	Deposited during the year.	Withdrawn during the year.	Dividends credited.	Total am't of deposits.
1857......	6,900	$431,359	$576,739	$92,142	$1,529,192
1858......	7,164	523,412	394,042	90,559	1,749,122
1859......	7,642	567,234	481,176	127,802	1,962,982
1860......	8,362	627,481	492,436	117,635	2,215,663
1861......	8,623	616,689	605,110	131,623	2,358,866
1862......	9,561	845,479	554,750	140,279	2,789,875
1863......	10,420	928,680	694,800	166,909	3,190,664
1864......	10,888	1,137,957	979,576	192,734	3,541,780
1865......	10,574	802,637	1,301,114	210,084	3,253,388
1866......	11,305	1,146,380	878,260	226,193	3,747,702
1867......	12,047	1,200,350	941,663	262,072	4,268,462
1868......	12,559	1,229,721	1,048,452	298,956	4,748,687
1869......	13,299	1,306,839	1,193,325	332,735	5,194,936
1870......	13,860	1,279,963	1,203,286	366,882	5,638,496
1871......	15,021	1,610,484	1,233,966	401,785	6,429,802
1872......	16,412	1,705,951	1,350,748	457,099	7,242,979
1873......	17,448	1,783,307	1,740,632	508,672	7,794,327
Total...	....	$22,983,446	$20,094,192	$4,905,072	....

Whole number of accounts opened...........	58,571
" " " " closed............	41,023
Amount deposited, including dividends........	$27,888,519

SPRINGFIELD INSTITUTION FOR SAVINGS.

Incorporated and commenced business in 1827.

The following extracts from a report of the managers of the institution, made in 1858, gives a sufficiently detailed account of its operations during the first thirty years of its existence. It exemplifies the extremely moderate growth of this interest in this country during the early years of its history.

"This institution was first incorporated in 1827, and was one of the earliest Savings Banks in the State. During the first seventeen years of its existence its growth was slow in the extreme, and in 1844, its deposits had only reached the sum of $49,415.22. That its progress had not been greater was owing to various causes. The great benefit and value of these institutions had not, then, been completely apprehended and appreciated, and the most successful mode of managing them had not been adopted. During these first seventeen years of its existence, its entire deposits were loaned to the Springfield Bank at five per cent per year, and its whole business hardly amounted to any thing more than an open account at that bank. In 1844, the Springfield Bank declined longer to take and manage the funds of the institution, or to pay any thing for them, and, in consequence, a new organization of the institution took place, and the system of management was substantially adopted, under which it has reached its present position. The effect of this re-organization was immediately perceived in the rapid increase of its deposits and dividends. When the present mode of management was adopted in 1844, the amount of deposits received from the Springfield Bank as the result of seventeen years' operation, was $49,415.22. In December, 1849, when the business of the institution was finally removed from the Springfield Bank to its present location, its deposits had increased to $202,458, and from January 1, 1850, to May, 1857, they continued to accumulate till they reached the sum of $670,757. From 1844 to May, 1850, the institution paid an annual interest of four per cent, and since May, 1850, of five per cent, and, to those who have participated in the surplus dividend once in five years, the annual interest has averaged seven per cent.

This uninterrupted increase of its deposits, in face of the fact that, since 1850, four new Savings Banks have gone into active operation in the county, and three of them at points whence this institution had usually drawn a very considerable portion of its deposits, is certainly very satisfactory evidence of the continued confidence of the community in the institution, and of the fidelity, energy and economy with which its officers have managed its affairs.

Since its present organization was adopted, the institution has never lost a dollar of the funds intrusted to its care, with the exception of one or two small sums paid to persons who had become wrongfully possessed of depositors' books, and a depreciation in the value of the stock of the Grocers' Bank held by the institution, the extent of which has not yet been ascertained.

Statement of Operations from Organization in 1827 *to May* 1, 1858, 30 *Years.*

DURING YEAR ENDING MAY 1.	Amount received.	Amount paid.
1844 (Balance due this date)	$49,315	....
1845	82,432	$43,520
1846	67,651	33,413
1847	82,551	43,216
1848	89,991	68,706
1849	72,252	83,938
1850	87,913	96,674
1851	151,983	62,315
1852	178,030	112,215
1853	220,717	127,660
1854	247,818	150,137
1855	199,262	235,208
1856	184,345	191,487
1857	162,010	175,783
1858	121,120	208,235
Totals	$1,997,391	$1,632,604
Dividends credited to May 1, 1858	250,186	
Total credits to 8,547 depositors	$2,247,577	
Deduct amount paid to 5,804 depositors	1,632,604	
Leaving due to 2,743 depositors	$614,973	

We have not the details of growth during the subsequent years, but the aggregate from organization to the close of 1873, was kindly furnished by the treasurer, Henry S. Lee, in reply to my inquiries, and is as follows:

Number of accounts opened since organization..	43, 600
Number of accounts closed since organization...	29, 100
Number of open accounts..................	14, 500
Amount deposited, including dividends.......	$18, 259, 503
Amount withdrawn	13, 027, 207
Amount due depositors, Jan. 1, 1874.........	5, 232, 296
Amount of dividends credited...............	2, 283, 761

From the foregoing it appears that the deposits during the first sixteen years were less than $50,000. During the next fourteen years they were, not including dividends, not quite $2,000,000, and the dividends during that period $250,000; while since May, 1858, during a period of about fifteen and a half years, or half the former period, the deposits have been nearly $14,000,000, and the dividends over $2,000,000, or more than the entire deposits during the first thirty years; while there have been in operation in that city two other Savings Banks whose aggregate deposits in October, 1873, were nearly $2,500,000.

Worcester County Institution for Savings.

This Institution received its first deposit June 4, 1828. The following exhibits its condition in 1834, and at the beginning of 1874:

1834.

Open accounts..............................	1, 246
Amount on deposit..........................	$165, 542

1874.

Whole number of accounts opened...........	56, 014
" " " " closed.............	40, 842
Number of open accounts, Jan. 1	15, 172
Amount on deposit, Jan. 1	$5, 383, 756
" of interest (dividends) credited........	4, 583, 885

The treasurer, C. A. Hamilton, Esq., in reply to my circular for information, furnishes the above, and says:

"Of the first 5,000 accounts opened, 373 are still open. The whole amount deposited since organization cannot be ascertained without a great deal of labor, as in the beginning the accounts were not kept in a very lucid manner, the treasurer being at the same time cashier of a bank."

It is evident that the institution has long since outgrown that impediment.

A noticeable feature of the foregoing, is the amount of dividends, nearly equal to the amount now on deposit, showing that the balance remaining on deposit has been uniformly large.

Nantucket Institution for Savings.

Commenced business January, 1835.

Statistics January 1, 1874.

Number of open accounts	1, 635
Due depositors	$586, 554
Dividends since organization	544, 694

No other statistics given. The institution is located on an island whose inhabitants number about 4,200, about one-third of whom, it would appear, are depositors. Over 550 of the accounts are for less than $50 each.

Quincy Savings Bank.

Statistics January 1, 1874.

Date of first deposit, April, 1845.

Whole number of accounts opened	7, 466
" " " " closed	4, 421
Number of open accounts	3, 045
Amount on deposit	$1, 001, 139

The foregoing was furnished by the institution. The whole amount deposited and the interest credited are not given.

Wareham Savings Bank.

Statistics January 1, 1874.

Date of first deposit, April 19, 1847.

Whole number of accounts opened	4, 674
" " " " closed	2, 996
Number of open accounts	1, 678
Amount on deposit	$572, 284

The foregoing was furnished by the institution. The whole amount deposited and the interest credited are not given.

Waltham Savings Bank.

Statistics January 1, 1874.

Date of first deposit, June 1, 1853.

Whole number of accounts opened	9, 640
" " " " closed	5, 669
Number of open accounts	3, 971
Amount on deposit	$1, 204, 847

The above, furnished by the institution, omits the whole amount deposited, and the amount of interest credited.

Worcester Five Cents Savings Bank.

Statistics January 1, 1874.

Date of first deposit, July 1, 1854.

Whole number of accounts opened	12, 681
" " " " closed	6, 122
Number of open accounts	6, 559
Amount deposited, including interest	$2, 558, 260
" withdrawn	1, 343, 554
" on deposit	1, 214, 706
Interest credited	380, 122

The treasurer of the institution, George W. Wheeler, to whom I am indebted for the foregoing, also furnished me with a detailed statement of the deposits and interest credited for each year since organization, which will be found below. He also, during 1873, kept a statistical record of the number and amount of deposits made, classifying them according to their size from $5 upwards. A summary of these for the year is given, as possessing interest in connection with a topic concerning the ministry of Savings Banks, elsewhere discussed. I am further under obligation to Mr. Wheeler for some of the incidents recorded in that chapter.

Yearly Deposits and Interest credited in the Worcester Five Cents Savings Bank.

YEAR.	Deposits.	Dividends.
1854	$8,809 20	....
1855	14,412 32	$282 67
1856	15,999 53	790 78
1857	22,720 70	1,294 95
1858	24,257 19	1,968 29
1859	38,297 07	2,780 87
1860	53,198 34	4,254 11
1861	33,306 89	5,966 43
1862	62,084 53	6,884 19
1863	67,702 63	8,891 74
1864	75,572 70	10,710 65
1865	42,505 34	11,396 71
1866	64,422 39	10,800 87
1867	119,277 66	12,496 74
1868	172,283.08	19,965 03
1869	241,194 97	29,761 42
1870	226,900 85	36,479 66
1871	244,255 53	44,453 61
1872	284,902 58	52,343 91
1873	366,035 06	60,812 42
1874, six months	....	34,700 96
Extra, 1859, 1868	....	23,061 14
	$2,178,137 56	$380,122 25

Deposits in 1873.

CLASS.	Number.*	Amount.
Under $5	3,074	$5,905 71
Under 10 and not under $5	735	6,340 02
Under 25 " " " 10	932	17,607 79
Under 50 " " " 25	805	33,774 57
Under 100 " " " 50	600	50,439 43
Under 300 " " " 100	469	89,733 74
Over 300	272	162,233 80
Total	6,887	$366,035 86

* These are not identical with accounts; the same account receiving frequent deposits during the year.

NORTH BROOKFIELD SAVINGS BANK.

Statistics January 1, 1874.

Date of first deposit, September, 1854.

Whole number of accounts opened	2, 827
" " " " closed	1, 698
Number of open accounts	1, 129
Amount on deposit	$250, 969

The treasurer, Bonum Nye, Esq., says that the whole amount deposited and the interest credited cannot be given, owing to the destruction of the earlier records by fire.

PLYMOUTH FIVE CENTS SAVINGS BANK.

Statistics January 9, 1874.

Date of first deposit, July 3, 1855.

Whole number of accounts opened	3, 783
" " " " closed	1, 393
Number of open accounts	2, 390
Amount deposited, not including interest	$850, 522
Amount on deposit	462, 073

The above is furnished by the treasurer, D. J. Robbins, Esq., who says he is unable to give the amount of interest credited. This, of course, prevents me from making any deduction as to the amount withdrawn.

Boston Five Cents Savings Bank.

The following extract from the twentieth report of this institution, made to the corporation April 7, 1874, presents a complete view of its origin, progress and present condition.

The distinguishing feature of this institution is the low average amount due to each depositor, being but $189.22, while the average in all Savings Banks in the State is over $300. The depositors are more than twice the number in any other institution in the State.

Report.

In the month of November, of the year 1853, a few individuals met to consult upon the expediency of establishing an additional Savings Bank in this city, to induce the young and industrial classes to make a beginning to save, by encouraging deposits as small as five cents. The result of the deliberation was an application to the Legislature by the Rev. Edward Edmunds and others, for a charter providing for the receiving of small deposits, and giving minors the right to withdraw their money in person, without a guardian.

It is now twenty years since the charter of the Boston Five Cents Savings Bank was granted by the Legislature of Massachusetts.

From the time of its organization to the present, its prosperity has been uninterrupted; showing conclusively that such an institution was needed.

The growth and success of the bank, as may be seen by the tabular report herewith annexed, has been large and almost unceasing.

No year since it commenced business has the number of accounts closed exceeded the number of accounts opened; and at no time, during the several panics and financial disturbances which have overtaken the business community for the past twenty years, has the bank suffered embarrassment in any way in meeting all demands made upon it.

One of the most favorable features to be considered is, that during the great pressure in the money market of last year, though depositors had the privilege to withdraw all of their deposits without notice, the whole amount drawn from the bank, from the fifteenth day of September to the fifteenth day of December, was $107,793.06, less than was drawn in the corresponding months of the year previous.

The whole number of deposits and withdrawals since the bank was organized has been 1,331,152; whole amount deposited, $45,125,946.42; whole amount withdrawn, $33,708,734.84; and the total amount of interest paid depositors has been $5,475,381.20.

The number of depositors who have on deposit less than $50 is 36,529; $50, and less than $100, is 5,235; $100, and less than $500, is 14,416; $500 to $1,000 inclusive, is 9,441.

The subjoined table indicates the operation of the bank from year to year:

Years.	Annual gain in depositors.	Annual gain in deposits.	Annual amount deposited.	Annual amount withdrawn.	Dividends paid depositors.
1855....	6,583	$275,088	$370,533	$95,445	$5,013
1856....	3,222	289,637	513,251	223,613	17,249
1857....	2,771	315,293	654,930	339,636	30,710
1858....	1,990	220,789	709,754	488,965	41,677
1859....	4,153	663,077	1,142,212	479,135	*100,568
1860....	3,730	611,397	1,457,557	846,159	92,969
1861....	2,400	372,012	1,383,932	1,011,920	116,511
1862....	510	41,233	1,093,017	1,051,784	125,217
1863....	3,694	867,209	1,758,339	891,129	144,335
1864....	4,687	937,921	2,218,332	1,280,411	*257,897
1865....	2,645	111,496	2,579,272	2,467,776	202,312
1866....	1,753	†132,421	2,232,302	2,364,723	190,822

Years.	Anuual gain in depositors.	Annual gain in deposits.	Annual amount deposited.	Annual amount withdrawn.	Dividends paid depositors.
1867....	3,824	$977,676	$2,849,100	$1,871,423	$220,277
1868....	4,191	1,185,952	3,443,008	2,257,056	271,438
1869....	4,318	988,185	3,288,660	2,300,475	*795,190
1870....	4,263	1,024,973	4,474,623	3,449,649	367,886
1871....	2,429	673,763	3,714,135	3,040,372	414,263
1872....	3,320	764,478	3,875,128	3,110,650	452,976
1873....	2,359	598,808	3,809,320	3,210,511	486,442
1874....	2,779	630,638	3,558,532	2,927,893	*1,141,620
Total...	65,621	$11,417,211	$45,125,946	$33,708,734	$5,475,381

* Include extra dividends. † Decrease.

Stoneham Five Cents Savings Bank.

Statistics January 1, 1874.

Date of first deposit, October 6, 1855.

Whole number of accounts opened..............	3,116
" " " " closed...............	1,903
Number of open accounts......................	1,213
Amount on deposit............................	$256,874
Interest (paid)..............................	73,110

The above furnished by the institution does not give the whole amount deposited. The statement concerning interest is in terms as given, and is supposed to refer to so much as has been withdrawn, and not to the whole amount credited.

Natick Five Cents Savings Bank.

Statistics January 1, 1874.

Date of first deposit, October 4, 1859.

Whole number of accounts opened..............	3,515
" " " " closed...............	1,952

Number of open accounts........................ 1, 563
Amount deposited, including interest............ $921, 303
Amount withdrawn........................... 594, 749
Amount on deposit............................ 326, 554
Interest credited............................. 82, 984

The details of amount deposited, and interest credited for each year, are also furnished by the treasurer, James Whitney, Esq., as follows:

The first items are for 1859 and 1860. The last are for six months only.

	Deposits.	Interest.
1860	$10,443 70	$138 70
1861	3,321 68	210 84
1862	11,106 44	212 51
1863	15,490 58	591 52
1864	24,090 58	891 88
1865	18,489 34	1,017 11
1866	22,301 96	1,367 17
1867	37,587 43	2,174 81
1868	36,769 84	2,990 17
1869	93,467 83	5,516 08
1870	102,279 04	12,402 34
1871	110,685 02	12,177 22
1872	130,640 21	15,767 66
1873	114,491 45	17,709 97
1874	107,154 89	9,815 69
	$838,319 47	$82,983 67

Peoples' Savings Bank, Worcester.

Statistics January 1, 1874.

Date of first deposit, December 31, 1864.

Whole number of accounts opened............. 16, 226
" " " " closed............. 7, 252
Number of open accounts...................... 8, 974
Amount deposited, including interest.......... $7, 260, 280
Amount withdrawn........................ 4, 193, 227

Amount on deposit	$3, 067, 053
Interest credited	711, 887

The above was furnished by the institution and exhibits a remarkable growth for a period of only nine years.

West Boston Savings Bank.

Statistics January 1, 1874.

Date of first deposit, June 15, 1867.

Whole number of accounts opened	14, 469
" " " " closed	5, 869
Number of open accounts, about	8, 600
Amount deposited, including interest	$6, 095, 461
Amount withdrawn	3, 097, 250
Amount on deposit	2, 998, 211
Interest credited	488, 405

The foregoing was furnished by the treasurer, J. H. Wilder, Esq., who further attributes the success which in six and a half years has secured a deposit of nearly $3,000,000, to the following innovations upon previously existing methods.

1. Discarding extra dividends and dividing the full earnings every six months.

2. Commencing interest upon deposits on the first of each month, instead of quarterly. Other Savings Banks in Boston have been induced, by the success which has attended these changes in established usages, to copy the example of this institution.

Doubtless the result of the experiment serves to illustrate and enforce the principle for which we contend in another place, that varying practices concerning the payment of interest or dividends are desirable in order to meet varying necessities, or at least varying preferences on part of patrons.

South Weymouth Savings Bank.

Statistics January 1, 1874.

Date of first deposit, April 7, 1868.

Whole number of accounts opened	966
" " " " closed	232
Number of open accounts	734
Amount deposited, including interest	$383, 027
Amount withdrawn	133, 527
Amount on deposit	249, 500
Interest credited	56, 082

The foregoing was furnished by B. F. White, Esq., treasurer.

Webster Five Cents Savings Bank.

Statistics January 1, 1874.

Date of first deposit, August 10, 1868.

Whole number of accounts opened	2, 364
" " " " closed	824
Number of open accounts	1, 540
Amount deposited, including interest	$456, 151
Amount withdrawn	211, 171
Amount on deposit	244, 980
Interest credited	23, 393

The above was furnished by the treasurer, Edwin May, Esq.

Taunton Savings Bank.

Statistics January 1, 1874.

Date of first deposit, July 3, 1869.

Whole number of accounts opened	5, 453
" " " " closed	1, 629

Number of open accounts	3, 824
Amount deposited, including interest	$2, 188, 220
Amount withdrawn	832, 899
Amount on deposit	1, 355, 321
Interest credited	170, 157

The above was furnished by the institution.

Munson Savings Bank.

Statistics January 1, 1874.

Date of first deposit, June 1, 1872.

Whole number of accounts opened	548
" " " " closed	70
Number of open accounts	478
Amount deposited, including interest	$153, 187
Amount withdrawn	13, 491
Amount on deposit	139, 696

The above was furnished by the institution and is complete except the item of interest credited is not separately stated, but as this would be small it is not material.

Uxbridge Savings Bank.

Statistics January 1, 1874.

Date of first deposit, October 5, 1870.

Whole number of accounts opened	991
" " " " closed	211
Number of open accounts	780
Amount deposited, including interest	$303, 713
Amount withdrawn	122, 730
Amount on deposit	180, 983
Interest credited	27, 294

The foregoing was furnished by the treasurer, C. A. Taft, Esq.

North Avenue Savings Bank, Cambridge.

Statistics January 1, 1874.

Date of first deposit, August 31, 1872.

Whole number of accounts opened...............	129
" " " " closed................	16
Number of open accounts........................	113
Amount deposited, including interest.............	$30, 154
Amount withdrawn..............................	6, 154
Amount on deposit.............................	24, 000

The above facts were furnished by the institution. The interest credited on a deposit so small, for a period of a little over a year, could not exceed a few hundred dollars.

GENERAL STATISTICS OF GROWTH AND PROGRESS.

Having thus put on record such detailed statistics as I have been able to procure, there is nothing left to do but to fall back upon the published records for such further information as they contain, bearing upon the growth and development of the Savings Bank system in Massachusetts. Our starting point will be, of course, with the reports made in the year 1834.

Our first table exhibits the contrast in the condition of the 23 institutions in operation in 1834, with the condition of the same institutions as reported in 1873. It will be seen that the amount deposited in these 23 institutions in 1873, over $14,000,000, was more than four times the whole amount on deposit in 1834, that being less than $3,500,000. The amount held on deposit had, in these 40 years, increased over 21 times, and the number of depositors over eight times. Of course the growth of the system in the State at large greatly exceeds this, as will be seen from other tables.

TABLE showing comparative condition of Savings Banks in 1834, *and of same Institutions in* 1873.

Year of Incorporation.	NAME OF INSTITUTION.	1834.		1873.		
		Open Accounts.	Amount on Deposit.	Open Accounts.	Amount on Deposit.	Amount deposited in 1873.
1831	Barnstable	142	$17,160	3,868	$1,502,572	$243,926
1816	Boston, Provident	11,495.	1,686,202	31,885	12,787,700	1,665,593
1833	Boston, for Seamen[1]	272	32,937	18,212	6,842,947	1,303,439
1831	Dedham	538	61,166	3,476	1,039,940	148,755
1832	Fairhaven	102	9,102	1,410	766,347	243,154
1828	Fall River	335	46,692	11,128	5,274,998	1,019,859
1831	Gloucester[2]	240	20,014	......	....	....
1828	Haverhill	327	25,731	7,284	2,458,209	311,215
1829	Lowell	1,026	114,105	5,379	1,926,150	386,121
1826	Lynn	461	33,646	5,075	1,557,731	520,939
1825	New Bedford	1,162	207,764	17,327	7,778,586	1,761,961
1820	Newburyport	1,513	232,460	10,160	4,328,542	664,318
1831	Newton	61	1,829	1,690	316,342	142,186
1828	Plymouth	703	91,672	6,785	1,922,651	212,320
1825	Roxbury (Boston)	668	83,913	6,949	2,374,679	663,144
1818	Salem	2,205	360,852	16,079	5,796,214	807,717
1828	Salisbury and Amesbury	263	30,557	4,073	1,126,581	243,771
1827	Springfield[3]	......	....	14,322	5,137,141	1,457,375

1827	Taunton[4]	845	121,938	3,799	1,343,120	572,412
1829	Warren (Charlestown)	622	62,556	9,942	3,262,798	731,028
1834	Wellfleet[5]	4	832	1,007	305,188	100,953
1833	Weymouth	26	1,097	2,377	753,129	96,818
1828	Worcester County	1,246	165,542	15,207	5,185,506	822,203
	23 Institutions	24,256	$3,407,773	197,434	$73,787,091	$14,119,207

1 Name changed to Suffolk Savings Bank.

2 Failed in 1844.

3 Though organized in 1827 it appears not to have reported its operations in 1834. Probably deemed too limited to require notice. For statement of its growth, see *ante*, p. 95.

4 Original institution reporting in 1834, failed in 1843, and was succeeded, I suppose, by that found reporting in 1873.

5 Incorporated under the general law of that year.

The following table exhibits the condition of all the Savings Banks in Massachusetts reporting in 1834, as compared with all in 1873, in respect to the character of their investments, amount of surplus, and the per cent of interest paid, to the total amount on deposit. Of course the ratios are not exact, but approximate sufficiently near for all practical purposes. It will be seen that the banks in 1834 reported no surplus.

INVESTMENTS, ETC.	Aggregate 1834.	Aggregate 1873.	Per cent 1834.	Per cent 1873.
Public Funds	$2,000	$17,530,640	0	8
Loans on Public Funds	....	1,123,214	0	1-2
Bank stock	1,192,097	21,733,490	34	10
Loans on Bank Stock	557,930	1,572,687	16	7-10
Deposits in Bank	520,669	2,367,824	15	1
Railroad Bonds	....	6,098,435	0	3
Loans on Railroad Stock	....	495,237	0	1-5
Invested in Real Estate	....	2,273,749	0	1
Loans on Mortgage of Real Estate	387,396	100,406,767	11	48
Loans to Counties, Cities and Towns	 269,781	 14,722,283	7	7
Loans on Personal security	283,744	35,260,386	8	17
Cash on hand	24,953	2,125,490	7-10	1
Miscellaneous	169,203	....	5	0
Surplus	....	3,159,593	0	1 1-2
Amount of dividends	138,576	10,807,906	4	5

The growth and progress of the Savings Bank system in Massachusetts in its entirety, is best exhibited by the subjoined table, taken from the report of the Savings Bank commissioner. A table in this form was first compiled by the bank commissioners for the report made in 1861, from which we have elsewhere extracted so largely. Its great value in presenting at a glance the condition and growth of Savings Banks from year to year, has led to its continuance as a feature of the annual reports. Two columns, one of the population of Massachusetts at different periods and the other giving the total expense of conducting the business of Savings Banks in the State, have been omitted in order to reduce the table to the dimensions of our smaller page. These are not material, however, as the ratios derived from them are retained, and these contain all of real value which the omitted aggregates would furnish.

TABLE exhibiting the number, condition and progress of the Savings Banks of Massachusetts, in each year, from 1834 to 1873, inclusive.

YEAR.	Number of banks.	Number of deposit accounts.	Increase in number of accounts over previous year.	Percentage of increase.	Amount of deposits.	Increase in amount of deposits over previous year.	Percentage of increase.	Average to each account.	Deposits to each person of population.	Percentage of expense to total deposits.
1834	22	24,256	......	......	$3,407,773 00	....	.....	$140 09	$5 58	.33
1835	27	27,232	2,976	12	3,921,370 00	$513,597 00	15	143 99	.....	"
1836	28	29,786	2,554	9	4,374,578 00	453,208 00	11 1-2	146 19	.....	"
1837	30	32,564	2,778	9 1-2	4,781,426 00	406,848 00	9 1-3	146 51	.....	"
1838	30	33,063	499	1 1-2	4,869,393 00	87,967 00	2	147 27	.....	"
1839	30	36,686	3,623	11	5,608,159 00	738,766 00	15 1-4	152 86	.....	"
1840	31	37,470	784	2	5,819,554 00	211,395 00	3 3-4	157 98	7 88	.29
1841	30	41,423	3,953	10 1-2	6,714,182 00	894,628 00	15 1-2	162 08	.....	"
1842	..	42,587	1,164	2 2-3	6,900,451 00	186,270 00	2 3-4	162 03	.....	"
1843	31	43,217	630	1 1-2	6,935,547 00	35,095 00	1-2	160 40	.....	"
1844	31	49,699	6,482	15	8,261,345 00	1,325,798 00	19	166 23	.....	"
1845	33	58,178	8,479	17	9,813,288 00	1,551,943 00	18 2-3	168 56	.....	"
1846	38	62,893	4,715	8	10,680,933 00	867,645 00	7-8	169 82	.....	"
1847	39	68,312	5,419	8 1-2	11,780,813 00	1,099,880 00	10	172 45	.....	"
1848	41	69,894	1,582	2 1-3	11,970,448 00	189,635 00	1 1-4	171 26	.....	"
1849	43	71,629	1,735	2 1-2	12,111,554 00	141,106 00	1 3-4	169 08	.....	"
1850	45	78,823	7,194	10	13,660,024 00	1,548,471 00	13	174 57	13 73	.26
1851	45	86,537	7,715	9 2-3	15,554,089 00	1,894,065 00	14	179 73	.....	"

1852	53	97,353	10,816	12 1-2	18,401,308 00	2,847,219 00	12	189 01	.....	"
1853	60	117,404	20,051	20 1-2	23,370,102 00	4,968,794 00	27	199 05	.....	"
1854	73	136,654	19,250	16 1-2	25,936,858 00	2,566,756 00	11	189 88	.....	"
1855	80	148,263	11,609	8 1-2	27,296,217 00	1,257,359 00	4 2-3	18[illegible] 10	24 12	.28
1856	81	165,484	17,221	11 1-2	30,373,447 00	3,077,231 00	10 3-4	18[illegible] 15	.....	"
1857	86	177,375	11,891	8	33,015,757 00	2,642,310 00	8 2-3	186 13	.....	"
1858	86	182,655	5,280	3	33,914,972 00	899,215 00	2 2-3	185 67	.....	"
1859	86	205,409	22,754	12 1-2	39,424,419 00	5,509,647 00	16	191 93	.....	"
1860	89	230,068	24,659	12 1-4	45,054,236 00	5,629,817 00	14 1-3	195 83	35 59	"
1861	93	225,058	5,010*	2 1-6*	44,785,439 00	268,797 09*	3-5*	198 99	.....	.27
1862	93	248,900	23,842	10 1-2	50,403,674 00	5,618,235 00	12 1-2	202 50	.....	"
1863	95	272,219	23,319	9 1-3	56,883,828 00	6,480,154 00	12 4-5	208 92	.....	"
1864	97	291,616	19,397	7	62,557,604 30	5,673,775 75	10†	214 52	.....	.29
1865	102	291,488	128*	.....	59,936,482 52	2,621,121 78*	4 1-5*	205 62	47 29	.33
1866	102	316,853	25,365	8 2-3	67,732,264 31	7,795,281 79	13	213 76	.....	.32
1867	108	348,593	31,740	10	80,431,583 71	12,699,319 40	18 2-3	230 73	.....	.31
1868	115	383,094	34,501	10†	94,838,336 54	14,406,752 83	18†	247 55	.....	"
1869	130	431,769	48,675	12 3-4†	112,119,016 64	17,280,680 10	18 1-5	259 67	.....	.30
1870	139	488,797	57,028	13	135,745,097 54	23,626,080 90	21	277 71	93 14	.27
1871	160	561,201	72,404	14	163,704,077 54	27,958,980 00	20 1-2	29[illegible] 52	.....	.26
1872	172	630,246	69,045	12 1-3	184,797,313 92	21,093,236 38	12 7-8	293 21	.....	.25
1873	175	666,229	35,983	5 2-5	202,195,343 70	17,398,029 78	8 1-2	303 49	.....	.26

* Decrease. † Nearly.

The increase in deposits it will be seen is quite variable from year to year, fluctuating between a loss of four and one-fifth per cent, and a gain in one year of as high as 27 per cent, a variation of 31 and one-fifth per cent. A better idea of the growth of the system will be derived from a comparison in periods of about five years. As the term for which the record is made is not divisible by five, we make the first period four years; we have then the following:

1834 to 1838.....	Increase,	$1, 461, 620 =	42.9 per cent.
1838 to 1843.....	"	2, 066, 154 =	42.4 "
1843 to 1848.....	"	5, 034, 901 =	72.6 "
1848 to 1853.....	"	11, 399, 654 =	95.2 "
1853 to 1858.....	"	10, 544, 870 =	45 "
1858 to 1863.....	"	22, 968, 856 =	67.7 "
1863 to 1868.....	"	37, 954, 508 =	66.7 "
1868 to 1873.....	"	107, 357, 007 =	115.3 "

The results in the above form are so astounding, that if they stood alone, or were exceptional in their character, their correctness would challenge investigation. But so far from being exceptional, we shall find as we proceed, that in other States a like wonderful growth has been maintained.

The topics suggested by these exhibits are not local or special in their character, and are consequently reserved for consideration until the facts and figures concerning the development of this interest in other States are produced, and combined so far as practicable with the foregoing, and a common line of deduction and discussion derived from their united testimony can be entered upon.

The unexpected delay in completing this work enables me to give a summary of the progress of Savings Banks in Massachusetts during the year ending October, 1874, as the same is found in public journals.

Number of depositors	702, 099
Amount of deposits	$217, 452, 120
Gain in number of depositors	34, 853
Gain in amount of deposits	$14, 389, 964

THIRD SECTION;

SAVINGS BANKS IN THE STATE OF CONNECTICUT.

CHAPTER XI.

GENERAL COURSE OF LEGISLATION.

Savings Banks had their inception in the State of Connecticut by the incorporation of the "Society for Savings," at Hartford, which act was approved June 1, 1819. Like the pioneer institutions in Massachusetts, New York and other States, it has, in practical results, immeasurably surpassed the hopes and expectations of its founders, and nobly justified the motives and purposes which called it into being. The charter will be found in full in the Appendix, from which the character of its provisions can be derived. The institution was organized and the first deposit received in July, 1819, the same month in which the first Savings Bank in New York was opened. The population of the county of Hartford, which we may assume to have been tributary to the support of the institution, was at this time about 47,000, and of the State about 275,000. In 1870 the population of the county of Hartford was 109,000, an increase of about two and one-third times in fifty years; and the population of the State was, at the latter date, 537,000, an increase of 1.95 times during the same period. On the first of December after the opening of the bank, the first dividend was declared, amounting to $37.31, and the amount remaining on deposit after the above credit of interest, was $4,352.77.

It is said that the incorporation of this society was vigorously opposed by members of the General Assembly from the rural districts, upon the ground that its tendency would be to draw away money from the country and concentrate it in the city of Hartford. Theirs was a misreading or a misapplication of the scripture: "There is that scattereth, yet increaseth; and there is that withholdeth more than is meet, but it tendeth to poverty."

The order of incorporation of the first twelve Savings Banks in this State was as follows:

Society for Savings, Hartford	1819
Savings Bank of New Haven *	1820
Norwich Savings Society	1824
Middletown Savings Bank	1825
Savings Bank of New London	1827
New Haven Savings Bank	1838
Plainfield Savings Bank (closed)	1839
Savings Bank of Tolland	1841
Bridgeport Savings Bank	1842
Willimantic Savings Institute	1842
Derby Savings Bank	1846
Salisbury Savings Society	1848

* Appears never to have organized; was succeeded by the incorporation of the New Haven Savings Bank, in 1838.

In tracing the course of legislation in this State, concerning Savings Banks, we shall find no material modification in the form of charters, except in the direction of imposing some form of limitation concerning the manner in which the moneys received should be used and employed by the corporation for the advantage of depositors, which will be considered in its proper place.

ORGANIZATION.

The charter uniformly named the first corporators, and empowered them to increase the number at pleasure. In some later charters the corporators were required to elect associates to fill vacancies, so that the number of corporators should not be reduced below a certain limit, varying from ten to twenty-five. Seven corporators, one of the same being an officer, constituted a quorum. It would seem, from the provisions of section six of the charter of the Society for Savings, that it was not contemplated that the general control and management of the institution should be exercised by the entire body of corporators, as is the case in New York, but that the same might be delegated, with full powers, to the officers and "trustees" chosen by the corporators for that purpose. Such provision would seem to be a necessary incident to the power to increase the number of corporators indefinitely, as under such practice the corporation might become too unwieldy to exercise executive functions with efficiency and dispatch. The power to delegate authority to conduct the operations of the institution to a subordinate board, would further be rendered necessary, if but one meeting of corporators should be held in each year, as under the same section might be done. In some charters, however, the number of corporators was limited.

No provision for involuntary vacancies seems to have been made by law until 1871, when it was enacted, that neglect to attend meetings for three years without reasonable excuse, or a conviction of crime, should vacate the office of a corporator, on the same being declared by a unanimous vote at an annual meeting. Rather a tedious process, one would think, for getting rid of the association of a convicted criminal! There was, however, less occasion for a regulation creating vacancies otherwise than by death or resignation, where the number comprising the body of corporators was, or might be by act of the members, unlimited. By an amendment to the charter of the Norwalk Savings Society, the corporators were required each year to chose nine directors to serve for one year, but no corporator could serve as director more than three years out of four.

NOTICE OF INCORPORATION.

An act in 1858 provided, "that no petition for the incorporation of any Savings Bank shall be heard by the general assembly, unless public notice thereof shall have been given by advertisement setting forth the proposed location of such Savings Bank, in some newspaper published in the county where such Savings Bank is proposed to be located, at least two weeks before the first day of the session in which such hearing is to be had."

We have no means of knowing whether this act shared the fate of a similar effort in the State of New York, to check the rapid increase in the number of Savings Banks, by restricting the consideration of the legislature to such as should give promise of success by challenging public criticism. I suppose there was nothing in this act that could bind any subsequent legislature that might choose to consider and pass a bill of incorporation that had not been introduced pursuant to the forms prescribed in the above act.

But the passage of the act shows at least, that occasion was found for interposing some impediment to ill-considered acts of incorporation, which experience was doubtless common to all the States; and it further shows that one legislature was found sufficiently alive to the importance of well-considered action, to make an effort at least to secure it.

By an act in 1870 notice was required to be given of annual and special meetings of corporators; and it was also deemed important this year to prohibit the removal of any Savings Bank to another town without the consent of the general assembly.

INVESTMENTS.

The first Savings Bank charter in this State appears not to have recognized the principle of investments as now understood and provided for, as we find that in this charter provision was only made for *loaning* the moneys received by the corporation, and the same was left to the discretion of the managers, subject only to the requirement that the loans should be made in a manner consistent with the laws of the State. In the following year, however, the Savings Bank of New Haven was incorporated, with similar powers in regard to loaning the deposits received, and was further authorized to *invest* the same in the purchase of bank stock or any other public stock of any State or of the United States, but it does not appear that a bank was ever organized under this charter; and in 1821 the like privilege was accorded to the Society for Savings, by an amendment to its charter. The reference above made to "other public stocks," after the words "bank stock," suggests the inquiry whether *calling* bank stocks public stocks, even in an act of legislature, *makes* them such?

Though, under the general power conferred to loan the moneys received on deposit, Savings Banks might unquestionably accept the mortgage of real estate as security, this form of security was not specifically mentioned in any charter until 1827, when the Savings Bank of New London was incorporated, with power to loan the moneys received, by order or consent of a majority of the directors, on mortgage of real estate or other undoubted security, or to invest the same — as previous charters had authorized — in the stock of any bank in the State of Connecticut, or in the public stock of any State or of the United States. Though in the charter of the Savings Bank of New Haven, the investment in bank stock was not in terms limited to the stock of Connecticut banks, the uniformity with which, in other charters, this limitation was expressed, leads to the conclusion that the same was implied in case of the New Haven Savings Bank. In 1832, however, the privilege was accorded to the Norwich Savings Society, and to the Savings Bank of New London, to invest in the stock of any banks in the cities of New York, Boston, or Providence, also in the stock of the Bank of the United States. Thereafter there was little change of importance to notice in the powers of Savings Banks, concerning investments, until the same were modified by a general act relating to these institutions, passed in 1843.

This act prohibited the investment of the moneys or funds of Savings Banks in the stock of any bank of discount, or in the stocks or bonds of any State, city, or other corporation, or in post notes, except such investment was necessary in order to obtain the payment of a debt previously contracted and owing to any Savings Bank, and which could not be otherwise obtained. Loans, also, were prohibited unless secured by mortgage of unincumbered real estate within the State (a limitation not previously imposed), equal in value to double the amount of the loan. From this prohibition concerning loans, however, ten per cent of the amount of deposits in any Savings Bank was excepted. The perversity and inconsistency of modern legislation is exemplified in the fact that the very first charter, and, for that matter, all subsequent charters, granted after the passage of this act, conferred privileges in the matter of investment, in direct contravention of the foregoing provisions. Thus, the Derby Savings Bank, incorporated as the Derby Society for Savings, in 1846, was authorized to invest twenty-five per cent of the deposits in bank stock or United States stocks, or to loan the same on *undoubted personal security;* and the Norwich Savings Society was, by an amendment to its charter in this same year, authorized to subscribe to the stock of the Merchants' Bank. In short, Savings Banks were incorporated with powers and privileges utterly at variance with the provisions of the general law, which, so far as imposing any restraints is concerned, might as well have never been enacted.

In the charter of the Derby Savings Bank, above mentioned, there was introduced, for the first time, a feature which subsequently became as nearly the settled policy of the State, concerning the investments of Savings Banks, as any thing so capricious as legislation could become. This was an implied requirement to invest at least three-fourths of the deposits in mortgages of real estate. Subsequent charters contained, some of them a provision requiring one-fourth, others two-thirds, some one-half, to be thus invested, while many were not restricted as to the amount.

The act of 1843, above referred to, was modified, in 1847, by providing that where the deposits of any Savings Bank were less than $120,000, such Savings Bank might loan not exceeding $30,000 on such personal security as the trustees, directors or managers should approve, but not more than one-half the deposits were to be so loaned. In 1851 the act was further amended by authorizing one-half of the deposits in any Savings Bank to be loaned on personal security, all other loans to be on mortgage of real estate within the State.

Neither the act of 1843, nor this amendment in 1851, provided for any investments except in mortgages; but the charters uniformly authorized the purchase of bank stocks and United States stocks, and some of them the stocks of other States. It should have been noted, that in 1848 the Bridgeport Savings Bank was authorized to invest 15 per cent of its deposits in the bonds of the city of Bridgeport. This was the first specific recognition of municipal bonds as a desirable investment for Savings Banks, and this, as will be seen, was made in the face of the explicit prohibition in the act of 1843 concerning such investments.

After this time, a common form of authorizing investments in Savings Bank charters was in these words: "to loan or invest in a manner not inconsistent with the laws of this State," etc. Frequently, however, this would be coupled with specific provisions concerning investments, at variance with the general laws, whereby the latter would, in some of their features at least, be rendered nugatory. Thus, the Collinsville Savings Bank, besides loans on mortgages to the amount of one-fourth of the deposits, was authorized further "to invest in the stock of any banks in the State, or any other public stock of any State or of the United States, or of the cities of this State, New York, Albany, Boston or Providence, or undoubted personal security, or in a manner not inconsistent with the laws of this State," etc. Not all charters were as liberal in their provisions concerning investments as this one, but in very few of them were they held to the uncompromising strictness of the general law.

In 1858 the loans authorized on personal security were restricted to one-third of the deposits, but were restored to one-half in the following year. By the same act, in 1858, the portion of deposits (one-third, subsequently one-half) allowed to be loaned on personal security were permitted to be invested "in the public stocks of the New England States, New York, Ohio, Pennsylvania and Kentucky, or of the United States; in the stock of any bank in this State, New York city or Boston, in the public stock of any incorporated city, town or borough in this State, or of the cities of New York, Boston, Providence or Albany."

It will be seen that this was a very marked and decided enlargement of the powers of the general law, in fact exceeding the powers specifically conferred by any previous charters, except in the matter of State stocks, introducing many securities for investment not before recognized. In 1862 Savings Banks were authorized to invest a still larger proportion of their deposits in the Stocks of the New England States and of the United States, or in those of municipalities in Connecticut; and in 1868 the range of investment was extended so as to embrace the stocks of New Jersey, Ohio, Michigan, Indiana, Illinois, Wisconsin and Iowa, and of the cities of Brooklyn, Troy, Rochester and Buffalo, in addition to those previously enumerated.

It will appear from a review of the foregoing provisions, that despite the desultory and incongruous action of the legislature concerning the investments of Savings Banks, the general policy was toward the encouragement of loans upon mortgages of real estate within the State of Connecticut, in preference to other forms of investment. The impracticability of effecting such loans advantageously was doubtless the occasion of frequent appeals from the managers of Savings Banks for a removal of the restrictions imposed, and resulted, according to the temper of varying legislaures, in the changeable and capricious provisions which we have noticed.

The deposits in bank we must presume to have been made under the general powers, always sufficiently liberal for the purpose, of making loans, as there appears to be no special provision in any charter or general law upon this subject, except in case of the Norwich Savings Bank, which by an amendment of its charter in 1840, was authorized to loan moneys to any bank, notwithstanding the corporators were stockholders therein. This was done doubtless to remove the implied prohibition against such loans, found in nearly all charters, which forbid the corporators directly or indirectly to borrow the funds of the Savings Bank with which they were connected. Doubtless loans to or deposits in any bank in which such corporators were stockholders, were not commonly regarded as a violation or evasion of this provision, as we find no other instance in which the action of the legislature was invoked to remove such implied disability, though it can hardly be possible that similar conditions did not exist in many other localities.

PURCHASE OF REAL ESTATE.

Few of the original charters contain any provision authorizing the purchase of real estate for any purpose. But, as the occasion would arise with the growth and expansion of any institution, rendering the possession of a banking house desirable or necessary, the legislature was petitioned for authority to make such purchase, which was commonly conceded, but upon terms limiting such investment to a specific sum, varying, we may presume, according to the condition, ability and needs of the institution. The first act of this kind, of which I find any record, was in 1833, when the Society for Savings, at Hartford, was authorized to expend in this way not exceeding $7,000. Of course the institution has long since outgrown the facilities which such a sum would procure, and doubtless has, without difficulty, obtained the desired relief from the legislature. A few charters are found, in which a limited sum is authorized for this purpose, and one in which there is no limit, except that the investment shall only be for the use of the institution in the transaction of its business, in this respect conforming more nearly to the prevailing practice in the State of New York.

LATER LEGISLATION.

The latest legislation concerning investments, had in 1873, is in the direction of prohibition; the first excluding railroad stocks or bonds, and the other forbidding the purchase of any note, bill, draft, check, or other mercantile paper on which only one person or firm shall be holden — technically known as "one-name" paper. This seems to have been enacted in deference to the opinions of the bank commissioner, who had reported adversely to such investments. There would seem to be no occasion for the first prohibition mentioned above, as the general laws conferred no authority to make such purchases as are there excluded; nor is the power to invest in railroad securities found in but two charters, unless it is to be inferred from the broad provisions of the earlier acts of incorporation. It is evident, however, that the power to make such investments was claimed and exercised somewhat generally, and it was deemed expedient to correct, by specific prohibition, what might become, if it was not already, an abuse of discretion. The commissioner's report for 1873, indeed, shows investments in railroad stocks and bonds amounting to $1,254,707, or one and seven-tenths per cent of the assets of all Savings Banks in the State.

Two Savings Banks were in 1869 authorized to invest in the bonds of any *school district* in the State, the only instances of the kind brought to my notice.

The requirement to invest a given proportion of the deposits in any specific security had, as we have seen, been directed to mortgages of real estate, as high as three-fourths being by many charters required in this form; but in 1872 the Operatives' Savings Bank of New Haven was incorporated, and one of the provisions of its charter required one-fifth of its deposits to be invested in United States, Connecticut or New

Haven city bonds, as a special fund to meet extraordinary demands of depositors; but the total amount of this fund was limited to $100,000. This partakes somewhat of the character of what is known in New York charters as an available fund; with the advantage, however, of being limited to investment in truly available securities, and not left, as in the latter State, to be loaned on call, at the discretion of the trustees, upon the *least* available securities in the market. This departure is, however, significant only of the disposition of the legislature, and has no practical bearing, as it does not appear that the bank was organized.

SURPLUS.

None of the charters of Savings Banks in Connecticut contain any provision for the accumulation of a surplus, from which to make good any losses arising from bad debts or depreciated securities. The necessity for some provision of the kind seems first to have attracted the attention of the legislature in 1847, when it was enacted that any Savings Bank might reserve out of its surplus earnings — whatever these may be presumed to be! — "such sums as might, from time to time, be conveniently reserved, not exceeding the sum of five thousand dollars for the sum of two hundred and fifty thousand dollars of deposits," which would be two per cent upon that amount. Where the deposits of any Savings Bank exceeded the sum of $250,000, such bank might reserve one per cent upon such excess, but not to exceed in all the sum of $15,000. This was called by the act a "contingent fund," but its object was clearly the same as that of the surplus fund of the New York Savings Banks. It was further provided that the banking house or other fixtures for the use of the bank or society should form a part of said contingent fund, though such a requirement would seem to be altogether aimless and inconsequent. Yet, perhaps not more so than many other features of legislation concerning these institutions, which, like other human interests, must take their chance of being legislated upon oftentimes by bodies of men who are profoundly ignorant of their nature, purpose and needs.

In 1854 the amount of surplus or contingent fund authorized to be reserved was increased to two and one-half per cent of the total deposits; and in 1868 it was made five per cent, the banking house and fixtures to be a part of the same, as before.

LIMITATION OF INDIVIDUAL DEPOSITS.

Every Savings Bank charter in this State, I believe, has limited to a definite sum the amount that might be received from any one depositor, not in the aggregate, but in one year; and, upon the whole, this seems to be a more rational method of restricting the operations of Savings Banks to their legitimate purpose, than the New York policy of trying to limit the aggregate that may be received, but allowing that aggregate to be received in a single deposit. If one is so favorably circumstanced that he can save from his earnings $1,000 annually, it does not seem to be good policy to allow him to deposit this sum for five years in the institution of his choice, and then compel him either to withdraw and otherwise invest this accumulation, or seek a new depository for his surplus earnings thereafter. And the common and perfectly valid objection to deposits of large sums, that in time of a run their withdrawal depletes the resources of the bank too rapidly, applies with little force to large deposits which are the accumulation of a long period. I believe it will be found that the depositors who, by good fortune in business, combined with frugality, have in a series of years, accumulated very considerable sums in Savings Banks, are extremely tenacious in their hold upon the depository they have chosen. Many instances have been narrated to me by Savings Bank officers in New York, in accounting for a larger deposit than they were authorized by law to hold, of the persistence of such depositors in refusing to withdraw and invest their money, even though offered assistance in obtaining a good bond and mortgage yielding a higher rate of interest than the bank would pay. It is the large deposits in large sums, commonly placed in Savings Banks for safety and profit until a desirable form of investment presents itself, that are so sensitive in time of general financial insecurity. I cannot believe that the accumulation of quite large sums, the gradual savings of years of honest labor and fair good fortune, would subject Savings Banks to any considerable embarrassment nor to any peril.

The limit that may be received from any depositor in one year varies in the different charters, commonly from $200 to $500. In 1850 it was fixed by general statute at $400, and thereafter most charters named the same limit; some simply referred to the general law defining the limit, while a few confined the deposit to the original sum of $200. In 1872, however, the limit was fixed by general statute at $1,000. This seems, under the changed conditions and relations of things as compared with those existing when the original limit of $200 was applied, to be a very fair and rational provision.

DIVIDENDS OR INTEREST TO DEPOSITORS.

The profits of Savings Banks, credited from time to time to depositors, are called, interchangeably, interest or dividends. These profits are mainly derived from interest on investments and loans. So are those of banks of issue or joint-stock banks. The profits of the latter, distributed to shareholders, are called dividends, while those of the former, distributed to depositors, are frequently called interest. I see no good reason for this distinction in terms, applied to essentially the same thing produced in essentially the same way. Interest has a special, legal and technical signification. It is always fixed and determinate in advance, either by law or by agreement of parties. Dividends are indeterminate until earned and declared, or should be so, and bear some defined ratio to profits, as no profits, no dividend. All the characteristics of dividends attach to the distribution of profits to depositors; they have none of the characteristics of interest. I prefer, and shall therefore employ the term dividend as being more significant, truthful and appropriate.

The provision in the original charter of the Society for Savings, that the income or profits of the deposits "shall be applied and divided among the persons making the deposits, their executors or administrators, in just proportion, with such reasonable deduction as may be chargeable thereon," is substantially preserved in all subsequent charters.

This uniform provision was modified by a general act in 1847, in the following words:

"All the increase, profits and earnings on the deposits and on the contingent fund in any Savings Bank or Society, after defraying the expenses of said bank or society, as provided in its charter, and after deducting the losses of said institution, shall be semi-annually divided and applied among the depositors in the said institution, their executors or administrators, in just proportions; *provided*, no dividend need be made on any other fraction than one-half of one per cent."

TAXATION OF DEPOSITS.

As early as 1846 the deposits in Savings Banks were made the subject of taxation. The policy was to tax them as personal property, as other property was taxed; but only deposits in excess of $250 were made liable. The secretaries of the several Savings Banks were required to return to the assessors of the towns in which the depositors resided, the names of such depositors and the amount of their deposits. Non-resident depositors were also taxed in common with residents, the tax being, we presume, paid by the institutions holding the deposits, and the same was paid into the treasury of the State.

In 1852 this mode of taxing the deposits was changed, and the Savings Banks were required to pay to the treasurer of the State one-eighth of one per cent on the total amount of their deposits, which was to be in lieu of all other taxes upon the institutions or depositors therein. This tax was in 1857 increased to three-sixteenths per cent, in 1859 to one-fourth per cent, in 1862 to one-half per cent, and in 1864 to three-fourths per cent; but, under this last increase, the real estate of any Savings Bank, over and above that required and used by the institution in the transaction of its business, was also subject to taxation. In 1869 this latter rate of taxation was re-imposed, but with an exception of United States bonds, exempt from taxation, and certain bonds of the State on which the tax was one per cent.

In 1872 the rate of taxation was still further modified, so as to be one-half per cent on the deposits loaned on real estate, and one per cent on the amount of all other deposits not invested in untaxable securities, as United States bonds. The encouragement thus given to loans on real estate will be noticed.

COMPENSATION TO OFFICERS.

Under the provisions of the various charters of Savings Banks, no president, vice-president or trustee could receive any compensation for his services. This prohibition was somewhat relaxed by a general law in 1868, which authorized Savings Banks, whose deposits exceeded $500,000, to pay the president such compensation as the trustees might deem just and reasonable;

but in 1873 the salary, which any Savings Bank might pay its president, was limited, after the next annual election, to $300. Of course, merely nominal service was expected for such merely nominal pay.

BORROWING FUNDS.

One salutary provision runs through all the charters of Savings Banks in this State, as in the State of New York: "That no member of the corporation shall be the hirer or borrower, or surety for any hirer or borrower of the funds of the corporation, or any part thereof." In excluding the corporators from the relation of suretyship, the statutes of Connecticut were in advance of those in New York State.

PENALTY FOR VIOLATION OF LAW.

The act of 1858, defining what should be the loans and investments of Savings Banks, was enforced by a provision making those trustees who assented to a violation of the provisions of the act, jointly and severally liable to the Savings Bank for any loss that might result therefrom; and the penalty for violating the provisions of the act of 1873, prohibiting the taking of more than seven per cent interest upon loans, or investing in railroad stocks or bonds, was a fine of not less than $1,000 nor more than $5,000.

RATE OF INTEREST RECEIVABLE ON LOANS.

In 1873 Savings Banks were prohibited from taking more than seven per cent per annum on loans, either as bonus, commission or tax, or in any other way, directly or indirectly; but were allowed to deduct six months' interest in advance.

Why such a prohibition should be necessary, in view of a general usury law, which must have been operative upon Savings Banks as well as upon individuals, is not very clear; but it may be presumed that real or supposed abuses had grown up, which the existing laws failed to correct, as the penalty of forfeiture could only be enforced at the will of the borrowers, who, as is well known, are not prone to become parties to such a proceeding. The penalty for violating this provision, besides that of forfeiture — which we suppose still to have been operative under the general usury laws — was not less than $1,000 nor more than $5,000, and we suppose this might be sued for by the State prosecuting officer; and, as it was made the duty of the bank commissioner to require strict conformity to the provisions of the law on the part of Savings Banks, there was perhaps some likelihood that violations of the law might be detected and punished, or, what is better, prevented altogether. Still there is left unsolved the doubt why Savings Banks should have been selected for more stringent discipline in this matter than other corporations or than private individuals. The act seems to have been incited by the recommendation of the bank commissioner, as will hereafter appear, which shows, at least, that he was an independent and honest official, and not at all blind to the faults of Savings Banks, nor backward in exposing them and seeking to have them corrected.

WITHDRAWAL OF DEPOSITS.

The Savings Bank charters in this State quite uniformly contain a provision to the effect that deposits may be withdrawn upon giving some defined term of notice, commonly four months. There is, perhaps, no special advantage between this and leaving the withdrawal subject to such regulations as the board shall prescribe, as in most other States. It is certain that the notice required, when left to the discretion of the trustees, has commonly been less than the above, as defined by the statute in Connecticut.

Practically, however, it makes very little difference, for the usage we presume to be alike in all cases, to pay on demand without notice, except in seasons of peculiar exigency, rendering such course impracticable. We know, as a practical fact, that the managers of Savings Banks are very reluctant to enforce the rule requiring notice before withdrawing deposits, and in our judgment there is far more danger to the welfare of depositors, in the disposition to pay without notice, than in any abuse of the discretion with which they are invested to require it.

The subject generally will be more fully considered hereafter.

SAVING AND BUILDING ASSOCIATIONS.

These were a modification of, or innovation upon the Savings Bank system, which for a time acquired some degree of popularity in the State of Connecticut, and doubtless had the effect somewhat to attract to themselves moneys that would otherwise have found their way to the regular Savings Banks. Their object and methods will best be seen by the following summary of the general act, passed in 1850, authorizing their formation:

They were "authorized to receive deposits in payment of shares of stock or otherwise, not exceeding $1,000 from one individual in one year; to loan to members, upon real or personal security, or upon pledge of stock in the association; to receive a bonus for such loans, as might be agreed upon, in addition to legal rate of interest; to loan to those not members, at the legal rate of interest; also to purchase, with such of its funds as could not be loaned to members on good security, the stock of any city, of any incorporated bank in this State, the stock of State of Massachusetts, New York, and of United States, and no others."

They were also required to make detailed reports of their operations to the general assembly. The bank commissioner says of them, in 1855: "Their object is to furnish a place of deposit for small sums; also to use deposits and capital in making loans to stockholders on terms that will enable them to own their own dwellings."

The highest deposit was reached in 1858, when it was $2,391,302, and the stock was $2,390,643.

The result of this experiment does not appear to have been satisfactory, for in 1858 their formation thereafter was prohibited, and provision was made for closing those already formed.

CHAPTER XII.

OF SUPERVISION AND REPORTS.

The first act of a general character relating to Savings Banks in this State was in 1833, and required these institutions to make a return annually to the comptroller of public accounts, under a penalty for neglect of $100, of all moneys belonging to each of them respectively, with a statement of the amounts belonging to residents and to non-residents separately. Whether these returns were required as a basis for taxation, or for statistical information only, does not appear. I do not find any of these returns in the public documents of that early day, and hence infer that they were destroyed or pigeon-holed by the officer to whom they were directed. Access to the State records failed to disclose any of these early returns, and, if preserved, the information gleaned from them would doubtless be very meager and unsatisfactory.

In 1837 provision was made for the appointment of two bank commissioners, but the act conferred no powers or duties upon these officers in connection with Savings Banks. I do not find such powers specifically conferred until 1853; but the commissioners report, in 1846, that they had required statements from and had examined every Savings Bank in the State. They speak of their appointment "last year" (1845), and also refer to the same in "1844." In this report —

apparently the earliest published document on the subject, the commissioners make a few judicious and timely observations concerning Savings Banks; but the bulk of the text, as also of the tabular statistics, relates to banks of issue. There is indeed no summary made of the statements of Savings Banks. These will be found in their appropriate place in this volume, and form the starting point in the statistical history of these institutions in this State.

As we cannot suppose the bank commissioners would have charged themselves with this duty without authority, it is perhaps fair to presume that I have somehow overlooked the act conferring it, although I have diligently and carefully examined the statutes to find when the relation thus assumed was instituted, and find nothing until the act of 1853, above noted.

The act of 1843, which we have before cited under the topic of Investments, further made it the duty of some officer of every Savings Bank, annually, on or before the second Wednesday of May, "To transmit to the general assembly a statement, under oath, of the condition of the institution of which he is treasurer, secretary or clerk, on the first day of April, specifying the number of the present depositors, the amount of deposits, the amount deposited in the past year, and the amount of deposits withdrawn, the amount and rate of dividends, the balance of profit and loss, the amount of expenses for the year, the amount of interest due and unpaid, the amount loaned on real estate, the amount loaned on stocks and other personal estate, the amount loaned on notes not secured, the amount invested in real estate and the locality thereof, and the amount invested in stocks, bonds, or other personal estate, specifying the name and quantity thereof; and if the treasurer, secretary or clerk of any Savings Bank or Savings Society shall neglect or refuse to make such statement as aforesaid, he shall forfeit and pay to the treasurer of the State a sum not less than ten nor more than one hundred dollars, according to the nature and circumstances of the case."

I have no means of knowing how fully this requirement was complied with, as the returns, if made, were not published. I have a conviction that they were generally made, and filed without notice or any action thereon. I found in the office of the secretary of state, at Hartford, the original returns for the years 1848, 1849 and 1851. The returns for 1850 could not be found, nor for previous nor subsequent years. Yet it is very possible that they are somewhere in his office, and will be brought to light when, upon the completion of the new State house, now in progress, the removal of his office to more commodious quarters shall afford opportunity for filing, arranging and depositing such documents in proper order and accessible place, which, in his present crowded and overflowing apartments, is simply impossible. Every facility for the prosecution of my search, which his office afforded, was freely extended to me; and for the interest manifested and the assistance rendered by the *attaches* of the office, I desire to express my grateful acknowledgments.

The report of the bank commissioners for 1847 I have been unable to find among any of the published documents of that State; but the report of these officers, made in 1855, refers to it, and gives the number of depositors and the amount on deposit, as stated in that report — the former being 22,663, and the latter

$3,221,591. It is only in this way that I have been able to give, by even *quasi* authority, these items for that year. The corresponding items for 1848, 1849 and 1851 were obtained, as above stated, by copying from the original returns of Savings Banks, made to the general assembly in those years.

Finding no returns for 1850, I was compelled to make an estimate from the best data I could procure. These I found in the report of the comptroller of public accounts, who in his report in 1852, remarks that the deposits of Savings Banks reported to the legislature of 1851 was very nearly $4,500,000. As the reports made for April 1, 1851, show a deposit of nearly $5,500,000, I infer that the report to which he alludes must be that showing the condition of Savings Banks in 1850.

That he was not referring to the returns for 1851, is evident from the fact that he estimates these, not yet returned, at $5,000,000, which, as will be seen, was nearly half a million short of the true amount.

On the strength of that statement of the comptroller of public accounts, I estimate the deposits in 1850 at $4,450,000, which besides being in accord with his statement, corresponds with a rational presumption founded upon the rate of growth in former and in subsequent years.

For the years 1852 and 1853, I found no returns from Savings Banks, but the report of the comptroller of public accounts gives the amount of deposits on the 1st of July in each of these years, as returned for taxation, and I have used the figures as given by him, though I am not sure whether these represent the total deposits or only those in excess of $250. I am inclined to believe, from the correspondence in the aggregates, with what might be presumed to be the rational increase from year to year, that they represent the entire deposits. In the first of these years, however (1852), the deposits of the Waterbury Savings Bank are not included, though the bank was certainly in operation, having reported in 1851 and being reported by the comptroller in 1853. Comparing the returns of these two years, being respectively $11,544 and $31,084, I estimate its deposits in 1852 at $20,000, and have so changed the aggregate of the comptroller's returns for that year. The number of open accounts for these years are estimated at 40,000 in 1852, and 45,000 in 1853, the same being reported in 1851 at 37,808, and on the 1st of January, 1854, at 50,950. My estimates are, therefore, upon these data, clearly within the facts. In this way I am enabled to fill the period from 1846 to 1854, for which there are no returns of Savings Banks in the volumes of documents published in this State. Indeed, it was not until after 1850 that there was any uniformity or system pursued in printing and publishing, still less in preserving legislative or other documents.

In 1854, and thereafter, the returns of Savings Banks form a permanent feature in the documentary volumes of the State, and from these the aggregates in our tables are thereafter derived.

At the legislative session in May, 1848, the joint committee on banks report that the deposits in Savings

Banks amount to nearly $4,000,000, the amount as will be seen from our table was $3,686,805, and they recommend that these institutions be placed under the supervision of the bank commissioners. It would appear from this that they were not under such supervision in 1848, whatever may have been their status in 1846.

As has been already stated, this recommendation received legislative sanction in 1853, when the bank commissioners were authorized to visit and examine Savings Banks, and were required to report the results to the general assembly.

The first published report concerning Savings Banks after that already noted in 1846, was made for the 1st of January, after the passage of the above act. This gives the year of incorporation, the number of depositors, the amount deposited and withdrawn during the year, the amount due depositors, and the surplus of each institution in the State. From this it appears that the amounts deposited and withdrawn during 1853 were, respectively, $2,471,721 and $1,278,928, and the surplus reported $101,034; other items will be found in the tables herewith.

The text of the commissioners' report, in the year 1855, contains nothing of interest. In 1856 they call attention to the fact that some Savings Banks have failed to comply with the law requiring one-half of the deposits to be loaned upon the security of real estate, and deprecate the investment of so large a proportion, as is the practice with some institutions, in miscellaneous stocks and bonds.

In 1857 the report shows that more than half the deposits were loaned on mortgage, and the remainder nearly equally divided between various bonds and stocks and loans on personal security, the latter preponderating. The commissioners again express their disapproval of these investments, and especially oppose the practice of loaning money out of the State in order to realize seven per cent. The same topics form the staple of successive reports, and more stringent legislation is recommended to correct the practices complained of, which resulted in the passage of the act, in 1858, regulating the loans and investments of Savings Banks in accordance with the recommendations of the commissioners. The commissioners also comment on the careless and negligent methods in the transaction of business which characterized certain institutions, such as taking stock collaterals without having the same transferred, and discounting notes without the indorsement of the parties in whose favor or for whose benefit they were discounted.

In 1859 the condition was reported to be much improved, though the making of loans outside the State and buying business paper at considerable discount was still prevalent. The commissioners express, in this report, a doubt of the ability of Savings Banks to continue paying to depositors so high a rate of dividends as six per cent, which appears at this time, and for some time previous, to have been the prevailing rate.

In 1860 the commissioners use the following language:

"The laws upon our statute books relating to Savings Banks are, in the opinion of the commissioners, inadequate to the proper protection of their depositors. Their hitherto good management has been secured more by the character and integrity of the persons who had them in charge than from the protection which has been afforded them by our laws."

They also make various recommendations which in their judgment will add to the security of depositors, some of which were incorporated into subsequent legislation. Reference is again made, by the commissioners, to the dangers attending the effort to pay six per cent to depositors, and a limitation to five and one-half per cent recommended; and the same subject engages their attention the following year.

The act of 1862, giving to Savings Banks a wider range of investments, is referred to by the commissioners in their report, in 1863, as having proved salutary in practice, and they declare that no further legislation is necessary. It should also be noted, in this connection, that the legislature of 1862 required from Savings Banks much more full and complete returns than they had made hitherto, and these were now to be made to the bank commissioners, and not to the general assembly. In these returns they were to present a complete balance-sheet of their transactions, which would of course reveal, not only the amount of moneys received from all sources, but what had been done with them in the way of investments, losses and expenses. Any form of Savings Bank reports that falls shorts of this is, in so far as it falls short, defective.

In 1864 the commissioners report an improvement in the condition and workings of Savings Banks generally. Much of this was doubtless due to the facilities which the time afforded for making safe and profitable investments in the securities of the United States government; and the same conditions had greatly stimulated the increase of deposits, which now amounted to nearly $27,000,000.

A summary of the assets of Savings Banks is given in the report, as follows:

Loans on real estate	$12, 850, 258
Loans on stocks and bonds	1, 994, 657
Loans on personal security	1, 306, 026
Invested in bank stocks	1, 598, 014
Invested in railroad stocks and bonds	868, 715
Invested in United States government securities,	6, 481, 530
Invested in real estate and other	1, 666, 500
	$26, 765, 700
Deposits reported at	$26, 954, 802

This would seem to show a deficiency, which may arise from reporting assets at cost which, taken at their market value, would produce a surplus.

In 1865 we gather from the commissioners' report the following items of general interest: Of the 48 institutions reporting, one paid dividends at the rate of six and one-half per cent; 20, of six per cent; nine of five and one-half per cent; and 18, of five per cent. The amount of taxes paid to the State was $178,310.77, and to the United States $65,734.37, making a total in taxes of $244,045.14, being about eight-tenths of one per cent on their deposits. With such dividends and such a burden of taxation, it is not surprising that there should be a deficiency in the assets, at *cost*, to meet the liabilities. This burden of taxation does not escape the notice of the commissioners, who recommend a change in the system whereby large depositors may be made subject to local taxation, like the owners of other personal property, and small depositors be exempted altogether.

The report made in 1866 of the operations in 1865, comments upon the very considerable decrease in the deposits, amounting to nearly $2,000,000, and accounts for it upon the ground of the favorable opportunity for investing in government securities commanding a higher profit than Savings Bank deposits. But this cause had been equally operative during the two or three years previous, while the deposits had been steadily increasing. A more rational explanation of this decrease, which was by no means confined to the State of Connecticut, is to be found in the fact of the return to their homes of thousands of soldiers, who, before leaving for the war, had deposited their bounty money in the Savings Banks, and now withdrew it to use in business or for other purposes. Very many of them, besides their bounty money, managed to put by a part of their wages, and on their return had a very considerable capital with which to commence business. In this year, the duties of commissioner were, at the June session, devolved upon a single officer, and were so performed down to and during the remaining period covered by this history.

The investments of Savings Banks then stood as follows:

Loans on real estate	$11,491,197
" " stocks and bonds	1,470,786
" " personal securities	1,281,456
Invested in bank stocks	2,041,519
" " railroad stocks and bonds	784,973
" " United States bonds	8,194,220
" " real estate	194,239
	$25,458,390
Deposits	27,319,013
Apparent deficiency	$1,860,623
United States tax paid	$153,436
State tax paid	192,128
Total	$345,564

In 1867 the commissioner reports that several Savings Banks pay seven per cent dividends, and recommends that they be restricted by law to six per cent. The loans on real estate, otherwise mortgages, had risen to over $13,000,000, and the investments in United States stocks to over $9,000,000.

In the following year these had become, mortgages, $16,787,715, and United States bonds, $10,191,713. The commissioner recommends that a surplus of five per cent be authorized, and that the commissioner have power to make such discretionary order as he may deem expedient where he finds the business of any Savings Bank conducted in an illegal or unsafe manner. This seems to have been suggested by a similar recommendation in the New York report of the previous year. These recommendations were favorably considered by the legislature, and laws to give effect to the same were enacted. Another recommendation made by the commissioner, was favorably considered by the legislature in the enactment of a law requiring the trustees of each Savings Bank annually to appoint not less than two auditors, not trustees, to examine the books, accounts and securities, and make a sworn statement of the condition of the institution, in January of each year, one copy to be forwarded to the bank commissioner and one to be placed on file in the bank examined.

In 1869 the loans on real estate had increased to $21,031,619, or more than one-half of the assets, and the investment in United States bonds amounted to $10,585,029. The amount of State tax paid was $340,332, and to the United States government $61,516.

In 1870 the loans on real estate had increased to $26,081,162, and there was a small reduction in the amount of government bonds. The amount of taxes paid to the State was $312,000, and to the government, $73,706.

Attention is called, in the report of 1871, to the evils arising from granting special privileges to certain Savings Banks, in their charters, and uniformity is recommended. From this it appears that the disposition of managers of Savings Banks, and the pliancy or negligence of legislators, were very much the same in Connecticut as in other States. Various infractions of the law are commented upon, and more stringent penalties recommended. A limitation of dividends to six per cent is again urged, and that the surplus allowed be increased to ten per cent. This report contains a summary of the condition of the Savings Banks in New England at the close of 1869, except in the State of Vermont, in which Savings Banks never attained a high degree of efficiency. This summary we will reproduce here, as follows:

	Number of banks.	Number of depositors.	Amount of deposits.
Massachusetts	131	431,769	$112,119,016
Rhode Island	25	67,238	27,067,072
Maine	36	39,527	10,490,368
New Hampshire	45	71,536	18,759,461
Connecticut	58	165,692	47,904,834
	295	775,762	$216,340,751
Add Vermont, as derived for this History	11	11,000	2,740,278
Total	306	786,762	$219,081,029

The report in 1872 attributes the rapid increase of deposits to the disregard of the law limiting the amount receivable from one person, and discountenances the deposit of large sums. The commissioner fails to give any data for his conclusions, and the increase in the aggregate of deposits does not of necessity establish any infraction of the law, which, by permitting deposits of $400 from any depositor in one year, would allow of a much greater increase than that made. In this year, as we have elsewhere noted, the amount receivable from one depositor was increased to $1,000. It appears from the report, also, that the practice of discounting what was known as "one-name paper" was not wholly discontinued.

In 1873 we find a somewhat interesting *résumé* of the progress of Savings Banks in the State, from which it appears that the whole number of depositors since the organization of the earliest Savings Bank in the State, down to first January, 1873, was 541,887, or more than the entire population of the State in 1870. It is much to be regretted that we could not have also a statement of the total deposits and of the interest credited since the first Savings Bank was organized. In 1872 there was deposited, including interest, $21,-864,553, and withdrawn $15,979,628. Sixty per cent of the deposits was loaned on real estate, amounting to $43,174,000. The State tax paid in 1872 was $448,567, and to the United States $173,912.

The report opposes the practice of investing in railroad bonds as being against the perfect security of depositors, which should be the first consideration. It is also stated that, since the repeal of the usury laws, some Savings Banks are charging eight per cent for loans on real estate, and the practice is strongly condemned.

The failure of the Staffordville Savings Bank is noted, as the necessary consequence of investments and loans — railroad and personal securities — not authorized by law.

CHAPTER XIII.

STATISTICS OF GROWTH AND PROGRESS.

The following statements embrace all the statistics of growth and progress which I have received from Savings Banks in answer to my inquiries for information thereon. It will be found that these are in many cases incomplete, the amount deposited and the total amount of dividends credited not being included. As there is no source of information from which these facts can be derived, outside of the institutions themselves, the record is as nearly complete as it could be made. I regret that it covers the transactions of so few institutions in the State, and that concerning so many of these it is defective in the respects indicated. Perhaps in some future edition of this work it may be practicable to make good the deficiencies herein acknowledged and apparent. We will at least indulge such hope.

STATISTICS FURNISHED BY SAVINGS BANKS.

Society for Savings, Hartford.

Statistics January 1, 1874.

Date of first deposit, June 14, 1819.

Whole number of accounts opened	90, 468
" " " " closed	66, 619
Number of open accounts	23, 849
Amount on deposit	$7, 135, 608

Whole amount deposited, and of dividends, not given.

WILLIMANTIC SAVINGS INSTITUTE.

Statistics January 1, 1874.

Date of first deposit, June 28, 1842.

Whole number of accounts opened	7,398
" " " " closed	4,633
Number of open accounts	2,765
Amount on deposit	$753,032

Whole amount deposited, and of dividends, not given.

The treasurer, H. F. Royce, Esq., says the institution has never failed to make regular semi-annual dividends, which is not, however, an exceptional experience, and that it has always paid depositors on demand without notice. It did this even during the panic of 1873, when over one-eighth of its deposits were withdrawn, nearly all of which was returned within the next three months. It claims a surplus of nearly ten per cent, seven and three-tenths, which is unusually large in that State.

DEEP RIVER SAVINGS BANK.

Statistics January 1, 1874.

Date of first deposit, July 29, 1851.

Whole number of accounts opened	2,551
" " " " closed	1,500
Number of open accounts	1,051
Amount deposited, including dividends	$749,487
Amount withdrawn	446,704
Amount on deposit	302,783
Amount of dividends credited	154,546

The foregoing was furnished by the treasurer, R. P. Spencer, Esq.

GROTON SAVINGS BANK, MYSTIC RIVER.

Statistics January 1, 1874.

Date of first deposit, July 14, 1854.

Whole number of accounts opened..............	3, 750
" " " " closed...............	2, 275
Number of open accounts.......................	1, 475
Amount on deposit............................	$562, 466
Amount of dividends credited...................	311, 721

Whole amount deposited not given.

CONNECTICUT SAVINGS BANK, NEW HAVEN.

Statistics January 1, 1874.

Date of first deposit, July 8, 1857.

Whole number of accounts opened........ about	20, 000
" " " " closed......... "	15, 344
Number of open accounts......................	4, 656
Amount on deposit..........................	$2, 045, 430

The above are all the items furnished.

WESTPORT SAVINGS BANK.

Statistics January 1, 1874.

Date of first deposit, September 1, 1860.

Whole number of accounts opened............	773
" " " " closed..............	416
Number of open accounts......................	357
Amount deposited, including dividends	$210, 001
Amount withdrawn	127, 943
Amount on deposit..........................	82, 058

The amount of dividends credited is not given; but, on so moderate a sum deposited in thirteen years, these must be small.

Mechanics' Savings Bank, Hartford.

Statistics January 1, 1874.

Date of first deposit, January 4, 1862.

Whole number of accounts opened	5, 198
" " " " closed	2, 722
Number of open accounts	2, 476
Amount deposited, including dividends	$2, 384, 457
Amount withdrawn	1, 416, 015
Amount on deposit	968, 442
Amount of dividends	276, 797

Savings Bank of New Britain.

Statistics January 1, 1874.

Date of first deposit, August 26, 1862.

Whole number of accounts opened	4, 783
" " " " closed	2, 528
Number of open accounts	2, 255
Amount deposited, including dividends	$1, 751, 839
Amount withdrawn	1, 141, 028
Amount on deposit	610, 811
Amount of dividends credited	159, 027

The treasurer, S. Rockwell, Esq., who furnishes the data for the above, deprecates the "tinkering" of the Savings Bank laws by the legislature, from year to year, with little knowledge of their character, condition or needs, as calculated to create distrust of their soundness in the minds of depositors. He favors the fostering care of the State through intelligent and well-considered legislation, guarding against abuses, but not embarrassing by onerous requirements and restrictions that do not conduce to security.

DIME SAVINGS BANK OF NORWICH.

Statistics January 1, 1874.

Date of first deposit, September 27, 1869.

Whole number of accounts opened (new)	5, 893
" " " " closed.............	1, 315
Number of open accounts....................	4, 578
Amount deposited, including dividends........	$1, 108, 500
Amount withdrawn	358, 294
Amount on deposit..........................	750, 206
Dividends credited..........................	78, 534

MOODUS SAVINGS BANK.

Statistics January 1, 1874.

Date of first deposit, September 3, 1870.

Whole number of accounts opened...............	498
" " " " closed...............	76
Number of open accounts......................	422
Amount deposited, including dividends	$85, 433
Amount withdrawn...........................	27, 871
Amount on deposit............................	57, 562
Amount of dividends credited	5, 749

The institution suffered a loss by robbery in April last, but passed a dividend and went on.

DIME SAVINGS BANK OF HARTFORD.

Statistics January 1, 1874.

Date of first deposit, October 1, 1870.

Whole number of accounts opened.............	10, 268
" " " " closed..............	2, 683
Number of open accounts....................	7, 585
Amount deposited, including dividends........	$1, 323, 472
Amount withdrawn........................	823, 846
Amount on deposit..........................	499, 626
Amount of dividends	44, 398

Windsor Locks Savings Bank.

Statistics January 1, 1874.

Date of first deposit, August 15, 1871.

Whole number of accounts opened	411
" " " " closed	106
Number of open accounts	305
Amount deposited, including dividends	$83, 344
Amount withdrawn	42, 166
Amount on deposit	41, 178
Amount of dividends credited	3, 990

Cromwell Dime Savings Bank.

Statistics January 1, 1874.

Date of first deposit, October 2, 1871.

Whole number of accounts opened	356
" " " " closed	117
Number of open accounts	239
Amount deposited, including dividends	$116, 471
Amount withdrawn	73, 654
Amount on deposit	42, 817
Amount of dividends credited	5, 061

Woodbury Savings Bank.

Statistics January 1, 1874.

Date of first deposit, July 11, 1872.

Whole number of accounts opened	315
" " " " closed	29
Number of open accounts	286
Amount deposited, including dividends	$32, 572
Amount withdrawn	4, 114
Amount on deposit	28, 458
Amount of dividends credited	1, 201

Stafford Savings Bank.

Statistics January 1, 1874.

Date of first deposit, ————, 1872.

Whole number of accounts opened	549
" " " " closed	55
Number of open accounts	494
Amount deposited, including dividends	$167,498
Amount withdrawn	23,093
Amount on deposit	144,405
Amount of dividends credited	3,725

This young and small institution makes three and one-half per cent semi-annual dividends.

GENERAL STATISTICS OF GROWTH AND PROGRESS.

The growth of Savings Banks in the State of Connecticut will be seen from the following tables, made up, so far as the material of the reports would admit, after the plan of those showing the growth of the system in Massachusetts. The percentage of increase in accounts and deposits for each year is not sought to be given here, as there is no material significance in these minute expressions of change, and the percentage in periods of five years gives a much more clear and satisfactory view of the growth of this interest than the same for each year. This will be apparent upon referring to the corresponding table for the State of Massachusetts, *ante*, pp. 114, 115, where the yearly percentage of growth is given.

In the following table is exhibited a comparison between the conditions of the institutions first reporting in Connecticut in 1846, and of the same institutions as reported on the 1st of January, 1874, also a comparison of the amount on deposit at the former period and the amount deposited during the year 1873, in the same institutions.

NAME OF INSTITUTION.	CONDITION APR. 1, 1846.		CONDITION JAN. 1, 1874.		Amount deposited in 1873.
	Open acc'ts.	Amount due depositors.	Open acc'ts.	Amount due depositors.	
Bridgeport....	761	$125,791	7,013	$2,860,240	$629,914
Middletown...	3,478	548,308	8,972	5,502,074	1,427,936
New Haven...	2,294	403,238	12,000	3,757,983	1,049,001
Norwich......	2,448	357,708	12,744	7,320,524	1,205,541
New London..	1,246	240,779	5,954	2,868,520	460,239
Plainfield.....	125	18,610	closed	....	....
Tolland.......	559	52,437	766	284,313	50,581
Sav. So. Hart..	7,898	976,963	23,849	7,135,608	1,389,606
Willimantic...	215	22,128	2,765	753,032	220,663
9 Institutions.	19,024	$2,745,965	74,063	$30,482,294	$6,433,481

Our next table presents a comparison of the investments of Savings Banks in 1846 and in 1873. The percentage of the different classes of securities preserves a remarkable uniformity. The same is true of the surplus, while the rate of dividends exhibits a material increase, corresponding with that in other States:

INVESTMENTS.	April, 1846.		January, 1874.	
	Amount.	Per cent.	Amount.	Per cent.
Bonds and mortgages......	$2,203,046	77.7	$47,226,893	63
Public funds, viz:	45,175	1.6	10,857,519	14.7
U. S. bonds..............	13,000	....	4,039,564	.....
State bonds..............	3,000	....	....	.....
City, county and town....	29,175	....	*6,817,955	.....
Bank and railroad stocks and bonds...............	171,112	6	4,877,370	6.6
Real estate................	7,000	0.2	519,840	0.7
Loans on bank and other stocks	69,405	2.4	4,061,936	5.5
Loans on personal security..	231,434	8.2	4,534,881	6
Cash on hand	78,724	2.8	1,403,023	2
Miscellaneous	11,627	0.4	196.117	0.3
Surplus	71,467	3	2,756,767	3.7
Dividends..................	120,915	4.4	4,202,649	5.9

* State, city, etc.

TABLE exhibiting the number, condition and progress of Savings Banks in Connecticut from April, 1846, to January 1, 1874.

DATE.	No. of banks.	Open accounts.	Gain in open accounts.	Due to depositors.	Gain in deposits.	Gain in Accounts in Periods of 5 Years. Amount.	Gain in Accounts in Periods of 5 Years. Per cent.	Gain in Deposits in Periods of 5 Years. Amount.	Gain in Deposits in Periods of 5 Years. Per cent.
April, 1846	9	19,024	....	$2,745,965	....	First period from April, 1846, to January, 1854, 7¾ yrs.		First period from April, 1846, to January, 1854, 7¾ yrs.	
" 1847	9	22,663	3,639	3,221,591	475,526				
" 1848	9	26,557	3,894	3,686,805	465,214				
" 1849	10	28,675	2,118	3,962,680	275,875				
" 1850	....	32,000	3,325	4,450,000	487,320				
" 1851	15	37,808	5,808	5,466,444	1,016,444				
July, 1852	20	40,000	2,192	6,698,158	1,231,714				
" 1853	21	45,000	5,000	8,135,016	1,436,858				
Jan'y, 1854	23	50,950	5,950	8,883,397	748,381	31,936	168	$6,137,432	223
" 1855	26	54,589	3,639	10,006,131	1,122,734				
" 1856	28	56,000	1,411	10,844,933	838,802				
" 1857	29	61,392	5,392	12,162,136	1,317,203				
" 1858	29	48,027	—13,365	12,562,594	400,458				
" 1859	35	66,709	18,682	14,052,181	1,489,586	15,759	31	5,168,784	58
" 1860	37	75,792	9,083	16,565,284	2,513,103				
" 1861	44	84,614	8,822	19,377,670	2,812,386				
" 1862	45	88,373	3,759	19,983,959	606,287				
" 1863	49	103,727	15,354	23,146,936	3,162,979				
" 1864	48	116,681	12,954	26,954,802	3,807,886	49,972	75	12,902,621	92
" 1865	49	121,682	5,001	29,142,288	2,187,486				

"	1866	50	107,572	— 14,110	—27,319,013	1,823,275				
"	1867	54	127,004	19,432	31,224,464	3,905,451				
"	1868	54	138,846	11,842	36,283,460	5,058,996				
"	1869	55	149,919	11,073	41,803,681	5,520,221	33,238	28	14,848,879	55
"	1870	58	165,692	15,773	47,904,834	6,101,153				
"	1871	64	177,887	12,195	55,297,705	7,392,871				
"	1872	73	189,087	11,200	62,717,814	7,420,109				
"	1873	78	201,742	12,655	68,523,397	5,805,583				
"	1874	79	204,741	2,999	70,769,407	2,246,010	54,822	37	28,965,726	70

The decrease in accounts during 1857 and 1865, and in the amount of deposits during the latter year, will be noted. That in the accounts in 1857 is inexplicable in view of the gain, though small, in the amount of deposits. That there should be some decrease in the number of accounts, though a gain in the deposits, is not remarkable; but so large a difference as that found above — over 13,000 — does not seem reasonable. Very possibly the 48,027 is a misprint for 58,027, which would make the decrease 3,365 only. But the figures are as reported for that year, and I have no data, except conjecture, for correcting them. The decrease in both accounts and deposits, in 1865, is rational, and the causes are considered elsewhere.

The report for January 1, 1875, shows the following: Number of banks, 86; open accounts, 206,274; increase, 1,533; due depositors, $73,783,802; increase, $3,014,394; surplus, $2,992,219; increase, $235,452.

— Decrease.

FOURTH SECTION;

SAVINGS BANKS IN THE STATE OF RHODE ISLAND.

CHAPTER XIV.

INCEPTION AND COURSE OF LEGISLATION.

The first Savings Bank incorporated in the State of Rhode Island was "The Savings Bank of Newport," in June, 1819, the charter of which will be found in the appendix.

In October of that year the Providence Institution for Savings was incorporated, the charter of which, though less minute and elaborate, conferred substantially the same powers as the former.

The Bristol Institution for Savings was incorporated also in the same year, with substantially the same provisions in its charter as the Providence, but appears not to have organized under that charter. It was re-incorporated in 1841. Thus the smallest State in the Union had, in 1819, incorporated three Savings Banks, while no other State, except Massachusetts, had chartered more than one. The two institutions which organized are in a flourishing condition at this time, and have worthily fulfilled the expectations founded upon them.

Their condition at the date of their last annual statements, December 4, 1873, was as follows:

Savings Bank of Newport.

Resources.

Mortgages	$1,050,117 72
Stock investments	216,940 00
Invested in bonds	2,227,890 00
Loaned on public bonds	79,000 00
Cash on hand	38,321 94
Banking house	30,000 00
Total resources	$3,642,269 66

Liabilities.

Due depositors	$3,510,758 76
Profits (surplus)	131,510 90
Total liabilities	$3,642,269 66

Number of depositors, 4,897. Rate of last dividend, six months, three and one-half per cent. Average rate of annual dividends last three years, seven per cent.

Providence Institution for Savings.

Resources.

Mortgages	$3,016,916 20
Stock investments	333,400 00
Invested in bonds	1,553,000 00
Loaned on personal security	1,390,854 47
Loaned on collaterals	537,300 00
Cash on hand	135,804 89
Real estate	30,000 00
Total	$6,997,275 56

Liabilities.

Due depositors	$6,739,579 06
Profits	257,696 50
Total	$6,997,275 56

Number of depositors, 17,415. Rate of last dividend, six months, three and one-half per cent. Average rate of annual dividends, last three years, seven per cent.

No more Savings Banks were incorporated until 1828, when the Pawtucket Institution for Savings was chartered, with powers substantially the same as those conferred on the Providence Institution. The institution, however, did not organize until 1836, under a re-enactment of substantially the old form of charter. The amount of deposits which it might in the aggregate receive was limited in the act to $100,000, which limitation was extended in 1846 to $300,000. Subsequent legislation must have been invoked to remove this restriction also, for in December, 1873, it held deposits amounting to more than $2,000,000. Indeed, the restriction thus very commonly imposed in charters must have been as commonly removed.

In 1832 the Warren Seamen's Friend Society was incorporated with power to receive deposits, and the surplus was to be devoted to the general and benevolent objects of that society. As might have been anticipated, the institution did not succeed as a Savings Bank, for the reason, probably, that when people put money in a bank they expect to derive some profit therefrom, and most people like to select their own objects of charity.

The Warwick Institution for Savings, and the Woonsocket were both incorporated in 1845.

FORM OF ORGANIZATION.

The policy adopted in Rhode Island as well as in some of the other States, was to provide for a large body of corporators, who were to choose from their number the president, vice-presidents, and a designated number of directors, who together should constitute a board of trustees, to whom the management of the affairs of the institution was committed. In the case of the Providence Institution the corporators were 126 in number, but seven of these constituted a quorum.

Such a form of organization doubtless has certain advantages over that of a smaller number of corporators, who are themselves the board of trustees, and directly control the management of the institution.

Among these advantages is the association of a larger number of persons of character and influence, having a responsible connection with the institution, and being in a degree interested in its success and prosperity. The name, fame and credit of the institution will thus be more widely extended than if limited by the association therewith of a smaller number of names.

We can easily enough perceive other incidental advantages attending this form of organization, such as the ease with which the responsible management can, at each recurring anniversary meeting, be re-formed, and discordant elements eliminated. We do not see how the corporators could have any personal interest to serve, incompatible with the interests of the institution. Their power in connection with the direction was exercised only in the election of the board of trustees. The annual recurrence of this duty would bring in review the character of the previous management, and result in a vote of confidence or lack of confidence, according as the duties devolving upon the board of trustees had been well or ill discharged, which would naturally be indicated by their re-election or the election of others in their places. In any event, the fact that the management was thus liable to review at each recurring annual meeting, could hardly fail to exert a wholesome, restraining influence.

Under the form of organization which commits the control and direction of affairs to the whole body of corporators, instances are not unfrequent, in which ambitions, jealousies, and sometimes mere perversity of disposition, have seriously impaired the effectiveness of administration which ought to prevail, and which, but for these discordant elements, might prevail. If in such cases there were an intelligent constituency, of character and influence, sufficiently numerous to remove all likelihood of being controlled by interested motives, yet not so numerous as to destroy all sense of personal responsibility, to whom the existence of such conditions could be made known, and who might quietly bring to bear that powerful remedial agent in such cases, the silent vote, we can but think many of the evils and annoyances that attend the permanent form of corporate control, as at present exercised in some States, would cease to exist, and, when found interposing themselves, would easily — almost unconsciously — be removed.

In these respects, therefore, if in no others, we think this form of organization superior to that which commits to the body of corporators the direction of affairs, and invests each corporator with functions, for the indiscreet exercise of which he can never be called to account. What disadvantages such a system may possess, the writer has no means of knowing from any personal acquaintance with its practical workings.

INVESTMENTS.

It will be seen, from the provisions of the earliest charters, that, while an effort was made to give legislative direction and limitation to the investments of Savings Banks, or at least an indication of preference concerning their character, by designating "public stocks, either of the United States, this State, or some of the towns thereof," and also bank stock, as those among which it should be the duty of the trustees to invest, the practical force of this as a limitation was quite broken and destroyed by the further mention of "private securities, at the discretion of a standing committee of the board," which practically left the range of investments quite unlimited.

The various charters subsequently granted do not appear to have varied materially, in this respect, from the foregoing; whence we may infer that the discretion conferred was so far wisely exercised as not to invite criticism. The departures from the provisions above set forth were more in the form of statement than in any essential broadening or narrowing of the powers conferred, as where the phraseology which we have noted as common in other States was sometimes adopted, of requiring the moneys deposited, "to be used and improved to the best advantage."

While, therefore, the form of charters was somewhat varied, there was not such difference in the powers really conferred as to give to any one institution any considerable advantage over others, and we find a very considerable degree of uniformity in the classes of investments reported by the different banks.

Not until 1858 was there any general law designed to promote uniformity in respect to investments, and to impose upon all Savings Bank alike, certain defined limitations to their discretion. This was sought to be effected by the following provisions of sections 56 and 57 of chapter 273, Laws of 1858:

"SEC. 56. All institutions for savings may, and shall hereafter, invest their receipts in such public stocks of any State, or of the United States, or in any bank stock, or in notes or bonds of any town or city, or other public securities, as they may deem safe and secure; or they may discount, in accordance with the provisions of sections 24 and 25 of this act, the notes, bonds or drafts of individuals or corporations, secured by the public notes, by bonds or stocks aforesaid, or by mortgage of real estate.

"SEC. 57. Not more than one-half its receipts shall be invested in notes, bonds or drafts of individuals, or corporations, unless secured as above; but such reasonable amount as is customary, or may be deemed proper, may be deposited in bank, payable on demand, whether drawing interest or not."

In one direction the foregoing extended the area of investment to quite a large number of Savings Banks which by their charters were prohibited from investing by not being permitted to invest in the public securities of other States. As we have seen, all were not thus limited, being permitted to exercise absolute discretion as to the character of their investments, under the elastic phrase "to be used and improved to the best advantage." But by the foregoing the securities of any State were, in specific terms, authorized for investment.

REPORTS AND SUPERVISION.

The earliest action of the Rhode Island legislature looking in the direction of making the trustees of Saving Banks account to the State for the manner in which their trust was executed, was the adoption of a resolution by the general assembly at the June session in 1848, requiring these institutions to make a return of their condition on the first Monday in July following. There were then seven institutions in operation, if we include the Warren Seamen's Friend Society which had a merely nominal existence, and was half bank and half a charitable association. Of these seven institutions, all except the Bristol reported their condition under the above-mentioned resolution; and at the October session of the general assembly the secretary of State was directed to publish the same. These reports being so few in number as not to greatly encumber this history, are elsewhere given in detail.

In 1849 the action of the general assembly took the more defined and permanent form of a legislative act, requiring returns from these institutions of their condition on the first Monday in October to be made annually to the general assembly.

Such returns were to embrace the following particulars:

Amount of deposits.

Number of depositors.

Number whose deposits were under $100; between $100 and $200; between $200 and $500; between $500 and $1,000; and those of $1,000 and over.

Largest amount due to any depositor.

Amount invested in bonds and mortgages.

Amount invested in stocks, specifying the same, with names of institutions (or corporations) in which stocks were held, with the respective amounts.

Amount loaned on personal security.

Amount of cash on hand.

Amount of profits on hand.

Amount and rate per cent of last dividend.

Average rate of dividends for the last three years.

Amount of reserved profits at time of last dividend.

Amount of deposits not liable to be claimed.

This last item is returned by only three out of the 37 institutions reporting in 1873, and these, of course, return "none," just as, if called upon to return the name of the depositor who would probably be first to withdraw money from the bank on the next day, they would say "don't know!"

These items have not been materially changed since 1849, except that, concerning the size of deposits, only the number of those of $500 and under $1,000, and those upwards of $1,000 are now required to be reported. In 1857, besides the amount which the treasurer might have a suspicion any depositor had generously though silently donated or devised to the institution, he was required to return the names of those whose deposits had remained unpaid for twenty or more years, and in 1858 this term was reduced to five years. Though I do not find that this last requirement has been repealed, it does not appear to be very faithfully regarded, for we look in vain for any information of the kind in any of the published reports from Savings Banks in this State. The subject of "unclaimed deposits," and the principles properly governing the same, will be found fully discussed elsewhere; hence, further comment at this point is not called for.

In 1856 these returns were required to be made to the secretary of state, who was directed to designate some day between November 15 and December 15 as the day for which the return was to be made; and he was also directed to prepare and publish an abstract of the returns. In 1857 the returns were directed to be made to the bank commissioners, and in 1858 their direction was again changed to the State auditor, to whom they have since been and are now made.

It does not appear whether any official examination of these institutions is in fact made, nor that the auditor has any powers concerning them, except to designate the day for which they shall make up their returns, and, we must presume, incidentally some power to compel compliance with the law. The bank commissioners were, in 1857, authorized by law to visit and examine Savings Banks, but to what extent the power conferred was exercised, the public records do not disclose.

The bank commissioners compiled the returns of Savings Banks but once — in 1857 — and made but brief comment concerning them, recommending only that they be prohibited from making mortgage loans upon property in other States than Rhode Island.

DIVIDENDS.

The provisions of law concerning dividends are found only in such charters as contain reference to this subject, there being no general law regulating the matter. These may therefore be presumed to reflect, in every instance the views of the corporators, rather than any settled policy of legislation. It will be noticed that the rules and regulations of the Savings Bank of Newport are incorporated into and made a part of the charter. The same is true of the Providence Institution and of some others. In this way, what in other States, particularly in New York, are a part of the by-laws, and subject, of course, to revision and alteration by the trustees, are here a part of the fundamental law, and can be changed only by the legislature; for, though the act authorized the corporation to modify the by-laws, it is difficult to see how such power could be exercised in such manner as to affect any of the regulations embodied in the act of incorporation. The provisions which will be noted in the charter under consideration, are substantially those that prevail in other institutions in the State, and, for that matter, in most other States. The noticeable features are that, in order to be entitled to a dividend, moneys must be on deposit at the time that a dividend is declared — in other words, moneys withdrawn between dividend periods are entitled to nothing for the portion of time which they remained during such periods — also, that dividends shall be declared only for full periods of three or six months.

The rate per cent of such dividends is commonly left to the discretion of the trustees, and there seems to be nothing to prevent this discretion being exercised in paying a low rate of dividends regularly, with such higher rate, from time to time, in the form of extra dividends, as they may deem proper. Whether, under the law, the trustees can so discriminate between deposits of a given amount and those of a larger sum, as to pay different rates upon such different sums, admits of question; an immaterial question, however, practically, as it would seem from the returns made, that the rates are uniform on all sums. It is also evident that the rate is not uniform at different periods, as the semi-annual dividends are frequently found to be at a different rate from the average of three years. The high rate of these dividends in late years is quite remarkable, but one institution reporting an average of less than seven per cent, and many of them as high as eight per cent. Such rates show a wonderful success, and are evidence, also, of strict economy in management; perhaps, also, of something else!

An exception to the prevailing rule concerning the discretion of the trustees in regulating the rate of dividends, will be noted in the charter of the Savings Bank of Newport, where the rate is fixed at two and one-half per cent, semi-annually, with extra dividends once in three years. But it would seem as though all these restrictions and limitations were repealed in later years, as they no longer seem to control the action of this corporation.

LIMITATION OF AMOUNT OF DEPOSITS.

We have already noticed the effort made in many of the charters to limit the aggregate amount of deposits which institutions might receive, as $100,000, $400,000, etc., and the futility of the effort as manifested by the fact that the prescribed limit had long since been reached and passed.

Limitations as to the amount which any person might deposit in the aggregate, or within a certain period of time, will be found in various charters, but these do not appear to have been very effectual, as single deposits above $60,000 are reported, and the average to each depositor in the State is exceptionally high, being $500.59. We must presume, therefore, that this limitation, like that concerning the aggregate deposits of any institution, has been abrogated. The exceptionally high rate of dividends paid, doubtless has much to do with inducing large deposits, as seven per cent or even more, with the privilege of withdrawing the principal at any time, must be a strong temptation to capital in large amounts. Some allowance must also be made for the fact, that, no legal impediment being offered to the deposit of large sums, there is less occasion, than there would be otherwise, for a depositor to open a large number of accounts for what is in fact a single deposit, so that the number of accounts more truly represents the number of actual depositors, and the average to each depositor is more truthfully stated than in those States where the restriction upon deposits is evaded by the devices we have mentioned.

WITHDRAWAL OF DEPOSITS.

The restrictions upon the withdrawal of deposits, which will be noted in the 14th rule under the charter of the Savings Bank of Newport, we must presume to have been greatly modified in practice, and, probably, also by an amendment to the charter. Such a provision is well to have in reserve, but as a binding obligation could not fail to be embarrassing to depositors to a degree that would seriously impair the prosperity of any institution enforcing it. A like restriction upon the withdrawal of deposits was incorporated in other charters, but we presume it to have been removed from all. Thus the Providence Institution for Savings has the same restriction in its original charter, but is not governed by it now, and during the panic in 1873 paid its depositors as usual on demand without notice.

PROHIBITIONS.

The prohibition against loaning any of the moneys of the institution to trustees is enforced in the most practical and salutary manner, by making all who even by their presence and silence countenance such loan, personally responsible for the same.

In at least one charter, loans are prohibited even to corporators, but this does not seem to be the import of the prohibition in charters generally. In some, or at least one, even the trustees are not excluded from the privilege of borrowing the moneys deposited, but this is altogether exceptional.

DEPOSITS OF MARRIED WOMEN AND MINORS.

The policy of protecting the deposits of females from the claim of husbands, appears to have first found favor in the State of Rhode Island, which in 1841, by an amendment to the charter of the Providence Institution for Savings, provided substantially as follows: that "Every person making any deposit personally, may withdraw the same and the interest thereon, notwithstanding such person be a married woman; and the receipt of such married woman shall be a sufficient discharge of said corporation for the sums so withdrawn." The same principle was recognized in the original charter of the East River Savings Institution of New York, in 1848, and was supposed by the corporators of that institution to be the earliest legislative sanction of such a policy, and I had conceded to that institution the priority in the direction of such beneficence, until I chanced to find the above in the statutes of Rhode Island. In 1850 a similar provision was embraced in the charter of the Wakefield Institution for Savings, and it was in the same year that the principle was recognized by a general law in the State of New York. It is now believed to be a common feature of Savings Bank legislation in all the States. Similar protection to the deposits of minors was extended by law in New York as early as 1820, as elsewhere set forth, but I do not find any thing of this nature in the laws of Rhode Island prior to the above charter of the Wakefield Institution, which places the deposits of minors on the same footing, as regards protection, as those of females. Since that time the provision has become a common though not uniform feature of Savings Bank charters in this State.

No other distinguishing features have marked the legislation of this State concerning Savings Banks, if we except from such designation the taxation of the deposits of these institutions, which is fixed at twenty-five cents upon each $100 of such deposits and of reserved profits.

So far as I have been able to discover, but a single charter authorizes the accumulation of any surplus, and this but three per cent; though, as there is no absolute requirement that all the profits shall be divided among the depositors, the subject of dividends being left to the discretion of the trustees, the power to hold a portion of the profits in reserve to meet contingencies may doubtless be fairly inferred. It is evident the managers have so regarded their powers, as the last annual report shows a surplus of nearly four per cent.

CHAPTER XV.

STATISTICS OF GROWTH AND PROGRESS.

It is now in order to present such statistics as we have been able to procure, illustrating the growth and progress of Savings Banks in Rhode Island. Our effort to procure details concerning each Savings Bank have not been more successful here than in other quarters; but such as have been furnished, in reply to my inquiries, are here produced as a matter of justice to those who have seconded my efforts, and also in the hope that they may furnish the basis from which, in some future edition of this History, more full and complete details may be made.

Replies to my inquiries were made by seven out of the thirty-seven institutions in the State, and not all of these were able or willing to give a statement of the aggregate work accomplished, as shown by the whole number of accounts opened and the total amount of deposits received. Of course, such fragmentary details as I have received do not admit of tabulation for the purpose of exhibiting aggregates or making comparisons, and for these we must look to the more full and connected, though imperfect, records compiled from the annual statements.

The statistics given of the Providence Institution for Savings were furnished by the treasurer, S. C. Blodgett, Esq., at a visit made by me to that institution while in the city prosecuting my researches at the capitol; and for these, as for other valuable information furnished by that gentleman, I desire to express my acknowledgments.

Columns of cents were used in making up totals, though omitted from the table.

STATISTICS FURNISHED BY SAVINGS BANKS.

Providence Institution for Savings.

[Incorporated and supposed to have commenced business in 1819.]

TABLE exhibiting the growth of the institution from 1846 *to* 1869, *inclusive, and for the year* 1873–4.

YEAR.	Number of open accounts.	Receipts from depositors.*	Payments to depositors.	Amount of deposits.
1846	3,714	$160,394	$123,774	$534,425
1847	4,133	202,316	156,555	603,757
1848	4,381	193,537	179,063	644,176
1849	4,673	211,743	192,912	692,011
1850	5,426	284,611	183,973	822,223
1851	6,356	345,859	217,364	993,728
1852	6,827	347,060	263,789	1,127,007
1853	8,007	398,168	270,448	1,312,822
1854	8,718	450,347	363,203	1,473,307
1855	8,962	420,370	405,431	1,562,768
1856	9,642	439,290	386,469	1,738,822
1857	9,149	495,481	573,835	1,695,849
1858	9,156	356,206	451,214	1,758,728
1859	10,338	518,410	290,757	2,085,059
1860	11,295	556,770	383,008	2,372,303
1861	10,608	393,988	508,464	2,373,163
1862	11,902	478,565	376,157	2,658,976
1863	12,667	594,621	402,607	2,971,486
1864	13,198	743,074	611,237	3,248,305
1865	13,312	787,531	807,253	3,420,783
1866	14,637	1,062,398	659,303	4,083,177
1867	15,879	1,005,876	737,207	4,601,421
1868	16,247	920,926	898,632	4,918,188
1869	16,551	845,676	1,017,357	5,017,130
1874	18,992	1,567,402	1,275,428	7,556,882

* Do not include dividends.

The statistics of growth prior to 1846, the treasurer informs me, cannot be given, owing to a partial destruction of the records by fire. We have nothing concerning the operations of the institution between the years 1869 and 1874, except what might be compiled from the annual reports, which do not give the receipts from, and payments to, depositors.

Woonsocket Institution for Savings.

First deposit received August 23, 1845.

Number of accounts opened, to close of 1873....	17,770
Number of accounts closed	11,001
Number of open accounts....................	6,769
Amount deposited, including dividends, since organization..............................	$8,615,459
Amount withdrawn	5,749,911
Amount due depositors at close of 1873	2,865,548
Amount of dividends	1,431,217

The following table, furnished by the treasurer, L. W. Ballou, Esq., exhibits the amount received from depositors. and the dividends credited in each year since organization. The per cent of dividends being, to 1849, five per cent; from 1850 to 1863, six per cent; thereafter, seven per cent, until 1873, when it was seven and one-half per cent. The columns of cents are omitted, though used in making up the totals.

YEAR.	Deposits.	Dividends.	YEAR.	Deposits.	Dividends.
1845......	$20,066	$286	1860.....	$137,838	$29,212
1846......	32,515	1,651	1861.....	106,005	28,944
1847......	31,730	1,649	1862.....	178,491	33,038
1848......	19,303	2,793	1863.....	204,548	36,996
1849......	21,962	3,035	1864.....	195,407	50,295
1850......	30,409	3,831	1865.....	309,579	54,257
1851......	41,336	4,956	1866.....	476,524	72,381
1852......	57,249	6,223	1867.....	498,616	89,846
1853......	86,889	9,247	1868.....	599,973	102,140
1854......	80,496	11,194	1869.....	654,952	118,697
1855......	104,123	14,315	1870.....	648,717	134,704
1856......	128,315	17,832	1871.....	767,390	156,279
1857......	86,531	17,867	1872.....	812,118	178,276
1858......	133,483	19,796	1873.....	573,692	205,643
1859......	155,972	24,919			
			Total..	$7,184,242	$1,431,217

People's Savings Bank, Providence.

First deposit received December 1, 1851.

Open accounts at close of 1873............... 6,009

Amount deposited, including dividends, since organization.......................... $11,552,086

Amount withdrawn since organization......... 7,553,255

Amount due depositors at close of 1873........ 3,998,831

Wickford Savings Bank.

First deposit received August 1, 1855.

Number of accounts opened since organization... 2,610

Number of accounts closed since organization... 1,545

Number of open accounts at close of 1873....... 1,065

Amount, including dividends, deposited........ $1,432,762

Amount withdrawn 955,867

Amount due depositors at close of 1873 476,895

Amount of dividends credited 261,139

Franklin Savings Bank, Pawtucket.

First deposit received June 3, 1857.

Number of accounts opened................. 3,880

Number of accounts closed.................. 1, 602
Number of open accounts at close of 1873..... 2, 278
Amount deposited, dividends included........ $2, 298, 844
Amount withdrawn 854, 481
Amount due depositors at close of 1873....... 1, 444, 363
Amount of dividends since organization 442, 529
Average rate of dividends for the last three years, 8 per cent. per annum.

Pascoag Savings Bank.

First deposit received October 1, 1864.
Open accounts at close of 1873................ 1, 011
Amount due depositors at close of 1873 .... $550, 354

The above is all that was furnished in reply to my circular of inquiry, all of which, except the first item of information, could be obtained from the annual report of the auditor.

Producers' Savings Bank, Woonsocket.

First deposit received June 26, 1868.
Number of accounts opened since organization, 703
Number of accounts closed since organization... 236
Number of open accounts at close of 1873 467
Amount due depositors at close of 1873....... $255, 072
Amount of dividends since organization 42, 106

Hopkinton Savings Bank, Wyoming.

First deposit received July 15, 1870.
Number of accounts opened since organization.. 882
Number of accounts closed since organization.. 156
Number of open accounts at close of 1873 726
Amount deposited, including dividends $217, 997
Amount withdrawn 5, 677

Amount due depositors at close of 1873.......	212, 320
Amount of dividends since organization	32, 582

It seems hardly credible that but $5,677 should have been withdrawn from a total deposit of $218,000 in three years and a half; but the amount deposited and the amount remaining due, as given by the institution and stated above, will produce no other result.

GENERAL STATISTICS OF GROWTH AND PROGRESS.

Next in order we will present in detail the condition of the Savings Banks in this State on the first Monday in July, 1848, as shown by their statements, made for the first time on that day, pursuant to a resolution of the general assembly, as previously noted.

Returns made by Savings Institutions in Rhode Island in 1848.

PROVIDENCE INSTITUTION FOR SAVINGS.

Number of depositors, 4,385.

Amount due depositors	$640, 011 08
Surplus	46, 440 39
	$686, 451 47

Resources.

Public funds (U. S. stocks)......	$34, 600 00
Bank stock....................	190, 050 00
Loans on railroad bonds	50, 000 00
Loans on mortgage, real estate...	298, 045 00
Loans to city of Providence.....	50, 000 00
Loans on personal security	20, 000 00

Loans on personal security and collateral	$12,400 00	
Loans to Butler Insane Hospital	14,000 00	
Cash on hand	17,356 47	
		$686,451 47

The difference of about $4,000 between the above deposits and those for the same year found on page 183, *ante*, is to be accounted for by supposing the statements to be made at different dates in the same year; the above being for July and the former for September.

Warwick Institution for Savings.

Number of depositors, 574.

Amount due depositors		$107,524 36

Resources.

Bank stock	$27,000 00	
Loans on real estate mortgage	75,100 00	
Loans on bank stock	1,000 00	
Paid for premiums	1,278 12	
Paid for expenses	61 68	
Overdrawn on interest account to pay dividend	65	
Deposits in bank	3,083 91	
		107,524 36

Savings Bank of Newport.

Number of depositors, 786.

Amount due depositors	$108,958 18
Surplus	1,633 27
	$110,591 45

Resources.

Loans secured by mortgages	$26,495 23	
Notes of manufacturing companies,	20,820 22	
Bank stock (in eighteen banks)...	62,080 00	
R. I. bridge stock..............	1,196 00	
		$110,501 45

PAWTUCKET INSTITUTION FOR SAVINGS.

Number of depositors, 767.

Amount due depositors		$130,828 67

Resources.

Bonds and mortgages..........	$85,780 00	
Bank stock.....................	18,000 00	
		103,780 00

The above exhibits a deficiency for which I am unable to account, as the institution, in its report, claims a surplus of over $2,000. The error must arise from the inadvertent omission of some items of assets by the institution, or from mistake by the printers in setting the copy.

WOONSOCKET INSTITUTION FOR SAVINGS.

Number of depositors, 443.

Amount due depositors		$66,941 31
Surplus		852 54
		$67,793 85

Resources.

Bank stock.....................	$53,016 00	
Bonds and mortgages...........	56,800 00	
Notes and bills	9,875 00	
Cash in bank..................	2,102 85	
		$67,793 85

WARREN SEAMEN'S FRIEND SOCIETY.

Four depositors, to whom is due	$185 05

To the foregoing should be added the Bristol Institution for Savings, not reporting, from whose returns — made the next year — we derive the following estimates for 1848:

Number of depositors, 150.
Amount due depositors $20, 000 00

Summary of the foregoing.

NAME OF INSTITUTION.	Number of depositors.	Amount due depositors.
Bristol (estimated)	150	$20,000
Newport	786	108,958
Pawtucket	767	130,828
Providence	4,385	640,011
Warren	4	185
Warwick	574	107,524
Woonsocket	443	66,941
Total	7,109	$1,074,447

For the purpose of comparison, we present the following summary of the condition of the same institutions, as reported in 1873. The Warren Seamen's Society, as its condition foreshadowed, closed soon after its statement was made, in 1849.

NAME OF INSTITUTION.	Number of depositors.	Amount due depositors.
Bristol	1,033	$261,127
Newport	4,879	3,510,758
Pawtucket	3,866	2,063,972
Providence	17,415	6,739,579
Warwick	2,523	1,360,373
Woonsocket	6,615	2,871,058
Total	36,331	$16,806,867

Increase in 25 years: Depositors, five times; deposits, nearly 16 times.

The returns in this State do not state the amount deposited during the year.

Comparing the investments of the two periods, we make the following table, in which, of course, all the Savings Banks reporting at each period, respectively, are represented. The increase in amount and per cent of surplus, also in the amount of dividends and per cent of the same on the whole amount of deposits, is given.

INVESTMENTS.	Aggregate, 1848.	Aggregate, 1873.	Per cent, 1848.	Per cent, 1873.
Mortgages of real estate ...	$552,220	$24,338,982	50	50
Bank and other corp'n st'ks,	300,146	2,576,333	27	5 1-3
Nat'l, State, and mun'pl b'ds,	84,600	6,266,774	7 1-2	13
R. R. and other corp'n b'ds,	56,196	1,707,813	5	3 1-2
Notes of cities, towns, etc..	....	365,500	.....	1-2
Loans on personal security,	30,875	10,637,429	3	22
Loans on collaterals.......	44,220	1,853,846	4	4
Cash on hand and in bank,	29,726	648,791	2 1-2	1 1-3
Real estate................	....	216,533	.....	1-3
Surplus...................	23,436	1,780,430	2 1-5	3 4-5
Dividends	24,012	1,701,864	4 1-2	7 1-5

The following table exhibits the growth of the system from year to year, from the time of making public record of the condition of Savings Banks to the close of 1873. The labor involved in making up this record can only be appreciated by any one who shall attempt to duplicate it from the original records. He will then find that there is not in the State library, nor in the office of the secretary of state, nor, so far as I could ascertain, in any other public or private library at Providence, a complete set of the reports from which this table is compiled.

TABLE exhibiting the number, condition and progress of Savings Banks in Rhode Island from 1848 *to* 1874.

YEAR.	No. of banks.	No. of open accounts.	Increase in acc'ts.	Amount due to depositors.	Increase in am't due depositors.	INCREASE IN PERIODS OF FIVE YEARS. Depositors' increase. Number.	Depositors' increase. Per cent.	Due depositors. Amount of increase.	Due depositors. Per cent.
1848	7	6,960	......	$1,074,447	....	....	...	....	...
1849	8	7,983	1,023	1,209,075	$134,628				
1850	....	9,295	1,312	1,495,545	286,470				
1851	9	11,161	1,866	1,907,233	411,688				
1852	10	13,396	2,235	2,474,109	566,876				
1853	12	16,989	3,593	3,308,769	834,660	10,029	158	$2,234,322	208
1854	14	20,338	3,349	4,104,091	795,382				
1855	15	23,229	2,891	4,834,312	730,221				
1856	18	27,002	3,773	5,797,857	963,545				
1857	18	27,259	257	6,079,053	281,196				
1858	20	27,643	384	6,349,621	270,568	10,654	63	3,040,852	92
1859	21	31,833	4,190	7,765,771	1,416,150				
1860	21	35,405	3,572	9,163,760	1,397,889				
1861	22	34,807	—598	9,282,879	119,119				
1862	21	37,774	2,967	9,560,441	277,562				
1863	21	40,827	3,053	11,128,713	1,568,272	13,184	48	4,779,092	75
1864	23	44,752	3,925	12,815,097	1,686,384				
1865	23	45,574	822	13,533,062	717,965				
1866	25	52,859	7,285	17,751,713	4,218,651				
1867	25	59,071	7,212	21,413,647	3,661,934				
1868	25	63,501	4,430	24,408,635	2,994,988	22,674	55	13,279,922	120

TABLE—(Continued).

YEAR.	No. of banks.	No. of open accounts.	Increase in acc'ts.	Amount due to depositors.	Increase in am't due depositors.	Increase in Periods of Five Years.			
						Depositors' increase.		Due depositors.	
						Number.	Per cent.	Amount of increase.	Per cent.
1869	25	67,238	3,737	$27,067,072	$2,658,437				
1870	26	72,891	4,553	30,708,501	3,641,429				
1871	33	79,676	6,785	36,289,703	5,581,202				
1872	36	88,664	8,988	42,583,538	6,294,835				
1873	37	93,124	4,460	46,617,183	4,033,645	29,623	46	$22,208,548	91

After 1848 the statements, until 1855, were made up for October; in 1856 and 1857, for December; from 1858 to 1867, for November, and thereafter for December. It will be observed that the progress of the system was never interrupted, except that in 1861 there was a decrease of 598 in the number of depositors.

Since the above table was prepared, the report for December, 1874, has been received, as follows: Number of banks, 37; number of open accounts, 98,539; increase, 5,415; amount due depositors, $48,771,501; increase, $2,154,318; surplus, $1,665,902. Two of the 37 institutions are in process of liquidation.

FIFTH SECTION;

SAVINGS BANKS IN THE STATE OF NEW HAMPSHIRE.

CHAPTER XVI.

INCEPTION AND HISTORY OF FIRST SAVINGS BANK.

The subject-matter of Savings Banks was considered in the legislature of New Hampshire as early as 1819, for, in the Senate Journal of that year, we find the following record: "A bill entitled 'An act to incorporate the Portsmouth Provident Society' was brought up, read a second time, and on motion voted that the further consideration of said bill be indefinitely postponed." This was probably the earliest consideration given to Savings Banks in this State, but fortunately it was not the latest; and in 1823 the effort was successfully renewed, and the Portsmouth Savings Bank incorporated.

The charter of this institution will be found in the Appendix, where we have collected all the earlier charters for the purpose of exhibiting the special features which characterized the inception of Savings Banks in the several States.

HISTORICAL SKETCH OF THE PORTSMOUTH SAVINGS BANK.

The following extract from the report of the treasurer, J. F. Shores, Esq., made to the board of trustees on the fiftieth anniversary of the institution, has been kindly furnished by that officer for incorporation into this History. The consideration of the subject of chartering a Savings Bank, above referred to, doubtless had its inception in the movement spoken of in the following extract as having originated in 1818, culminating, as elsewhere set forth, in the charter of the Portsmouth Savings Bank, in 1823.

Extract from the Treasurer's Report, made this day (Aug. 6, 1873), being the fiftieth anniversary of the establishment of the Bank.

"I cannot close this report of our doings for the past year without some reference to the fact that we now enter upon the second half century of our existence as a Savings Bank.

"The first Savings Bank in this country was opened in Philadelphia in 1816; the second in Boston in 1817; the third in New York in 1819. The founders of the latter, when they presented their petition to the New York legislature, asked for an act of incorporation 'to ameliorate the condition of the poor,' under the name of 'The Society for the Prevention of Pauperism in the City of New York.' *

"In 1818 — fifty-five years ago, and one year previous to the establishment of the New York Savings Bank — a meeting of gentlemen interested in the subject was held in this town, and an association was formed for establishing a Provident Institution, as will be seen from the original paper now hanging on the wall of our room.

---

* Not strictly correct. The founders applied under the name of the "Society for the Prevention of Pauperism," etc. (an association already formed), for the incorporation of a Savings Bank, and one of the recognized objects of such an institution was "the amelioration of the condition of the poor," and this was specifically recognized by the legislature in the preamble to the act of incorporation. (See Appendix.)

"An act of incorporation was not obtained till June, 1823, when the Portsmouth Savings Bank was chartered 'for the purpose of enabling industrious persons of all descriptions to invest such parts of their earnings as they can conveniently spare in a safe and profitable manner.'

"The first meeting of the corporation was held July 23, 1823, at the office of the New Hampshire Fire and Marine Insurance office (now the Athenæum). There were present, Jeremiah Mason, Enoch G. Parrott, Jas. Rundlett, Nathan Parker, John McClintock, Jacob Cutler, Ichabod Bartlett and John W. Foster. The act of incorporation was accepted, and a committee appointed to prepare a set of by-laws. The meeting adjourned to July 30, when the committee reported and the by-laws were adopted. A final organization of the corporation was made August 7, 1823, by the choice of Nathaniel A. Haven as president, Samuel Lord as treasurer, and as trustees, Levi Woodbury, Enoch G. Parrott, James Rundlett, Edward Cutts, John Haven, Hunking Penhallow, Henry Ladd, Samuel Lord, N. A. Haven, Jr., Jacob Cutler, Peyton R. Freeman, Alexander Ladd, John W. Foster, Ichabod Bartlett, Nathaniel B. March and Timothy Upham.

"A circular was then prepared and published, setting forth the objects of the bank and the good expected to result from its operations, a copy of which now hangs on the wall of our room.

"The bank was first kept, as the circular expresses it, 'in the northerly chamber, over the New Hampshire Bank; enter at the left hand door and go up stairs.' The New Hampshire Bank then occupied *this building*. In 1824, on the establishment of the Piscataqua Bank, the Savings Bank was removed to the corner of State and Pleasant streets; in 1835, to the room formerly occupied by the United States Branch Bank (now occupied by the New Hampshire National Bank); then, in 1844, to our present location, which we held in common, first with the Piscataqua Exchange Bank and afterward with the First National, till 1869, when the building was divided and this bank took the northerly half and enlarged it to suit its business purposes.

"The bank was opened for business on the 20th of August, 1823, and on that day the following persons made deposits:

No.	Name	Amount
No. 1.	Rebecca Hardy	$16
2.	Hezekiah and Hannah P. Kimball	65
3.	Augustus Morrison	20
4.	Isaac T. Frye	20
5.	Synthia Langton	5
6.	Elizabeth Walker	240
7.	Maria Walker	240
8.	Susan Parker Badger	10
9.	Elizabeth Ann Badger	10

"Of these books, No. 6 is the only one now in existence, being the property of the North Parish, to whom it was bequeathed by Miss Elizabeth Walker. The original deposit was $240, which, in 1838, was reduced to $188. During the fifty years the dividends on this deposit have amounted to $1,191.71, of which there has been withdrawn $871.49, leaving the present deposit $560.22.

"Nathaniel A. Haven was president eight years, 1823–31; Henry Ladd was president eight years, 1831–39; Jas. Rundlett was president one year, 1839–40; Robert Rice was president four years, 1840–44; William M. Shackford was president 25 years, 1844–69; William Simes has been president since 1869.

"Samuel Lord was treasurer 46 years, from 1823 to 1869; James F. Shores has been treasurer since 1869.

"The bank started with the promise to pay five per cent per annum, semi-annually; but a year's experience taught them that the promise could not be fulfilled, and in July, 1824, it was reduced to four per cent, and continued at that rate till January, 1871, and since then it has been five per cent.

"The extra dividends have been: In 1828, 13.90 per cent; in 1833, eight per cent; in 1838, 17 per cent; in 1843, 10.50 per cent; in 1848, 12.55 per cent; in 1853, 14.38 per cent; in 1858, 12.50 per cent; in 1863, 11.50 per cent; in 1868, 20.30 per cent; in 1873, 9.67 per cent; total, 130.30 per cent. The regular dividends have amounted to 202¼ per cent.

During the first year the deposits amounted to...	$28,319	58
Of which there was withdrawn during the year..	2,101	28
	$26,218	30
The two dividends of the year amounted to	471	94
Amount of deposits at close of first year...	$26,690	24

"To show the increase of the business of the bank, I will give the figures of the first five years and of the five years just closed:

At the close of the first five years there had been deposited..........................	$115,020	34
Regular dividends had been	9,100	34
Extra dividend, fifth year	4,352	95
	$128,473	63
Withdrawals during the five years..........	42,893	49
Balance on deposit	$85,580	14

During the five years just closed there has been deposited..........................	$1,116,036	57
Regular dividends have been	341,087	35
Extra dividend	120,062	34
	$1,577,186	26
Withdrawals during the five years..........	919,391	02
Increase during the five years..........	$657,795	24

During the fifty years there has been deposited	$4, 905, 374 36
Regular dividends have been	1, 122, 087 15
Extra dividends have been	527, 128 47
	$6, 554, 589 98
The withdrawals have been	4, 473, 216 51
Leaving on deposit	$2, 081, 373 47

"But, to show more fully the workings of the bank as a matter of profit to the individuals, and as giving the financial history of the bank, and also as an illustration of the value of money placed at interest at a low rate, I would cite the deposit of $20, made Dec. 17, 1823, four months after the bank went into operation:

After the extra of 1828	it amounted to $26.72 being simple interest at	8	per cent.
" " 1833	it amounted to $34.59 being simple interest at	6	"
" " 1838	it amounted to $47.95 being simple interest at	7 7/9	"
" " 1843	it amounted to $63.08 being simple interest at	6 1/3	"
" " 1848	it amounted to $84.51 being simple interest at	6 5/6	"
" " 1853	it amounted to $115.01 being simple interest at	7 1/4	"
" " 1858	it amounted to $154.13 being simple interest at	6 9/10	"
" " 1863	it amounted to $205.11 being simple interest at	6 6/10	"
" " 1868	it amounted to $291.58 being simple interest at	8 1/3	"
" " 1873	it amounted to $392.29 being simple interest at	6 9/10	"

"The regular and extra dividends amounting to 332.55 per cent, being an average at simple interest of 6.65

per cent; yet, by the power of compounding, the interest has amounted to 1860 per cent on the original deposit, or about 37 per cent per annum, simple interest."

In 1869, the solicitor of this bank, Hon. W. H. Y. Hackett, favored the writer with some interesting reminiscences of the institution, which, though covering in part the same ground as the foregoing, bring to view some features not therein commented upon, and justify their insertion here.

SKETCH FURNISHED BY MR. HACKETT.

"The Portsmouth Savings Bank was incorporated in June, 1823. It was the first Savings Bank incorporated or organized in this State. Neither the legislature which incorporated it nor the community in which it was to be located had much confidence in its beginning.

"It began in a small way, and gradually attracted the attention and secured the confidence and deposits of persons of small means, for whom it was organized. No deposit from any one person is received larger than $300, but the accumulation of interest on that sum is added to the principal and allowed to remain as long as the owner desires. The bank has uniformly refused to enlarge the amount which one person might deposit.

"Some time after this bank was organized other banks began to be organized, in other parts of the State, substantially upon the plan of this bank.

"The bank organized here soon after the Sunday school was established, and for the same purpose, and, to a considerable extent, by the same persons. It was essentially a philanthropic enterprise, intended to elevate the character and improve the condition of young people and people of small means. This bank and several others in the State have adhered to the original plan. The effect on this community has been decidedly favorable. It has improved the habits, as well as augmented the means, of those for whom it was established.

"The Savings Banks have, in their influence upon the people, greatly reduced the suits for the collection of debts. It is a fact that, though in this State the Savings Banks are liable to the trustee process, yet this bank, having had more than 25,000 depositors, has never been held as a trustee of a person who had a deposit in the bank.

"More recently several Savings Banks have been established with a view to become banks of discount and deposits, or as aids to stock banks, and are offering and paying larger rates of interest than this bank has paid.

"Without undertaking to predict what may be the result of this modification of the policy of institutions of savings, we have thought it better for our depositors, whose supposed interest has been our care and guide, to keep down the rate of interest and the amount of individual deposits. In this way every depositor is induced to leave his money at work for time as long as he can spare it, and no large depositors can have the power, in times of panic, to remove the available means of the bank to the prejudice of the small and confiding depositors.

The amount of deposits in the bank at the last quarter was	$1, 248, 925 82
The amount of surplus	150, 000 00

"Perhaps a few words and figures can give you a better history of the working of the bank, and to this end I would state the result of two deposits, made soon after the bank was organized, viz.:

Deposit No. 143, of $20, made December 17, 1823, amounted, July 18, 1868, to	$291 88
Deposit No. 343 of $20, made Aug. 4, 1824, seven	

months and 18 days later, amounted at the same time to	$268 88
Difference, more than the original deposit	$22 70

"Perhaps I may as well state that Wm. M. Shackford now is and has been president since August 14, 1844.

"Samuel Lord has been, ever since the organization of the bank, treasurer, and Wm. H. Y. Hackett has been for about the same time solicitor for the bank."

The order of the incorporation of Savings Banks in New Hampshire, down to 1846, was as follows:

Portsmouth Savings Bank	1823
Savings Bank of the County of Strafford (organized 1824),	1823
Exeter Savings Bank (not organized)	1828
New Hampshire Savings Bank	1830
Meredith Bridge (Laconia?) Savings Bank	1831
Connecticut River Savings Bank	1831
New Market Savings Bank	1832
Cheshire Provident Institution for Savings	1833
Franklin Savings Bank (not organized)	1833
Sullivan Savings Institution	1838
Somersworth Savings Bank	1845
Manchester Savings Bank	1846

Concerning the Exeter and the Franklin, noted above as not organized, I give only the presumption in the case. It is possible they were organized and failed or discontinued; but if so, it was prior to 1849, as they are not embraced in the commissioners' returns for that year. I give to the system the benefit of the doubt in enumerating them as not organized.

CHAPTER XVII.

COURSE OF LEGISLATION.

SUPERVISION, EXAMINATION, ETC.

Prior to 1847, it appears that no supervision by the State was exercised over Savings Banks, except that in 1845 an act was passed which defined the compensation to be allowed to commissioners making an examination of Savings Banks under the direction of the governor. From this it would appear that the governor might direct such examination when he thought proper; indeed, the power to examine was conferred upon the governor in the first charter. Of course there was, under this provision, no uniform or systematic examination of these institutions.

In 1847, however, it was made the duty of the bank commissioners, or one of them, at least once in each year, and oftener if the governor should require, without previous notice, to make personally a full examination of each Savings Bank in the State.

The first report of operations under this law was made in 1849. This report is made up from the reports of the examinations made by each commissioner, and, besides giving a statement of the condition of each institution examined, gives a brief summary of items of interest, historical and otherwise, which we cannot do better than transcribe in full to these pages, and the same will be found *post*, pp. 211–220.

Although this report of examinations made in 1849 is the first which I have been able to find amongst the published documents of the State, it would seem that the duty imposed by the law was discharged in 1848; for we find the deposits and accounts for that year in the summary of progress given in later reports. There are, however, some anomalies between the statements for the two years which I am unable to explain, as the falling off, from 1848 to 1849, of 342 in the number of accounts and $55,148.97 in the amount of deposits.

No specific form of examination, nor of reports of the results of examinations, appears to have been prescribed until 1869, when the commissioners were required to "give in their reports a detailed statement of all the items of expense of all Savings Banks, with the names of the treasurer and clerks and the salary of each; to report the kind and amount of stocks and bonds held by each of said banks, with the par value, the cost to said banks, and the market value at the date of examination; also the amount of the treasurer's bond, with all such information as will tend to give the true standing of the banks examined."

In addition to the examination by the commissioners, the trustees were required, by an act in 1872, to thoroughly examine their bank once in six months; and, where the deposits exceeded $500,000, they were required to make such examination four times a year, and to report the same to the bank commissioners.

The purpose of the legislature in the foregoing, as in its legislation generally, appears to have been to become apprised of the actual condition of the several

Savings Banks in the State from time to time. Hence no statistical information is called for. We are thus deprived of any means of knowing, from year to year, what number of persons has been reached and affected by the ministry of these institutions, and what amounts have been received and paid by them, and the amount or value of these savings as expressed in the form of dividends.

ORGANIZATION.

It will be seen from the charter of the Portsmouth Savings Bank (section 5), as also from explanatory comments of some of the following reports, that the form of organization differed from that in the State of New York and some other States, being more like that in Rhode Island.

Under this the board of corporators is somewhat large, usually numbering from 40 to 50 members, who elect from their number, annually or at other periods, a board of trustees, usually from 12 to 18 in number, to whom the affairs of the bank are committed.

The term of incorporation in the several charters was not uniform, some being perpetual and some limited to 40 and some to 20 years. Probably every institution whose term has expired has had its charter renewed, either in perpetuity or for an additional term.

There appears to have been less general legislation affecting Savings Banks in New Hampshire than in most other States, their powers being derived from and regulated by their charters and the amendments thereto.

INVESTMENTS.

Not until 1869 does there seem to have been any general provision directing and limiting the investments of Savings Banks. These were defined in that year by section 3 of chapter 4, amending chapter 58 of the general statutes, as follows:

"One-half of the deposits hereafter received in Savings Banks, and one-half the investments hereafter made by same, shall be invested in notes and mortgages of individuals residing or doing business and having a place of business in this State; in the stock of banking associations located in this State; in the first mortgage bonds of any railroad company incorporated under the authority of this State, which is in possession of and operating its own road, and which has earned and paid regular dividends for two years next preceding such investments, or in the bonds of any such railroad company which is unincumbered by mortgage; in bonds and loans of this State, or of any city, county or town therein, or in notes of individuals or corporations residing or doing business and having a place of business in this State, with sufficient sureties or collaterals."

The emphasis given to the restriction of loans to residents of the State would seem to indicate a special purpose in the act to correct a practice, which had doubtless grown up, of making loans outside of the State for the sake of higher interest attainable in this way. Beyond this, the measure in respect to the securities authorized would seem to enumerate those common to the various charters, and most in favor among the institutions of the State.

TAXATION OF SAVINGS BANKS.

Savings Banks in New Hampshire were early regarded as legitimate subjects of taxation by the State. As early as 1848 an act was passed requiring treasurers of Savings Banks to notify the assessors of all deposits in excess of $100, held by residents of any town, with the name of the depositor and the amount of each deposit. This, of course, was to give information to the assessors of personal property which they should include in their tax levy.

In 1865 Savings Banks were required to pay a specific tax of three-fourths of one per cent on the whole amount of deposits and accumulations, in lieu of all other taxes upon such deposits or against depositors on account thereof. In 1869 this was increased to one per cent. This tax was payable to the treasury of the State, and in 1871 a penalty of twelve per cent per annum was imposed for delay in paying over the same when due.

COMPENSATION TO OFFICERS.

It will be seen, from the charter of the Portsmouth Savings Bank, that trustees were prohibited from receiving compensation or other emolument, except that the treasurer or secretary might have a reasonable allowance made to him for his services. The same feature characterizes other acts of incorporation.

This was made the subject of general legislation in 1869, by requiring the salary of the treasurer and clerks to be fixed by the trustees annually, and by limiting the total expense of any institution, including the salaries, to not exceeding $4,000. In 1872 this provision was modified by authorizing Savings Banks having deposits in excess of $1,000,000 to incur expenses beyond the limit of $4,000, but not to exceed an amount at the rate of one-eighth of one per cent on the excess of deposits over $1,000,000. Thus, a Savings Bank with $2,000,000 of deposits could incur expenses amounting, first, to $4,000 — in common with all Savings Banks — and, in addition to that, at the rate of one-eighth of one per cent on the deposits in excess of $1,000,000, which would be $1,250, or $5,250 in all. It would seem that character, ability and fidelity to public trust were so common in New Hampshire as to call for no very flattering overtures to command their service, or the total expense attending the care and custody of $2,000,000 could not be reduced to a little more than one-fourth of one per cent upon that sum. It was also further provided that the duty imposed upon trustees of examining the affairs of the bank might be performed by a committee who should be entitled to receive proper compensation for the service. Of course this did not enlarge the amount of authorized expenditure, but changed the direction of it.

USE OF FUNDS BY TRUSTEES.

The charters of Savings Banks do not seem originally to have contained the restriction, quite common in other States, against the use of the funds or deposits in Savings Banks by the trustees or officers. Not until 1870 does this seem to have engaged the attention of the legislature, when very stringent provisions upon the subject were enacted, providing that no person indebted to any Savings Bank, as principal or surety, should be eligible to election as trustee, and that thereafter no Savings Bank should make any loan to any of its officers or receive them as surety for any loan, except with the unanimous consent of the trustees, given in writing and filed with the treasurer.

BONDS OF OFFICERS.

By the act of 1869, to which frequent reference is made, and which was a sort of revision and codification of provisions concerning Savings Banks, treasurers were required to give bonds in the sum of $25,000; and, where the deposits exceeded $100,000, the bond was to be increased in the sum of $5,000 for each $100,000 or fractional part thereof. These bonds were to be recorded at length, and an attested copy to be filed with the secretary of state.

The foregoing comprises substantially all the legislation in this State in relation to Savings Banks, which, as we have before remarked, is less voluminous than in most other States where these institutions have been established.

CHAPTER XVIII.

STATISTICS SHOWING CONDITION AND PROGRESS.

With the exception of the Portsmouth Savings Bank, no answer has been made by any Savings Bank in New Hampshire to my inquiries for facts, statistics, or incidents in their history. We have, therefore, only such facts as can be derived from the published reports, which exhibit the condition of these institutions from year to year since 1848.

As before remarked, the first published returns which I have been able to find were those of the bank commissioners made in 1849. These I subjoin in the form and in the order in which they appear in the documents of that year, the text or comments being that of the commissioners. These reports comprise, as will be seen, the returns of ten Savings Banks, and are as follows.

PORTSMOUTH SAVINGS BANK.

[Examined April 11, 1849.]

Investments		$390, 813 10
Deposits	$380, 119 92	
Last dividend	6, 827 12	
Surplus	3, 866 06	
		$390, 813 10

Incorporated June 26, 1823; charter perpetual. William M. Shackford, president; Samuel Lord, treasurer. No bad or doubtful investments; chiefly State and city stocks. Investments yielded at the rate of $22,460 per annum at date of examination. Annual expense last year, $1,202.24. Dividends four per cent per annum, and residue once in five years. Twenty dollars deposited Dec. 17, 1823, amounts now to $86.10, equal to 13 per cent, simple interest.* Thorough examination twice a year by committee. Number of accounts opened since bank commenced, 7,742.

Manchester Savings Bank.

[Examined April 17, 1849.]

Assets.

Seventy shares Merchants Bank..	$7, 098 75	
Ten shares Columbian Bank.....	1, 005 53	
Notes secured by mortgage......	10, 142 00	
Notes secured by pledge of stock,	400 00	
		$18, 646 28

Liabilities.

Due depositors	$14, 730 00	
Due Manchester Bank..........	2, 956 45	
Profits	959 83	
		$18, 646 28

Incorporated 1846; charter perpetual. Securities all good. Quarterly dividends at rate of four per cent per annum; earnings about six per cent. Trustees not indebted, either as principal or surety. Treasurer gives bond $3,000. Committee of trustees examine the affairs of the bank thoroughly once a year. Whole expenses since organization, $357.17. Number of depositors, 130.

* This famous deposit has become a prominent feature in the annals of this institution. It figures in the original History of Savings Banks of the State of New York, page 285, and its growth and progress will be found detailed in the historical sketch of this bank, *ante*, page 200, where it has increased to $392.29. It bids fair to out-rival the schoolboys' problem of the penny put at compound interest at the beginning of the Christian era! According to the assumption of those who fear that Savings Banks may ultimately absorb all the property of the country, this single deposit must, after the lapse of centuries, gather to itself all the property of the country, including that of all other Savings Banks! What would happen, then, if there were another such in another bank?

NEWMARKET SAVINGS BANK.

[Examined April 7, 1849.]

Below is the sworn statement of the treasurer, of its means and liabilities as they existed that day. His books appear to me, after a full examination, to be carefully and correctly kept, furnishing full means of ascertaining the condition of the bank without other aid. *I doubt not, therefore, the accuracy of his statement.**

Assets.

Due from town of New Market..	$2,909 04	
Due from New Market M'fg Co..	16,224 91	
Interest accrued	305 19	
Cash on hand	118 45	
		$19,557 59

Liabilities.

Due depositors	$18,812 27	
Interest account, four per cent, estimated......................	188 12	
Profits	557 20	
		$19,557 59

Incorporated 1832; perpetual charter. Trustees examine bank once in six months. First dividend December, 1832— one and one-third per cent for four months; since then regular semi-annual dividend at four per cent, and three extra, amounting to seven per cent in all; average for 16 years, a little less than four and one-half per cent. Expenses for 1848, $41.03. (Might not higher interest be obtained?) Number open accounts, 404.

* Significant as to the mode of conducting the examination!

CHESHIRE PROVIDENT INSTITUTION FOR SAVINGS.

[Examined May 5, 1849.]

Assets.

Debts due	$358, 392 79	
Cash on hand	860 89	
		$359, 253 68

Liabilities.

Due depositors	$358, 154 82	
Surplus.......................	1, 098 86	
		$359, 253 68

Incorporated July, 1833, for 20 years. Fifteen trustees chosen annually, from whom is chosen a board of investment of five persons. Corporators, 48; limited to 50. Number of depositors, about 2,300. Investments are, on mortgage of real estate, about one-half; bank and railroad stocks (loans), about one-ninth; $30,000 in railroad bonds, and balance on notes with personal security. No officer except treasurer has compensation. Dividends, five per cent, semi-annually, and extra once in five years; last extra dividend was nearly one and one-third per cent for each of the five years. Treasurer's account made up and examined weekly by one or more trustees, semi-annually by another committee, and annually by a third. Expenses in 1848, $523.11. One deposit over $3,000, one between $2,000 and $3,000, ten between $1,000 and $2,000, about 100 between $500 and $1,000.

SULLIVAN SAVINGS INSTITUTION.

[Examined May 9, 1849.]

Assets.

Amount of loans	$7, 840 34	
Cash on hand	87 00	
		$7, 927 34

Liabiliiies.

Due depositors	$7,833 05	
Surplus	94 29	
		$7,927 34

Incorporated June 26, 1838, for twenty years from that date; organized October 30, 1847. Corporators, 39; directors, 18. Present number depositors, 113. Loans made by monthly committees of three directors each. Nearly one-half loans on mortgage of real estate; balance, notes, with sureties. Debts due the institution all deemed good. Only treasurer receives compensation. But one deposit over $500. Two dividends been declared, two and one-half per cent semi-annually; extra once in five years to be declared.

CONNECTICUT RIVER SAVINGS BANK.

[Examined May 10, 1849.]

Assets.

All debts due	$124,827 55

Liabilities.

Due depositors	$118,056 25	
Due Connecticut River Bank....	1,820 50	
Surplus	4,950 80	
		$124,827 55

Incorporated June 16, 1831; charter perpetual. Corporators, 45; trustees, 18. Depositors, 660. Investments chiefly in notes secured by real estate or sureties; all deemed good but one note of $1,000, on which there will probably be a loss; this the only loss ever sustained. No real estate. Only treasurer receives compensation. Interest, five per cent, payable semi-annually; extra dividend once in five years.

New Hampshire Savings Bank, Concord.

[Examined May 11, 1849.]

Assets.

Debts due bank................	$175, 263 62	
Bank stocks....................	18, 559 50	
Interest due, not received	3, 214 56	
Cash on hand	2, 692 26	
		$199, 729 94

Liabilities.

Due depositors, principal........	$154, 362 00	
Due depositors, interest to Jan. 15,	28, 596 40	
Unclaimed extra dividend.......	248 15	
Surplus	16, 523 39	
		$199, 729 94

Incorporated 1830; perpetual charter. Corporators, 48; trustees, 18. Whole number of depositors from beginning, 5,391. Loans principally in notes secured by mortgage; balance on notes with sureties, or on bank, railroad or manufacturing stocks. Debts deemed good, except about $700. No real estate, except a tract estimated worth $150, taken for debt. Treasurer receives compensation; also investing committee, one dollar each for each meeting, weekly; also paid for time and expenses when out on business of the bank; this in violation of charter. Dividends, four per cent per annum. Surplus divided once in five years. Expenses of the year, including treasurer's salary, $600 = $948.02. One member of investing committee indebted to bank $500, contracted before his appointment.

SAVINGS BANK FOR COUNTY OF STRAFFORD.

[Date of examination not given.]

Assets.

Real estate:		
Brick building on Central street,	$4,625 00	
New Hampshire Hotel	5,425 00	
Lot on Orchard street	1,000 00	
		$11,050 00
Furniture in hotel		1,170 00
Deposits in Strafford Bank..................		1,677 17
Cash		326 76
Notes		287,142 45
Old Dover Bank stock		147 00
One hundred shares Strafford Bank...........		10,000 00
Albany city stock..........................		1,000 00
Railroad stock, to wit:		
328 shares Boston & Maine	$34,960 00	
129 shares Worcester	14,125 00	
228 shares Northern	22,800 00	
133 shares Old Colony.........	12,898 00	
200 shares Cocheco............	20,000 00	
		104,783 00
Total		$417,296 38

Liabilities.

Amount of deposits.............	$400,461 18	
Apparent surplus	16,835 20	
		$417,296 38

From the apparent surplus should be deducted:

Estimated loss on real estate......	$3,000 00	
Estimated loss on furniture.......	400 00	
For doubtful notes	757 00	
	$4,157 00	
True surplus		$12,678 20

Hardly probable that stocks will for some time bring above prices. No doubt, however, that bank can at any time pay depositors in full. Interest, five per cent. Number of depositors about 2,500; generally small amounts. Treasurer receives $700, which covers all expenses of institution. Incorporated 1823; organized 1824.*

Savings Bank of County of Strafford, Dover.

[February 12, 1872.]

Assets.

	Market value.	On books.
Loans on real estate	$252,457 13	$252,457 13
Loans on personal security	454,642 31	454,642 31
Loans on collateral security	11,535 00	11,535 00
Real estate	3,000 00	3,000 00
Corporations in New Hampshire	236,000 00	236,000 00
U. S. registered bonds	362,600 00	336,378 12
City of Dover bonds	100,000 00	98,000 00
City of Chicago bonds	99,000 00	96,437 50
Cincinnati city bonds	52,000 00	50,937 50
St. Louis city bonds	18,200 00	17,200 00
Boston & Maine R. R. stock	54,437 00	54,437 00
Northern R. R. stock	17,475 00	4,831 45
Boston & Albany R. R. stock	30,900 00	21,825 00
Bank stock	23,500 00	17,000 00
Town of Wolfeborough bonds	8,000 00	8,000 00
Town of Barrington bonds	7,800 00	7,800 00
Town of Farnham bonds	2,500 00	2,500 00
Town of Madbury bonds	6,000 00	6,000 00
City of Dover bonds	12,000 00	12,000 00
Deposited in Strafford Bank	39,873 04	39,873 04
Cash on hand	10 17	10 17
Totals	$1,791,929 65	$1,730,864 27

* The foregoing exhibit seems so unpromising, with an apparent surplus of about four per cent, an estimated surplus of about three per cent, and a class of investments almost certain, if forced upon the market, to wipe out the surplus and leave a deficiency, that we cannot forbear to cast our eye forward and see what the future has in store for an institution so environed; hence we subjoin the condition of this institution as reported in 1872, twenty-three years later. It illustrates the good sometimes wrought by judicious *letting alone.*

Semi-annual dividend, two and one-half per cent; an extra once in five years, the last being about eight per cent for the period.

Liabilities.

Due depositors	$1,593,219 55	
Surplus	137,644 72	
		$1,730,864 27
Add to surplus	$137,644 72	
Market value	61,065 38	
		$198,710 10
Doubtful loans	$8,000 00	
Protested	16,000 00	
Bad	1,650 00	
		25,650 00
True surplus		$173,060 10

Somersworth Savings Bank.

[Date not given.]

Assets.

Notes	$43, 346 14	
150 shares Great Falls Bank	15, 000 00	
50 shares Great Falls & Conway Railroad	5, 000 00	
Cash	237 40	
		$63, 583 54

Liabilities.

Deposits	$61, 665 21	
Balance profits	1, 918 33	
		$63, 583 54

Incorporated 1845; charter expires 1885. The above balance was the surplus after deducting dividend of January 1, 1849. Rate, two and one-half per cent semi-annually. Annual expenses $200, including treasurer's salary. Trustees liable as principals for $2,750, and as sureties for $6,721.39.

Meredith Bridge Savings Bank.

Assets.

20 shares Belknap County Bank..	$2,000 00	
U. S. six per cent stock	5,000 00	
Bond of B., C. & M. R. R......	500 00	
Notes	41,122 47	
Interest accruing	665 30	
Cash	2,057 79	
		$51,345 56

Liabilities.

Deposits......................	$50,346 25	
Reserved fund.................	527 95	
Profits on hand................	471 36	
		$51,345 56

Debts all deemed good. Interest, five per cent; extra in 1847 of $730, and 1842, one of $898.75. Treasurer, $160.

Below will be found a summary of the foregoing, and a comparison with the reported condition of the same institutions in 1874:

NAME OF INSTITUTION.	Open accounts, 1849.	Open accounts, 1874.	Due depositors, 1849.	Due depositors, 1874.
Cheshire...............	2,724	5,900	$358,154	$1,738,335
Connecticut River	660	1,176	118,056	257,799
Manchester............	130	5,152	14,730	2,504,845
Meredith Bridge*	380	1,996	50,346	537,372
New Hampshire........	1,187	3,461	154,362	1,064,909
New Market	404	245	18,812	39,337
Portsmouth............	2,930	7,056	380,119	2,110,049
Savings Bank of Strafford County	3,080	4,963	400,461	2,088,369
Somersworth	474	2,371	61,665	621,199
Sullivan	113	2,214	7,833	845,958
Ten institutions......	12,082	34,534	$1,564,540	$11,808,172

*Supposed to report in 1874 under name of Laconia Savings Bank.

Depositors' accounts increase a little less than three times. Amount of deposits increase about seven and one-half times in 25 years.

The following table exhibits a comparative view of the investments in 1849 and in 1873, in so far as the defective form of reporting the items for the former year would admit. It will be understood that, for that year, both the amount and the per cent of the several classes are approximations only, from the imperfect data given. I do not make the total investments in 1873 correspond with the amount given in the report for that year by some $300,000; but, as I use the items furnished, the result cannot be far wrong.

NAME OF SECURITIES.	INVESTMENTS, 1849.		INVESTMENTS, 1873.	
	Amount.	Per cent.	Amount.	Per cent.
Loans secured by real estate,	$804,000	50	$7,086,810	23 1-2
Loans on collaterals	175,000	11	2,496,519	8 1-5
Loans on personal security..	300,000	18	5,904,313	19 3-5
Public funds, viz.:				
U. S. and State bonds....	160,800	10	1,904,218	6 1-5
County, city and town b'ds and loans			5,440,630	18
Bank and railroad stocks and bonds	144,000	9	5,804,772	19
Cash on hand	20,000	1 1-5	632,892	2
Miscellaneous	4,200	2-5	791,562	2 4-5

The following table, exhibiting the number, condition and progress of Savings Banks in New Hampshire from 1848 to 1874, is derived from a table found in the annual report of the bank commissioners, made to the legislature in May, 1874. The column showing the increase in deposits from year to year was found to contain a number of errors, which are corrected in the table here given. The date for which the reported conditions are stated is in April or May of the year given, commonly the latter.

If the progress of Savings Banks in New Hampshire, as revealed by this table, is less striking than in some of the other States, it, nevertheless, when considered in connection with the growth in population and wealth, exhibits a very substantial growth, and is perhaps a fairer index of the development of the Savings Bank idea, pure and simple, than is found in some States whose merely financial exhibit is more wonderful than the following.

TABLE showing the growth of Savings Banks in New Hampshire from 1848 *to* 1874.

DATE.	No. of banks.	No. of open accounts.	Increase in open acc'ts.	Amount due depositors.	Increase in amount due depositors.	Increase in Periods of Five Years.			
						In number of open acc'ts.	Per c'nt of increase.	In amount due depositors.	Per c'nt of increase.
1848	9	12,424	....	$1,619,689	....	First period from 1848 to 1854, 6 yrs.		First per'd from 1848 to 1854, six years.	
1849	10	12,082	—342	1,564,540	—$155,149				
1850	12	13,031	949	1,641,543	77,003				
1851	13	14,316	1,285	1,776,768	135,224				
1852	15	15,771	1,455	2,009,617	232,849				
1853	16	18,105	2,334	2,507,909	498,292				
1854	16	20,145	2,040	3,222,261	714,351	7,721	61	$1,602,572	99
1855	17	21,300	1,155	3,341,256	118,995				
1856	19	23,489	2,189	3,537,363	196,106				
1857	20	24,786	1,297	3,748,285	210,922				
1858	21	23,463	—1,323	3,588,658	—159,627				
1859	23	26,762	3,299	4,138,822	550,164	6,617	33	916,561	29
1860	26	30,828	4,066	4,860,024	721,202				
1861	26	35,590	4,762	5,590,652	730,627				
1862	27	35,920	330	5,653,585	62,933				
1863	27	39,358	3,438	6,560,308	906,722				
1864	28	43,175	3,817	7,661,738	1,101,430	16,810	63	3,522,916	85
1865	29	43,572	397	7,831,335	169,597				
1866	29	42,894	—678	7,857,601	26,265				
1867	28	47,792	4,898	10,463,418	2,605,817				
1868	31	55,218	7,426	13,541,534	3,078,116				
1869	38	62,931	7,713	16,379,857	2,838,322	18,359	42	8,718,119	114

TABLE—(Continued).

YEAR.	No. of banks.	No. of open accounts.	Increase in open acc'ts.	Amount due to depositors.	Increase in amount due depositors.	Increase in Periods of Five Years.			
						In number of open acc'ts.	Per cent of increase.	In amount due depositors.	Per cent of increase.
1870	45	70,918	7,987	$18,759,461	$2,379,603				
1871	52	77,472	6,554	21,472,120	2,712,659				
1872	54	86,790	9,318	24,700,774	3,228,654				
1873	61	94,967	8,177	29,671,114	4,970,339				
1874	64	92,788	—2,179	28,829,376	—841,738	29,857	47	$12,449,519	75

By the courtesy of Hon. A. J. Fogg, chairman of the bank commissioners of New Hampshire, I am enabled to supplement the above table with the following statement of the condition of Savings Banks at the close of the examinations April 1, 1875: Number of banks, 68; number of depositors, 96,938; increase, 4,150; amount due depositors, $30,214,585; increase, $1,385,209; amount of surplus, $1,520,726.

— Decrease.

SIXTH SECTION;

SAVINGS BANKS IN THE STATE OF MAINE.

CHAPTER XIX.

INCEPTION AND DEVELOPMENT.

It seems like a singular coincidence that the impulse to the organization of Savings Banks should find culmination in legislative action thereon in so many States in the notable year 1819. In New York, Pennsylvania, Connecticut and Rhode Island, the first acts of incorporation date from this memorable year, and in New Hampshire the subject was considered, though not matured, whilst in Maryland the first charter was passed in December, 1818. In the same year (1819), and before its admission as a State in the Union, the legislature of Maine incorporated the "Institution for Savings of the Town of Portland," which entered on a prosperous career, but failed during the reverses of 1838, owing, it is said, to the nature of its investments. Unfortunately — as this event occurred before the era of Savings Bank disclosures, through examinations or reports to the legislature — we have no means of knowing what were the particular investments which precipitated this untoward result. So far as we know, this is the only instance in the country where the inception of the effort to establish Savings Banks ended disastrously. In all other States the first chartered institutions still remain, as worthy and substantial monuments of the wisdom and sagacity of their founders.

We have no data from which to derive any knowledge of the extent of injury wrought by this failure, there being nothing on record, unless it may be in the court of chancery and not easily accessible, showing the amount due to depositors nor the percentage of loss. But the total deposits could not, at this early period, have been large, and doubtless something must have been realized with which to make a dividend to depositors, who were thus preserved from total loss. As throwing some light upon the probable condition of the institution at the time of its failure, we may notice the fact that there were then but two other Savings Banks in operation, the Saco and Biddeford, organized in 1827, and the Gardiner, organized in 1834. The united deposits of these two institutions in 1855, seventeen years later, were but $419,610, and the total savings deposits in the State, at this latter date, were less than twice that sum, or in exact figures, $825,815. It is probable, therefore, that so early as 1838, the united deposits in the three institutions then existing, did not exceed $250,000, of which, if we concede to the older and more favorably located $125,000, we shall probably indicate the highest amount which even a total wreck of the institution, and unrelieved loss to the depositors, could have entailed; and, as total loss is not to be presumed, we may probably estimate the amount as considerably below $100,000.

But this amount at that time would, as we very well know, indicate a vastly greater degree of suffering and embarrassment than even twice the amount at the present day.

We deduce some interesting facts concerning the development of the Savings Bank interest in the State of Maine. As will be seen from the abstracts hereinafter presented, there were, in 1855, eleven Savings Banks in the State, with an aggregate of deposits amounting to $825,815, and a surplus of $41,316. As the aggregates in subsequent reports commonly embrace the deposits and surplus as so much belonging to depositors, we cannot, without great trouble and labor, separate these items; hence it will be understood, unless otherwise stated, that the term deposits embraces the profits earned and not yet divided. Of these eleven Savings Banks, one — the Randalls Savings and Benevolent Association — was a nondescript, of which some particulars will be found elsewhere. Three others — the Biddeford, Lewiston Falls, and South Berwick — were connected with banks of discount, or rather *were* banks of discount, with the privilege of receiving savings deposits, and all four were soon after discontinued; the Lewiston Falls being succeeded in 1860 by the Lewiston, a genuine and flourishing Savings Bank, and the Biddeford Savings Institution by the Biddeford Savings Bank in 1867, and the South Berwick by one of the same name in 1866, both apparently of substantial character. This leaves but seven Savings Banks in the State whose charters ante-date 1855, and but twelve out of the fifty-six with charters ante-dating 1866. Forty of the whole number of Savings Banks in the State are, or were in 1873, less than seven years old.

We find, further, that the seven Savings Banks organized prior to 1855 held, in 1873, $13,284,374 of the $29,556,523 of deposits and profits in all the institutions, or nearly half of the entire amount; and the twelve Savings Banks organized prior to 1866, which, of course, embrace the seven last mentioned, held $19,510,820, or about two-thirds of the total deposits in the State.

The order in which the fifty-six Savings Banks of Maine were organized was as follows:

YEAR.	No.	YEAR.	No.	YEAR.	No.
1827	1	1859	1	1869	9
1834	1	1860	2	1870	7
1848	1	1861	1	1871	6
1852	3	1866	4	1872	5
1854	1	1867	2	1873	2
1858	1	1868	9		

It will be noticed that an impetus was given to the development of the Savings Bank system in this as in other States, in respect to the number of institutions organized, very soon after the close of the late war, forty-four of the number having commenced after that period. The development in respect to the amount of deposits is equally remarkable. At the close of 1860 the deposits and profits were $1,539,257; in 1865 they were $3,336,828* (a falling off of $336,000 from 1864);

* Whether these embraced profits or not, does not appear; it is supposed they do.

whilst, as will be seen, in 1873 they had risen to the relatively enormous sum of $29,556,000. That is, from 1860 to 1865 the deposits had but little more than doubled in amount, while from the latter date to 1873 the increase was nearly nine times.

CHAPTER XX.

CHARACTER OF LEGISLATION.

The charter of the Saco and Biddeford Savings Institution, which will be found in the Appendix, was the model upon which subsequent acts of incorporation were framed. It will be seen that the organization was simple and natural, with very little in the way of machinery or conditions and provisos. A certain number of corporators were named, to whom was given the power of adding to their number at discretion, and upon this body of corporators all the powers and duties prescribed in the act of incorporation were conferred. These were, to receive deposits, to use and improve the same to the best advantage, and apply the net income or profits by dividing the same among the depositors in just proportion. Of course, under a form of organization so simple and free from complexity as this, much is intrusted to the character of those to whom so large powers and such wide discretion are committed. Indeed, more confidence seems to have been reposed in the wisdom and integrity of the corporators than in the restraints that might be imposed upon their actions by law.

The original charter of the Gardiner Savings Institution, granted in 1833, contained a provision requiring five per cent interest to be paid; but this clause was subsequently repealed, before the institution was organized, in 1834. Doubtless the organization was delayed by the presence of this obnoxious and unreasonable clause.

It was not until 1848 that the fourth act of incorporation was passed, that of the Augusta Savings Bank, with provisions similar to those in preceding charters. Meantime the original Portland institution, incorporated in 1819, had failed, as hereinbefore stated, leaving but two in operation upon the incorporation of the fourth. Thus a period of nearly thirty years, put in successful operation but three Savings Banks in the State.

In 1849 the Biddeford Bank, and in 1850 the South Berwick Bank, both banks of discount, and, we suppose, of circulation also, were authorized to receive deposits as Savings Banks, and in 1852 the legislature chartered the Lewiston Falls Bank and Savings Institution, with a capital of $50,000, conferring upon it, of course, the usual banking powers, with the right, also, of receiving deposits as a Savings Bank. The effort to combine the quite dissimilar objects and purposes of regular banks of discount and circulation and Savings Banks, does not seem to have been successful, as we find that the experiment was, after a few years, abandoned, and they were all superseded by genuine Savings Banks.

The Bangor Savings Bank, Portland Savings Bank, and Bath Savings Institution, were all incorporated in 1852, without any features that distinguished them from others, except that in the charter of the Portland Savings Bank there was a provision making it subject to examination by the bank commissioners at their discretion.

In 1854 the Hallowell Savings Institution was incorporated by an act which embraced but three sections, covering, however, essentially the same ground as previous charters in the use of the following language: "And to enjoy all rights and privileges incident to similar corporations."

In this year also, the Randall Savings and Benevolent Association was incorporated, with the unique feature that all of the profits over six per cent were to be devoted to some benevolent purpose. It maintained a feeble existence until 1861, when the trustees voted to close it up. Its condition in 1855 will be found in the reports of examinations made by the bank commissioners, hereafter introduced.

As no distinguishing features marked the course of legislation in the incorporation of Savings Banks thereafter, we will not further note the progress made in this direction.

MADE SUBJECT TO EXAMINATION.

Savings Banks generally, were first made subject to examination by the bank commissioners in 1855. These officers were first appointed under a provision of the Revised Statutes enacted in 1840, but their duties were by that act limited to banks of discount, which they were required to examine at least once in each year, and to make a report of the same to the governor and council. By the act of 1855 the same duties were imposed upon them concerning Savings Banks.

As this first examination constitutes the starting point of statistical information concerning the Savings Banks in this State, we shall transcribe the return of the same in full in a subsequent part of this section.

The two bank commissioners were in 1868 superseded by a single officer, denominated an examiner of banks and insurance companies, with powers concerning these institutions similar to those previously exercised by the bank commissioners, and subsequently the duties were divided between an examiner of banks and an insurance commissioner, and so remain at the present time.

GENERAL ACT OF 1869.

The first general act for the incorporation and regulation of Savings Banks was passed in 1869, and if it did not wholly derive its inspiration from, it was certainly stimulated by, the effort elsewhere narrated to enact a general law for the incorporation and management of Savings Banks in the State of New York in 1868. A general summary of the provisions of this act and the subsequent amendments thereto will serve our purpose of giving the latest status of Savings Banks before the law in the State of Maine.

Section 1 provides for the incorporation of Savings Banks, and grants the exercise of the powers conferred by this act and by the existing charters and general laws concerning corporations.

Section 2 provides for the election, annually, from the body of corporators, of five trustees, who shall have entire charge and control of the affairs of the institution, except as otherwise provided in the by-laws. Provides also for elections to fill vacancies in the board of trustees, and to add new members to the body of corporators.

Section 3 provides for the election of officers by the board of trustees, containing substantially the provisions of existing charters.

Section 4 requires an examination of the affairs of each Savings Bank by the trustees thereof as often as once in six months.

Section 5 directs the trustees to see to the proper investment of the funds of the institution, which investments are to be made in any manner which they may regard as perfectly safe, except that no loans are to be made on the security of names alone, nor, either directly nor indirectly, to any trustee, nor to a firm of which any trustee is a member.

Section 6 requires the net income (except as hereinafter provided) to be divided semi-annually to depositors of three months' standing, though deposits of a shorter time may be included; and the trustees are not required to divide earnings so close as to embrace a fraction of less than one-fourth of one per cent, the balance being carried to a new account for the next dividend. No deposit is to be received under any contract or agreement to pay any specified rate of interest or dividend for its use.

Section 7. Before making any dividend, one-fourth of one per cent of the net earnings of the dividend period is to be set apart as a reserved fund, to be kept constantly on hand, to secure the depositors against losses and contingencies until the same amounts to five per cent of the total assets (changed to ten per cent in 1871). All losses are to be charged to debit of the reserved fund account.

Section 8 defines the duties and powers of the treasurer.

Section 9 makes it the duty of the trustees to insure real estate held absolutely, or by mortgage, if the same is insurable

Section 10. Deposits of married women made payable to themselves. A general act in 1860 had made similar provision for the deposits of minors, where not fraudulent.

Section 11 makes it the duty of the treasurer to make an annual report of the condition of the institution to the bank examiner.

Section 12 prohibits any officer from using or appropriating any of the funds under penalty as for embezzlement.

SUPPLEMENTARY AND AMENDATORY.

In 1871 private banks, and banks of discount not organized in pursuance of law, were prohibited from holding themselves forth to the public as Savings Banks, a precaution found necessary in the State of New York as early as 1858.

In 1872 several additional and amendatory sections were enacted.

The first section imposed a tax of one-fourth of one per cent upon the deposits of Savings Banks, payable to the State treasury, for the use of schools.

Section 2 required dividends to be made once in six months, but not to exceed three per cent; the balance, except that set apart to the reserved fund, to be divided once in four years; changed to once in two years at the succeeding session of the legislature.

Section 3 provided that the examination required to be made by the trustees might be made by two or more of them, who should report to the bank examiner.

By section 4 the treasurer was required to return to the assessors the names of persons pledging bank stock as security for loans, and the amount of the same. The purpose, to reach these securities as personal property liable to taxation, is obvious.

Section 5 prohibited the trustees from investing the moneys deposited in unfinished railroads or roads whose net income was not sufficient to pay the interest on its funded debt; or in the bonds of any town or county, out of the New England States, issued in aid of any railroad.

By section 6 the trustees were authorized to receive a reasonable compensation for their services in making examinations and returns.

Some immaterial amendments were made in the following year, but nothing that modified the essential character of the general law concerning Savings Banks.

CHAPTER XXI.

CONDITIONS OF PROGRESS AS SHOWN BY REPORTS

We here present in full the first report of the examination of Savings Banks, made in 1855, and follow that with the aggregates in succeeding years, with such comments from the text of the reports as serve to reveal the conditions of this interest from time to time.

AUGUSTA SAVINGS BANK.

[September 30, 1855.]

Assets.

State and city stock	$15,600 00	
Notes secured by bank stock and city scrip	36,900 00	
Town note....................	1,320 00	
Thirty-three shares State Bank ..	3,300 00	
Yarmouth and Portland first mortgage railroad bonds	10,000 00	
Cash	3,073 00	
Mortgages	12,951 06	
		$83,144 06

Liabilities.

Due depositors	$80,582 00	
Profits	2,562 06	
		$83,144 06

Incorporated 1848. Regular semi-annual dividends, two per cent; extra dividends once in five years, the last being two per cent. Notes considered good.

BANGOR SAVINGS BANK.

[October 24, 1855.]

Assets.

City note	$5,000 00	
County of Penobscot note	4,000 00	
City of Bangor bonds	8,000 00	
Notes	3,300 00	
Deposited in bank	7,707 35	
Cash on hand	850 00	
Interest	164 30	
		$29,021 65

Liabilities.

Due depositors	$28,331 00	
Profits	690 65	
		$29,021 65

Incorporated 1852. Regular dividends, two and one-half per cent; extra dividends every five years. Notes deemed good.

BATH SAVINGS INSTITUTION.

[October 6, 1855.]

Assets.

Loans on notes	$13,514 00	
Town scrip	1,500 00	
Railroad bonds	1,275 00	
Bank stock	9,412 00	
Cash on hand	455 28	
		$26,156 28

Liabilities.

Due depositors	$23,113 55	
Interest	3,042 73	
		$26,156 28

Incorporated 1852. Semi-annual dividends, two per cent; balance of surplus divided annually. Notes regarded as well secured.

Biddeford Savings Institution.

[September 8, 1855.]

Assets.

Bank stock	$14,200 00	
Stocks	11,600 00	
Notes	60,003 08	
Cash	10,612 72	
		$96,415 80

Liabilities.

Due depositors	$90,424 78	
Balance	5,991 02	
		$96,415 80

Incorporated 1849. Semi-annual dividends, two per cent for two years, and two and one-half per cent for two years more. Stocks, quoted at par in the statement, are worth more. Notes all considered good. Connected with Biddeford Bank, which guarantees deposits if assets are insufficient.

Gardiner Savings Institution.

[October 5, 1855.]

Assets.

Bank stock	$17,750 00	
City, State and railroad bonds	72,000 00	
Guaranteed stocks	11,000 00	
Railroad stocks	28,400 00	
Notes of cities and towns	11,975 10	
Notes of individuals (estimated)	42,892 00	
Interest and dividends accrued	2,650 90	
Cash on hand	3,878 56	
		$190,546 56

Liabilities.

Due depositors	$182, 595 10	
Interest due	7, 951 46	
		$190, 546 56

Incorporated 1833; went into operation 1834. Regular semi-annual dividends, two per cent, and extra dividends once in five years; the latter always sufficient to average total interest to depositors more than six per cent, and during the last five years about eight per cent. Investments all regarded as perfectly safe.

Hallowell Savings Institution.

[October 5, 1855.]

Assets.

City of Hallowell scrip	$1, 700 00	
Interest (estimated)	35 00	
Notes secured by mortgage	997 00	
Cash on hand	4 62	
		$2, 736 62

Liabilities.

Due depositors	$2, 679 62	
Interest (estimated)	57 00	
		$2, 736 62

Incorporated 1854, and went into operation in July of that year. Semi-annual dividends, two per cent; surplus divided every five years. Investments safe.

Lewiston Falls Savings Institution.

[September 14, 1855.]

Assets.

Notes receivable	$18, 900 00	
Cash	940 01	
		$19, 840 01

Liabilities.

Due depositors	$19, 840 01

Notes secured as follows:

$12, 350 by $14, 500 bank stock.
3, 250 by indorsers.
3, 000 by $10, 000 manufacturing stock.
300 by $1, 000 railroad bonds.

Incorporated 1852. Semi-annual dividends, two per cent; no extra dividends provided for. Connected with Lewiston Falls Bank, which guarantees payment of depositors.

Portland Savings Bank.

[September 11, 1855.]

Assets.

State, city and county securities..	$14, 290 00	
Mortgages of real estate	38, 265 65	
Railroad bonds	20, 012 50	
Other securities (?)	3, 500 00	
Bank stock....................	1, 500 00	
Expense account...............	6 00	
Cash	390 99	
		$77, 965 14

Liabilities.

Due depositors	$77, 283 54	
Balance of profits.........	40 60	
Interest	641 00	
		$77, 965 14

Incorporated 1852. First dividend, May, 1853; five per cent per annum on periods of nine, six and three months; dividends since, at rate of six per cent per annum. Depositors receive net profits. *Trustees* deem moneys securely invested.

Randall's Saving and Benevolent Association.

Assets.

Bank stock....................	$4, 000 00	
Mortgages of real estate	838 53	
Estimated interest due..........	79 44	
Expense account................	50 00	
Cash on hand	1, 226 21	
		$6, 194 18

Liabilities.

Due depositors	$6, 020 02	
Estimated interest	99 23	
Surplus	74 93	
		$6, 194 18

Incorporated 1854. Receives deposits of five cents, and pays interest on two dollars; six per cent to be paid if so much accrue. After paying six per cent and expenses, any balance of profits is to be applied to benevolent objects. Treasurer is the depositary of his own bond! Moneys are received through agents appointed in different places. Notes good and amply secured.

Saco and Biddeford Savings Institution.

[September 9, 1855.]

Assets.

Bank stocks...................	$55, 564 05	
Railroad bonds and stocks	88, 244 05	
City and Portland and Bath bonds,	35, 145 83	
East Boston Ferry stock	100 00	
Loans on notes	74, 459 53	
Cash	129 08	
		$253, 642 54

Liabilities.

Due depositors	$237,015 39	
Profits	16,523 36	
Balance, suspense account	103 79	
		$253,642 54

Incorporated 1827. Oldest institution in the State. During first few years had only a small amount of deposits. Present number of depositors, 1,280.* Regular semi-annual dividends, two per cent; balance of profits divided every five years. Railroad stocks not in all cases worth par, but average dividends received by the institution from its investments is 6.47 per cent.

South Berwick Savings Bank.

[September 12, 1855.]

Assets.

Loans secured by indorsers	$76,239 75	
Bank stock	3,250 00	
Profit and loss	241 00	
Cash	1,813 02	
		$81,543 77

Liabilities.

Due depositors	$77,930 09	
Profit and loss	3,613 68	
		$81,543 77

Incorporated 1850. Semi-annual dividend of two per cent on deposits of less than one year, and two and one-half per cent on deposits of one or more years' standing. Connected with South Berwick Bank, which guarantees payment of depositors.

* The only institution concerning which this item is reported.

1856.

The next report of the bank commissioners was made under date of December 30, 1856, and presented the following

Summary.

Number of depositors	4, 947	
Due depositors (total assets)..................		$919, 571 85
Average to each depositor....................		185 88

The commissioners, at this early day, discern the need of uniformity in the provisions relating to the organization and government of Savings Banks, and recommend a general law for this purpose. They also comment unfavorably upon the intimate connection, in a few instances, of Savings Banks with banks of discount. We have previously noted that three of the institutions reported the previous year were only ordinary banks of discount and circulation, with Savings Bank powers superadded to their ordinary functions. Without legislative action, however, the connection appears not to have been sufficiently profitable to justify its continuance, and ceased after a few years.

The commissioners report the general condition of the Savings Banks examined as favorable.

1857.

The commissioners make but the briefest reference to that part of their duties connected with Savings Banks, and give no details, nor even a general summary. From other sources we gather that the total assets of Savings Banks were about $968,325, a gain over the previous year of a little less than $40,000. As at this time very little surplus had been accumulated, the reported assets represent very nearly the amount due to depositors.

1858.

The commissioners offer not a word concerning Savings Banks, and give no summary of their condition, which appears to have changed but little from the preceding year, the assets being estimated at $968,194.

1859.

In this year we have the following summary, without a line of comment:

Number of depositors	4,997	
Due depositors		$885,211 37
Profits		38,186 41
Total assets		$923,397 78

The above indicates a falling off from the two previous years; but the evident indifference of the commissioners to this part of their duties leads to a rational conjecture that they may not have been especially careful to secure accuracy in these results.

1860.

The commissioners, as usual, appear to find nothing in the condition or workings of Savings Banks worthy of comment, and negligently sandwich the aggregates of these institutions between the statistics of other banks and the text relating to the same. These aggregates are as follows:

Summary.

Number of banks	14	
Due depositors		$1,466,457 56
Profits		72,800 34
Total assets		$1,539,257 90

The above result more than confirms our suspicions that the aggregates, as given, of the two previous years must have been erroneous. That there should have been a falling off in 1858, resulting from the financial disturbances in 1857, would be reasonable; but it is also quite as reasonable that some part of the very large gain reported in 1860 should be credited to 1859. It is to be understood, however, that these aggregates relate to conditions not at the close of the year for which they are reported, nor on any uniform day, but at a period in the latter part of the year, commonly extending through October and November.

1861.

Summary.

Number of banks	14	
Number of depositors	9,818	
Due depositors		$1,620,270 26
Profits		88,691 40
Total assets		$1,708,961 66

The text of the report is brief, and refers to the gratifying fact that no failure of a Savings Bank has ever occurred in the State, the commissioners forgetting or not knowing of the failure of the first Savings Bank incorporated. They refer, also, to the passage in safety of the Savings Banks through the financial crisis of 1857, and comment favorably upon the economy with which these institutions are conducted, the expense being merely nominal. In this year the Randall Saving and Benevolent Association, whose peculiar character has been elsewhere noticed, resolved to close its operations.

1862.

In this year, the bank commissioners, Messrs. A. C. Robbins and Francis K. Swan, appear to entertain an intelligent and conscientious apprehension of their duties in relation to this rapidly growing interest. Their report for the year 1862, found in the documents of 1863, was by far the most elaborate, comprehensive and appreciative that had yet been made. In it they quote extensively from the report of the Massachusetts bank commissioners, made the previous year, and from which we have also taken liberal extracts in another part of this work. From their report we derive the following statement of the amount due to depositors in each of the fifteen Savings Banks doing business in the State:

Summary.

Augusta Savings Bank	$164,461
Bangor Savings Bank	120,076
Bath Savings Institution	88,760
Biddeford Savings Institution	118,308
Brunswick Savings Institution	23,609
Carried forward	$515,214

Brought forward	$515, 214
Calais Savings Bank	961
Gardiner Savings Bank	230, 315
Hallowell Savings Institution	27, 096
Lewiston Institution for Savings	69, 418
Portland Five Cents Savings Institution	87, 083
Portland Savings Bank	452, 088
Randall Saving and Benev't Institution (closing),	4, 228
Saco and Biddeford Savings Institution	373, 705
South Berwick Savings Bank	86, 551
York County Five Cents Savings Institution	29, 500
Total deposits (profits not reported)	$1, 876, 165

With a true and rational interest in the subject-matter with which they have been brought into official relations, the bank commissioners also present a summary of the aggregate deposits in the Savings Banks of the New England States and the State of New York in 1860, as derived from their returns to the proper departments as follows:

1860.

STATE.	Number of banks.	Due depositors.
Vermont	12	$1,145,263
Maine	14	1,466,457
Rhode Island	21	7,765,771
New Hampshire	26	4,860,025
Connecticut	64	18,132,121
Massachusetts	86	39,424,419
Total New England	....	$72,794,756
New York	72	67,450,397
Total New England and New York	....	$140,245,143

1863.

Summary.

Number of banks	15	
Due depositors		$2,641,476 41

Text brief, and not especially practical.

1864.

Summary.

Due depositors	$3,672,975 85

Items of Assets.

United States government securities	$1,072,636 52
State securities	232,913 00
City, town and county	582,831 00

Text brief, but satisfactory.

1865.

Summary.

Number of depositors	18,308	
Due depositors		$3,336,828 02
Decrease from previous year		336,147 00

The bank commissioners account for this decrease by the withdrawal of deposits to invest in government seven and three-tenths treasury notes. Doubtless this contributed somewhat to the result; but the return of many thousand soldiers, who had deposited their bounty money on going to the war, and now withdrew the same to engage in business, also had its effect.

1866.

Summary.

Number of banks	18
Number of depositors	19,786

Due depositors	$3, 946, 433 82
Increase from previous year	609, 605 80

Text practical and judicious. Comment on the alleged fact that not a dollar of loss had ever been sustained by depositing in Savings Banks. Whether we are to understand from this that the failure of the first incorporated institution was without loss to depositors, or that the statement was made without knowledge or in forgetfulness of that failure, we have no means of knowing.

1867.

Summary.

Due depositors	$5, 598, 600 00

Twenty banks reporting.

1868.

In this year we have the report of the first sole examiner of Savings Banks and insurance companies, under the late law. The position had been most fortunately and worthily conferred on Hon. A. W. Paine, whose industry, fidelity and intelligence in the discharge of this and other important public duties, have made his name familiar beyond the borders of his own State.

Summary.

Number of banks	28	
Number of depositors	30, 528	
Deposits and profits		$8, 032, 246 71

A summary of the investments is also given, as follows:

United States government securities	$1,726,146 00
State, county and municipal	1,294,511 00
Corporation securities	369,045 00
Real estate	176,551 00
Corporation stocks	449,561 00
Mortgages of real estate	1,811,241 00
Notes secured by collaterals	1,113,283 00
Notes secured by indorsers	775,285 00
Cash	309,571 00
Miscellaneous, furniture, safes, etc	2,048 00
Total	$8,032,246 00

The text of Mr. Paine's report discusses this important and rapidly-growing interest more fully and intelligently than any of his predecessors had done.

He points out serious defects in existing laws, referring to the various charters, which embraced nearly all the law there was for the government and control of these institutions. He recommends a limited number of trustees, to be selected, we suppose, from the body of corporators, as was subsequently provided for. His experience and observation had doubtless led to the conclusion that, where the management and direction of affairs was committed to a large body of corporators, the result was either general inefficiency or the concentration of too much power in the hands of a single managing officer. He would also require a bond of the treasurer, and that trustees make oath to the proper performance of their duties.

Concerning investments he takes conservative ground, maintaining that regard should be had to absolute safety. Security, he regards as primary and fundamental; profit, as only secondary and incidental. He also recommends that the purchase of real estate by any Savings Bank be limited to ten per cent of the deposits, though it is not made to appear that any serious abuse had arisen from investments in this direction. He favors mortgage security as exceptionally safe, and notes that not a dollar of loss had been sustained by the Savings Banks from the destructive fire at Portland; but, as a further precaution, recommends that trustees be required to insure mortgaged property. He does not favor personal security for loans, neither does he recommend legislation to prohibit it. He favors the accumulation of a moderate surplus, as a security against losses. He discountenances extra dividends, and would provide some means whereby trustees may be compelled to discharge the duties they have undertaken to perform.

The effect of this report is seen in the action of the legislature to which it was addressed, by whom the general law already noticed, and summarized on pages 233–235, was enacted, embodying many of the recommendations of the report.

1869.

Summary.

Number of banks.................	37	
Number of depositors.............	39,527	
Due depositors..........................		$10,839,955

1870.

Summary.

Number of banks....................	43	
Number of depositors..................	54,155	
Amount of deposits (including surplus)........		$16, 597, 888
Surplus..................................		768, 097
Leaving amount credited and due depositors,		$15, 829, 791

The commissioner, in commenting upon the average rate of dividends of Savings Banks in the State (seven per cent), suggests the propriety of requiring a larger amount to be credited to the reserve or surplus fund, against such time of financial depression as is likely to be attended by large demands upon the resources of Savings Banks, and a depreciation in the value of the securities from the conversion of which the demand must be met. The commissioner further says:

"The policy contemplated in the institution of Savings Banks was that of absolute safety to depositors, with such profits only as should be compatible with that condition. And, as they were designed to be permanent institutions, conducted for the benefit of persons of moderate means — for operatives, women and children, who have neither the time nor knowledge of business and of persons sufficient to judiciously invest their own funds — it is of the utmost importance that investments of unquestioned security should be sought, rather than those paying high rates, so as to insure moderate dividends and less fluctuation in the deposits. A large reserve would be of vast importance to this end."

The following comparison, illustrating the development of the Savings Bank system in the State, is made by the commissioner: In 1860 the deposits in Savings Banks averaged to each inhabitant of the State $2.33; in 1870 the deposits averaged to each inhabitant, allowing the same basis of population, $26.40.

1871.

Summary.

Number of banks	49	
Number of depositors	79, 411	
Amount of deposits and surplus		$22, 787, 802

1872.

Summary.

Number of banks	54	
Number of depositors	81, 320	
Amount of deposits and surplus		$26, 154, 333
Amount of dividends		1, 384, 510
United States tax paid		69, 779
State tax paid		119, 159
Added to reserve fund, at least one-half per cent.		

The text of the report recommends caution in organizing new banks; the first time, we believe, in which that matter receives attention. Investments in western securities are not favored.

1873.

Summary.

Number of banks	56	
Number of depositors	91, 398	
Amount of deposits and profits		$29, 556, 523 84
Gain in deposits from previous year		3, 402, 190 81

As this statement was made for the third day of November, at a time when the financial panic had wrought its worst results, we may say the exhibit is a remarkable one. The gain during the year had exceeded the gain of the previous year by more than $35,000, while a very considerable falling off might have been rationally anticipated. It will be seen that the gain in the State of New York was, on deposits, but $233,464, though to institute a fair comparison with the foregoing, the gain in assets in the latter State should be given, which was $2,259,399.

The bank examiner discusses various topics connected with the interest supervised by him with intelligence and good sense. He notes with favor the fact that the large deposits, which most unfavorably affect Savings Banks in time of financial difficulty, are diminishing, and favors a law, with proper restrictions, that shall prohibit Savings Banks from declaring any dividend on sums exceeding $2,000. He further recommends that Savings Banks be authorized by law to require sixty days' notice of intention to withdraw deposits. It would seem that, so far as the chartered institutions were concerned, they had all the power needed in the premises. See charter of Saco and Biddeford Savings Institution, section 3, last clause: Appendix.

The examiner calls attention to the fact that, notwithstanding the prohibition in the act of 1869, the reports show an aggregate of $358,828.74 loaned on names alone; and, though approving the policy of the law, and deprecating its violation, he suggests an abatement of its strictness by allowing some portion of the deposits to be thus loaned in preference to investing in Western securities, which he regards as altogether undesirable. He further recommends that dividends be limited to three per cent semi-annually, and that no extra dividends be declared until the reserve fund amounts to fifteen per cent of the deposits.

CHAPTER XXII.

STATISTICS OF GROWTH AND PROGRESS.

We will now present the condition and work accomplished by Savings Banks in the State of Maine, so far as these can be derived from their replies to my inquiries upon the subject, made in the same form in which they were submitted to other Savings Banks throughout the country. It will be seen that returns to my inquiries were in some form, more or less complete, made by ten of the fifty-six Savings Banks in the State. Where no other date is given, 1st of January, 1874, will be understood. These will be followed by the usual tables, showing the development of the system at large.

STATISTICS FURNISHED BY SAVINGS BANKS.

Augusta Savings Bank.

[Returns made for July 1, 1874.]

Date of first deposit, October 9, 1848.

Number of accounts opened	10, 744
Number of accounts closed................	5, 957
Number of open accounts..................	4, 787
Amount deposited, including dividends	$5, 236, 532 59
Amount withdrawn	3, 273, 537 85

Amount due depositors....................	$1, 962, 994 74
Dividends credited prior to July, 1874*	545, 700 47

About three-fourths of the whole number of open accounts are for less than $500 each.

Bath Savings Institution.

Date of first deposit, August 17, 1852.

Number of accounts opened to Jan. 1, 1874..	5, 747
Number of accounts closed.................	2, 777
Number of open accounts Jan. 1, 1874	2, 970
Due depositors at above date	$1, 585, 519 67

Amount deposited and amount of dividends, since organization, not given.

Calais Savings Bank.

Date of first deposit, August 29, 1861.

Number of accounts opened	1, 550
Number of accounts closed.................	752
Number of open accounts..................	798

Amount due depositors at periods mentioned below:

DATE.	Amount.	DATE.	Amount.
Aug., 1866...........	$8,180	Jan., 1871...........	$95,258
1867...........	8,049	1872...........	169,065
1868...........	29,922	1873...........	195,785
Jan., 1869...........	35,292	1874...........	232,384
1870...........	57,650	July, 1874...........	251,503

Dividends credited since organization, $39,648. Amount deposited since organization not given.

* Dividend earned, and to be credited Aug. 1, will increase the above to about $600,000.

Gorham Savings Bank

Date of first deposit, April 25, 1868.

Amount of first deposit, *ten cents.*

No items given concerning number of accounts opened or remaining open.

Amount deposited from organization to July 1, 1874, including dividends	$137,018 65
Amount withdrawn	56,142 41
Due depositors July 1, 1874	80,876 24
Dividends credited to depositors	11,431 12

The returns made to my inquiries state that the gross amount of deposits paid out is $44,711.29, which I suppose, however, to be exclusive of dividends credited and withdrawn. I deduce from other items that the amount of deposits and dividends withdrawn are as given above, $56,142.

Lewiston Institution for Savings.

Date of first deposit, July, 1860.

Amount deposited, including dividends	$3,668,380 08
Amount withdrawn	2,567,771 86
Amount due depositors	1,100,608 22
Amount of dividends	395,144 67

Average rate of dividends, 7.64 per cent.

No statement given concerning the number of depositors or accounts.

Maine Savings Bank, Portland.

This institution was chartered March 29, 1859, under the name of Portland Five Cents Savings Institution. In 1868 its name was changed to the above.

Date of first deposit, June 4, 1859.	
Number of open accounts	11, 551
Amount due depositors	$3, 664, 469 78

The treasurer of the institution, A. M. Burton, remarks that other inquiries made he is unable to answer, for the reason that the records, cash-books and journals of the institution were destroyed in the great fire of July 4, 1866.

NEWPORT SAVINGS BANK.

Date of first deposit, June 9, 1866.	
Number of accounts opened	1, 806
Number of accounts closed	912
Number of open accounts	894
Due depositors January 1, 1874	$191, 682 40

Treasurer states that the whole amount deposited cannot be given. The amount, however, from August, 1870, to November, 1873, is stated at $298,268.

PORTLAND SAVINGS BANK.

Date of first deposit, July 3, 1852.	
Number of open accounts Jan. 1, 1874	9, 700
Amount due depositors	$4, 066, 197
Amount of dividends credited since organization	1, 684, 749

The treasurer is unable to give further statistics of the work accomplished by the institution, owing to the imperfect system of keeping the books and records during the first years of the institution. The following extract, furnished by the treasurer, supplies some items of interest concerning the institution not otherwise attainable:

"Although not organized until 1852, it is the third oldest institution of the kind in the State,* the Saco and Biddeford Savings Institution having been organized in 1827 and the Gardiner Savings Institution in 1834. From various local causes the growth of the bank was very slow, and in May, 1862, it had only accumulated deposits to the amount of $408,363.27. In 1866 the bank began to feel the influence of the distribution of money among all classes by the business activities of the war, and for several years its net increase was over $600,000 per year, or the deposit increased $200,000 more in one of these years than in the ten years from 1852 to 1862. The deposits now amount to the sum of $4,003,588.89. The first president of the bank was Gov. Albion K. Parris, who, however, remained in office but a few months, and was succeeded by the late Phinehas Barnes, Esq., who resigned as president in October, 1863, although he continued to fill the important post of legal adviser of the bank until his death, in 1871. Oliver Gerrish, Esq., was chosen temporary president to succeed Mr. Barnes, and in May, 1874, the Hon. J. B. Brown was elected president, which office he still holds.

"The managers of the institution have been chosen, with scarcely an exception, from the most active and public-spirited men in the community, and the funds of the bank have been invested in such a way as to secure the greatest safety and at the same time assist in developing the various business interests of the city. At least one-half of the assets of the bank is loaned on

* This seems to be an error, as the Augusta Savings Bank, a large and flourishing institution, was incorporated in 1848, and the Bangor Savings Bank was organized March 27, 1852, about three months prior to the opening of the above. The Bath Savings Institution was incorporated in the same year (1852), but was not organized until August. It appears, therefore, that the Portland Savings Bank is the fifth in order of age of existing institutions, and not the third, as stated in the extract. It is, however, the largest.

mortgages and collateral securities to citizens of the city, while but a small proportion of the whole assets is invested in bonds of first-class cities and counties outside of Maine.

"The first treasurer of the bank was James Merrill, Esq., upon whose death, in 1859, Joseph C. Noyes, Esq., was chosen his successor. At this time, April 1, 1859, the deposits amounted to $161,825.62, and the bank had only been kept open on Wednesdays and Saturdays, between the hours of 11 and 1 o'clock. Under Mr. Noyes the bank was kept open every working day between those hours, and the office hours were gradually extended to the regular working hours. At his death, in July, 1868, the deposits amounted to $2,273,-266.11. He was succeeded by his son, Frank Noyes, who had been assistant treasurer.

"The bank, up to the time of the fire, occupied one of the small offices in the old Canal Bank building. It was then removed temporarily to Free street, until the completion of the building known as the Portland Savings Bank block, on Exchange street, in May, 1867.

"The rate of interest paid by the bank has never been less than six per cent, compound interest, and from May, 1866, to November, 1869, it was seven per cent, since which time it has paid six and one-half per cent, for 1870 and 1871, and under the new law pays six per cent for 1872.

"In this connection it is interesting to note the rapid accumulation of money at compound interest. The first deposit in the bank, July 3, 1852, of $100, was made by a gentleman, since deceased, for his daughter. This deposit has never been added to or subtracted from since. In November, 1862, it amounted to $181.60, and at this date the original $100 has increased to $374.56.

"Since the foundation of the bank, no money has been loaned on personal security. No money is loaned to any officer or manager, and the total losses from bad debts in the last twenty years has not exceeded $2,000.

Solon Savings Bank.

Date of first deposit, April 14, 1869.

Number of accounts opened since organization,	387
Number of accounts closed since organization,	124
Number of open accounts Jan. 1, 1874	263
Amount deposited, including dividends.....	$56, 865 57
Amount withdrawn	28, 288 72
Amount due depositors	28, 576 85
Amount of dividends credited	3, 309 29

West Waterville Savings Bank.

Date of first deposit, May 10, 1869.

Number of accounts opened...............	900
Number of accounts closed................	367
Number of open accounts.................	533
Amount deposited, including dividends	$234, 715 58
Amount withdrawn	137, 884 47
Amount due depositors...................	96, 831 11
Dividends credited.......................	16, 194 92

The village is largely manufacturing, and the population constantly changing, which makes the changes in deposits frequent and considerable.

The table below is constructed to show the progress made in eighteen years by the institutions whose earliest returns were made in 1855, when the total deposits in eleven banks were less than $1,000,000; and is, in brief, a summary of the reports for that year as heretofore given, with a comparison of their condition, as reported in 1855, with that of the same institutions existing and making returns in 1873.

NAME OF INSTITUTION.	Due depositors, 1855.	Due depositors, including surplus, 1873.	Open accounts, 1873.	Amount deposited 1873.
Augusta	$80,582	$1,927,241	4,643	$589,032
Bangor	28,331	2,341,205	5,728	683,819
Bath	23,113	1,704,531	2,908	468,761
Biddeford	90,424	Superseded	......	....
Gardiner	182,595	1,023,016	3,208	220,720
Hallowell	2,679	403,582	1,253	121,573
Lewiston Falls	19,840	Superseded	......	....
Portland	77,283	4,424,689	9,688	1,262,132
Randall's	6,020	Closed	......	....
Saco and Biddeford	237,015	1,460,107	3,755	338,473
South Berwick	77,930	Superseded	......	....
Profits or surplus	41,316	....	......	....
Eleven banks	$867,131	$13,284,374	31,183	$3,684,510

The number of depositors is not given in the report for 1855, but, as the number reported for 1856 was 4,927, we may estimate them for the previous year at 4,500, and in the seven institutions reporting in that year which reported in 1873, they may be estimated at 3,500. The deposits and profits in these seven institutions were $672,917. Comparing, then, the condition of the institutions reporting in 1855 with the conditions of the same institutions that continued in existence and reported in 1873, we have the following as the growth during eighteen years:

Increase in depositors or open accounts, from 3,500 to 31,183, or nearly nine times.

Increase in the amount on deposit, from $672,917 to $13,284,374, or about nineteen and one-half times.

As has been previously stated, the Biddeford, Lewiston Falls and South Berwick banks were subsequently closed, without loss, as we presume, and each has been superseded by an institution in active and successful operation at this time.

The Biddeford Savings Bank was organized in 1867, and had deposits and surplus, November, 1873, $533,662.

The Lewiston Institution for Savings was organized in 1860, and had deposits and surplus, 1873, $1,070,059.

The South Berwick Savings Bank was organized in 1866, and had deposits and surplus, 1873, $203,228.

The location of the Randall's Savings and Benevolent Association not being given, I am unable to determine whether it had any local succession. It never attained sufficient prominence to make its fate or survivorship of any considerable importance.

Below will be found a comparative table showing the amount and per cent of the different classes of securities in 1855 and 1873, as nearly as they can be made up from the data furnished by the returns of those years respectively. Those for the former period do not in all cases distinguish between loans on notes secured by real estate or other collateral and loans upon personal security alone; and the later reports include, among loans on collaterals, loans made directly to municipal corporations, which tends to confusion in an attempt to classify investments upon the basis of the nature of the security offered. So, loans on collaterals appear to embrace loans on personal security only. As the result is approximate and comparative only, the per cent is not carried to remote fractions.

SECURITIES.	1855.		1873.	
	Amount.	Per cent.	Amount.	Per cent.
Mortgages of real estate.........	$53,051	6	$7,319,777	25
U. S. bonds	....	..	974,104	3
State, county and city bonds.....	160,130	17	8,086,219	27
Bank stock......................	108,916	12	660,652	2
Railroad stock and bonds	184,531	21	4,566,199	15
Loans on collaterals and personal security	326,207	37	6,123,002	21
Real estate......................	....	..	231,581	1
Cash............................	31,071	3½	768,140	3
Miscellaneous	3,225	½	826,845	3

It will be seen that the changes in the course of eighteen years have been considerable, and that the tendency has been toward improvement in the class of securities in which investments are made.

The general progress of the Savings Bank system in Maine is shown by the following table. It will be observed that the wonderful development of the system is embraced within a period of about fifteen years.

The figures in the column "due depositors" will be found not to agree with those in a recent report showing the growth from 1860 to 1870. In that table the deposits sometimes included profits, and sometimes not. We have, for the sake of uniformity, sought to bring all to a common basis.

TABLE showing the growth and progress of Savings Banks in Maine from 1855 *to* 1874.

YEAR.	No. of banks.	No. of open accounts.	Increase in open accounts.	Amount due to depositors.	Increase in am't due depositors.	Increase in Periods of Five Years.			
						Increase in number of open acc'ts.	Per cent of increase.	Increase in amount due depositors.	Per cent of increase.
1855	11	* 4,500	......	$867,131	....	First period, three years.		First period, three years.	
1856	11	4,947	447	919,571	$52,440				
1857	11	* 5,500	553	968,325	48,754				
1858	12	* 5,600	100	968,194	—131	1,100	24	$101,063	12
1859	13	4,997	—603	923,397	—34,797				
1860	14	* 7,500	2,503	1,539,257	615,860				
1861	14	9,818	2,318	1,708,961	169,704				
1862	15	* 11,000	1,182	1,876,165	167,204				
1863	15	* 14,000	3,000	2,641,476	765,311	8,400	150	1,673,282	173
1864	15	* 18,000	4,000	3,672,975	1,031,499				
1865	15	18,308	308	3,336,828	—336,147				
1866	18	19,786	1,478	3,946,433	609,605				
1867	20	* 24,000	4,214	5,598,600	1,652,167				
1868	28	30,528	6,528	8,032,246	2,433,646	16,528	118	5,390,770	204
1869	37	39,527	8,999	10,839,955	2,807,709				
1870	43	54,155	14,628	16,597,888	5,757,913				
1871	49	69,411	15,256	22,787,802	6,189,914				
1872	54	81,320	11,909	26,154,333	3,376,531				
1873	56	91,398	10,078	29,556,523	3,402,190	60,870	200	21,524,277	268
1874	58	96,799	5,401	31,051,963	1,495,440				

* Estimated. — Decrease.

SEVENTH SECTION;

SAVINGS BANKS IN THE STATE OF VERMONT.

CHAPTER XXIII.

CONDITIONS OF DEVELOPMENT.

It is, perhaps, profitless to inquire what were the causes that delayed the inception and that have retarded the growth of the Savings Bank system in the State of Vermont, as compared with other New England States. But some of the more obvious causes that have tended to this result lie so nearly upon the surface of any investigation, that they may be briefly indicated. We can best call attention to these by instituting comparisons between Vermont and New Hampshire, which, to superficial eye, present so many features in common.

Thus, they are in juxtaposition, being separated only by the Connecticut river; possessing similar characteristics of surface, soil and climate, their respective northern and southern boundaries being, for all practical purposes of comparison, coincident.

They are of nearly identical area, New Hampshire having 9,280 square miles, Vermont having 9,056 square miles.

Their population respectively, from 1820, is shown by the following figures:

	1820.	1830.	1840.	1850.	1860.	1870.
N. Hampshire,	244,022	269,328	284,574	317,976	326,073	318,300
Vermont	235,966	280,652	291,948	314,120	315,098	330,551

The character of the population would seem to present, at least, no features of striking contrast.

Thus far the conditions which would seem favorable to the development of Savings Banks in the one State, would seem to concur equally in their promotion in the other. Yet, while we have seen that they had their practical inception in New Hampshire in 1823, the first act of incorporation in Vermont was in 1846, twenty-three years later, at which time the accumulations in the New Hampshire Savings Banks amounted probably to about $1,500,000.

The one condition favorable to the organization of Savings Banks is a concentrated population. It is obvious that a population of 5,000, in a manufacturing town, affords a more hopeful condition for the establishment of a Savings Bank than a population of 25,000 diffused over a county twenty-five miles square. And such a statement approximates the relative conditions existing in New Hampshire and Vermont, respectively, in 1820. At that time about one-fourth, certainly not to exceed one-third, of the area of New Hampshire, embraced more than four-fifths of its population, or 205,000 out of 244,000, and a much larger proportion of this was concentrated in the southern extremity of the State.

The population in Vermont, on the contrary, was more generally and evenly diffused over the entire area of the State. In New Hampshire there were but six counties in 1820, which is of itself an indication of a given population considerably concentrated in certain localities, and very sparsely diffused in other parts. Vermont, on the other hand, had, in 1820, thirteen counties, with its population quite evenly distributed among them; and but one county has been formed since in that State, while in New Hampshire there have been four.

We thus find that the condition of a concentrated population, favorable to the establishment and growth of Savings Banks, existed, and we may say still exists, in New Hampshire, in a much greater degree than in Vermont.

Another condition favorable to the institution and growth of Savings Banks is the development of those industries which employ large numbers of people at fixed rates of wages, paid promptly, regularly, and at short intervals, in money. Without going into any minute analysis of the subject, it is sufficient to say that, in this respect, manufacturing is far superior to agriculture. The development of manufacturing, upon any considerable scale, concentrates capital under the control of a few, who diffuse it among the many in the form of wages regularly and frequently paid, and so far remunerative as to give opportunity for saving, with corresponding regularity, for use in the future.

Agriculture, on the contrary, as a pursuit engrossing the attention of the mass of the population, diffuses capital among a larger number, who dole it out in wages to their help, at irregular and infrequent periods. The latter, receiving their wages in considerable sums, find it already pledged in payment for purchases made probably with less discrimination than would have been done with money in hand; or, unduly elated by the possession of so considerable wealth as the product of half a year's labor, they proceed to spend it with less discrimination than they would a much smaller amount received at frequent intervals. Whatever be the natural disposition toward economy and thrift, we think all will agree that the conditions of labor and wages in a manufacturing community are much more favorable to the exercise of these virtues than the conditions commonly prevailing in agricultural communities.

The application of the foregoing to the case before us is easily made. New Hampshire has developed a more diversified industry than Vermont. The manufactured products of the former are about double those of the latter.

Vermont exceeds New Hampshire in agricultural production. The one presents a favorable condition for the establishment and growth of Savings Banks; the other, an unfavorable one.

This argument goes no further, and makes no attempt to decide nor to indicate which condition is best for the general moral and material welfare of any people. Savings Banks had their origin in conditions and necessities absolutely abject and pitiful, and proved a most efficient auxiliary in the amelioration of those conditions. If a state of society is found in which Savings Banks do not flourish, it may be for the reason that there is no occasion for their ministry, or because there is no convenient opportunity for its exercise, or for some other reason. Our duty is ended when we have indicated the conditions which have proved unfavorable to the development of the interest in question. Whether the conclusion to be drawn from the fact be gratifying or otherwise, we will not seek to determine.

CHAPTER XXIV.

COURSE AND CHARACTER OF LEGISLATION.

The charter of the Windham Provident Institution for Savings, incorporated in 1846, will be found in the Appendix. It embodies the essential features found in all charters, except as modified by general laws, to be hereafter noted. This was followed by the incorporation of six Savings Banks in the following year, five of which were organized, and four are still in operation; after which there were no more charters until 1850, when the Rutland Savings Bank was incorporated.

INVESTMENTS.

It will be observed that section 3 of the charter of the Windham Provident Institution provides that "all deposits of money received by said corporation shall be used and improved to the best advantage," etc.; and this is the common form of direction in all Savings Bank charters in the State until 1867. Nor is there any restriction imposed upon the discretion of trustees concerning investments in any of the general acts relating to Savings Banks.

The change noted above as occurring in 1867 is in the charter of the Montpelier Savings Bank, which reads as follows:

"SEC. 5. All deposits of money received by said corporation shall be managed and improved to the best advantage by loaning the same, by order or consent of a majority of the directors, on mortgage of real estate, unincumbered, equal in value to double the amount of the loan secured thereon, except to an amount not exceeding one-half of the amount on deposit in said corporation; which said sum may be invested in the purchase of stocks of the United States or any of them, in bank stock in any bank in this State, or on undoubted personal security."

This was the second charter for a Savings Bank in Montpelier, neither of which resulted in any organization, at least no reports from any such institution are found. In 1870 the Montpelier Savings Bank and Trust Company was incorporated, which organized in 1871. As this was a capital stock company, it is not included in our review.

The foregoing provision appears also in subsequent charters, and is all the restriction that appears concerning investments in this State. The purpose of the legislature appears to have been to guard the management of these institutions through the exercise of what was deemed sufficient care in the selection of the original corporators.

CHAPTER XXV.

SUPERVISION AND REPORTS.

As early as 1849, three years only after the incorporation of the first Savings Bank in the State, the legislature made it the duty of these institutions, on the first Monday in September in each year, to report their condition to the auditor of accounts of the State, and this officer was directed to cause the same to be published in his annual report to the legislature.

Under this provision, of course, no uniformity in the statements could be expected, as each institution would simply report, in its own way, such facts as in its judgment expressed with sufficient fullness its financial condition.

In 1851, however, the provision was amended by specifying the items to be reported, as follows:

1. Number of depositors. 2. Amount invested in bank stocks, naming the banks. 3. Amount secured by bank stock as collateral. 4. Amount invested in public funds. 5. Amount loaned on public funds. 6. Amount of loans on mortgages of real estate. 7. Amount of loans on personal security, stating character of security. 8. Loans to counties and towns. 9. Loans on railroad, manufacturing, or other stocks, with character of stocks and condition of loans. 10. Amount of loans on pledge of bonds of any railroad, manufacturing, or other corporation. 11. Amount of

cash on hand. 12. Dividends for the year. 13. Annual expenses.

It will be seen that the statistical information required is very meager, nor, in the absence of the amount due to depositors — which item is not among those enumerated — does it appear how a very satisfactory financial exhibit could be made. The statements of some institutions are quite full, going beyond the requirements of the law, giving the deposits and the withdrawals, etc., during the year, though without absolute uniformity on the part of any institution, and many institutions fail fully to comply with the requirements of the law in their reports.

As early as 1847 the idea of subjecting Savings Banks to examination was embodied in legislation, two of the six Savings Banks incorporated in that year being made by their charters subject to the inspection of the bank commissioner, who was required to make an examination of these institutions upon an application made to him, in writing, by ten of the depositors, requesting him to do so.

In 1851 the bank commissioner was authorized to examine every Savings Bank whenever he believed the interests of depositors required it. In 1853, however, it was made the *duty* of the bank commissioner to visit and examine Savings Banks, and make a report to the auditor of accounts, giving, among other things, the number of depositors, the amount of the deposits, number and amount of dividends, etc.

Under these provisions of the law, reports have been made, commonly in September of each year, showing the condition of the banks reporting at various periods from July to September of each year. This enables us to bring the reported condition of Savings Banks in this State down to the summer of 1874.

The first reports were made in conformity with the very general and indefinite provisions of the act of 1849, but were from only two Savings Banks, the Bellows Falls and Black River; at least these are the only institutions from which returns were published, although four other Savings Banks were in operation at the time. In 1851, we find returns from only two Savings Banks, the Bellows Falls and the Windham Provident, the Black River not reporting. Meantime the Rutland Savings Bank had been incorporated and organized, but it made no report until the following year.

As the law invested the auditor with no power to demand these reports, but simply to publish such as were received by him, the negligence in making them must be imputed to the officers of the institutions, who might perhaps shield themselves under a plea of ignorance, for it does not appear to have been the duty of the auditor even to give notice to the institutions affected, of the requirements of the law in this regard. In 1852, however, five out of seven Savings Banks organized, and in 1853 seven out of eight reported to the auditor; and thereafter the banks generally, in some form, complied with the provisions of the law.

It will be remembered that in 1853 the duty of visiting, examining, and reporting to the auditor the condition of the various Savings Banks in the State, was imposed upon the bank commissioner, and this duty was discharged by that officer from 1854 until 1867, when the office of bank commissioner was abolished and the duty of simply publishing the reports received from Savings Banks was remitted to the auditor of accounts. It is noteworthy how much more acceptably this duty of supervision is performed when committed to an officer especially charged with it, than when imposed as an incident upon an officer whose time and attention are sufficiently engrossed with other duties, appertaining to his specific office. The published statements of the auditor of accounts are presumably mere copies of the returns made to him, unaccompanied by a word of text relating to the condition of the interest reported upon, or of suggestion concerning it, and with no summary even, or aggregate of the results or facts submitted by him. Whoever would know any thing of the condition of this interest in its general aspects in the State, must obtain it by himself summarizing, as best he may, the details of each institution, submitted without plan, uniformity or system, beyond the mere alphabetical order of their arrangement upon the pages of the auditor's report.

The bank commissioner, on the contrary, did not regard his duty as wholly discharged when he had reported in detail the condition of each Savings Bank examined by him, but accompanies the same with a summary of the increase or decrease in the assets of each institution, an aggregate of the assets of all the

Savings Banks in the State, and the first two reports are accompanied by a general review of the condition of the interest, the purposes to be accomplished by it, and the measures that will best contribute to such result, with reflections upon the defects in existing laws for the protection of depositors, and recommendations for their amendment. From the first of these reports — made in 1854 — I extract, as giving a view of the Savings Bank interest in this State at an early period of its history, the following. The commissioner says:

"The number of Savings Banks in operation is thirteen;* the amount on deposit, $895,370;† gain over previous year, $182,728.

"The importance to the public, of these and like institutions, can hardly be over estimated. They partake of the philanthropic in design and purpose. * * * * * They are designed peculiarly for the uninstructed in the arts of speculative investment — the weak, the feeble, the poor even, both men and women, and children as well; treasuries for administrators, guardians, trustees, where one may always be sure to find his own again. Safety, therefore, rather than large interest, should be the great idea of their administration, as it is of their design, if not in their actual constitution.

"It should be known that, as the law stands, the depositor has very little security beyond the confidence that may be due to the unrewarded vigilance, discretion and integrity of the trustees. * * * *

---

* There were in fact fourteen Savings Banks in operation at this time, the Burlington, which commenced business in 1847, not being included in the above, its condition and probably its existence being unknown to the commissioner.

† This amount includes about $90,000 of surplus, and the summary of the commissioner always includes the surplus in the amount of deposits. This will serve to explain differences between the reports and the figures in this volume, which do not embrace the surplus in the amount due depositors.

"Not only does the trustee's fidelity to his trust lack the stimulus of personal interest, but oftentimes his interest is adverse to the Savings Bank. Thus it appears that most of the Savings Banks are connected with banks of circulation, the cashier of the one being the treasurer of the other; and in some instances a majority of the trustees, or board of investment, are directors of, or otherwise interested in, the bank of circulation. It is apparent that, in such common management of both institutions, the temptation is to subordinate the interests of the Savings Bank to those of the bank of circulation. The occasions must not be unfrequent for transferring the debts of the bank of circulation to the Savings Bank. Against the temptation to make such exchanges, to the disadvantage of the latter, and to reduce it to a mere adjunct and convenience of the former, the law opposes nothing. Honor and fidelity in such case, which the law does not attempt to enforce, are but other names for self-sacrifice. Without implying that I have detected any thing wrong in practice in these respects, on the contrary, etc., * * * there seems to be a necessity for a revision of the laws upon this subject, for forming a system of regulations with more and other checks against injudicious investments and possible abuse of powers, and with better securities for faithful administration than are found in the several charters of these institutions.

"DANIEL ROBERTS,
"*Bank Commissioner.*

"MANCHESTER, *September* 15, 1854."

In his report for the following year, the commissioner notices the failure of two Savings Banks — the Black River and Middlebury — and renews his suggestions concerning a revision of the Savings Bank laws, "suggestions," as he says "to which the subsequent failure of two of these institutions has given an illustration and an emphasis."

The facts concerning the failure of these institutions will be found recorded elsewhere.

The recommendations of the commissioner do not seem, however, to have been regarded by the legislature, unless the following act, passed in 1857—three years after the recommendations were made—may be considered as incited thereby: "No president, vice-president, treasurer, secretary, trustee or officer of any Savings Bank shall be president, director, cashier, or hold other official position in a bank of discount."

The commissioner may well be excused from urging his views upon a legislature so indifferent, and thereafter the reports of this officer comprise simply the statement of the condition of Savings Banks, without any text or comments, except such, in connection with the report of any institution, as are necessary in explanation or amplification of its record.

As these returns, made by the bank commissioner, were from examinations made by him, we naturally look for uniformity in respect to the items reported, and their arrangement. But no such uniformity is found, and hence the difficulty in tabulating the facts for the purposes of this History. That there would be changes from year to year in the items reported, or in the order of their arrangement, might be anticipated; but the form and material of the reports of the different banks are not uniform in the same year. The only item found with persistent uniformity in all the reports is the amount due to depositors. The dividends are reported with a good degree of regularity, but not uniformly, and the manner of reporting them takes two forms: in the one, the dividends for the year are reported; in the other, the total amount of all dividends since organization is reported. Of course, under the latter form, the dividends for the year are easily derived. Sometimes one form will be pursued for a series of years in the reports, and then the other will be entered upon.

The number of depositors or accounts is reported with equal irregularity; in some cases and in some years the whole number of depositors, in others only the present number, and frequently not either will be given. In the case of a few institutions the whole amount of deposits from organization is given, and the whole amount withdrawn, and in a less number of cases the detail is so minute as to set forth not only the whole amount of dividends as part of the deposits, but what portion of the amount withdrawn is charged to dividend account and what to deposit account.

The want of unity and system in the statements of these institutions is apparent from the foregoing, and the difficulty of generalizing a mass of facts so heterogeneous is likewise evident. I have therefore tabulated for the successive years from 1850 only the one uniformly reported item of the amount due to depositors, for, to have constructed a table of other items, in which blanks would have been as common as figures, would be of little practical utility. The facts reported with sufficient uniformity to afford a basis for rational estimates, I have put in the aggregates of all the banks for the entire historic period of Savings Banks in this State. Under the head of the detailed progress of each institution, I have tabularized those items given with the greatest general uniformity, and have given other items incapable of connected arrangement, from which any one interested can work out all admissible generalizations.

We derive from these reports a general conclusion that the Savings Bank interest in Vermont not having assumed the gigantic dimensions and importance compared with other interests, which has characterized its development in other States, has been less an object of solicitude than it would otherwise be. The largest amount on deposit in any one bank was, at the date of the latest returns, made in 1874, $1,403,475, and the aggregate in all the banks in the State was but $5,011,831, or less than the amount in each of several Savings Banks in other States.

SUBSEQUENT LEGISLATION.

Other provisions of charter and of general law concerning these institutions present no marked nor unusual features demanding exposition. Officers of Savings Banks, as previously noted, are prohibited from holding, at the same time, official connection with banks of discount; the deposits of minors and married women are protected by the usual safeguards provided in other States, and deposits exceeding $250 are made subject to taxation by being returned, with names of the depositors, to the town clerk for that purpose.

The amount of real estate a Savings Bank is authorized to purchase or hold is commonly limited, by the charter of each institution, to a specific sum varying from $2,000 to $6,000.

The prohibition against loaning funds of the bank to trustees or officers, found in the charter of the Windham institution, is a common feature in all charters.

In 1869, and subsequently, we note the incorporation of a large number of institutions denominated "Savings and Trust," or "Trust and Savings," or "Savings Banks and Trust Companies." They are, whatever their name, a form of trust company, having a capital stock basis, varying from $25,000 to $100,000, only a portion of which is paid in; and the use of the term Savings Bank, in connection with them, is of course to attract a class of deposits which would not seek them under any other designation. I have not included these in the following summary, regarding them as outside of the Savings Bank system, as commonly understood. Where that system has no other representative in any State than organizations of this character, I have given to them such prominence as it seemed they were entitled to receive, as the best exponents of the system to be found; but, where the mutual form of organization prevails in any State, I prefer to confine this record to their exposition.

Notwithstanding the defects of legislation which render it impossible to present a clear and intelligible view of the Savings Banks of the State, as a system, and which we are constrained to believe have contributed, in some measure, to produce the unfavorable conditions upon which we have commented, it is not to be doubted that cautious and conservative management, guided by the strictest integrity, and resulting in such measure of success as the unfavorable conditions brought to view in the opening of this section would admit, find their exemplification in this, no less than in other States. Such institutions as the Windham Provident, the Rutland, and others that might be named, that have ministered to the public for a period of twenty-five or thirty years, have unquestionably won the public confidence by deserving it.

CHAPTER XXVI.

STATISTICS OF GROWTH AND PROGRESS.

The following tables, representing the growth of Savings Banks in the State of Vermont, are compiled from the annual reports already referred to, as indicated in our summary of the course of legislation. These reports are more full and detailed concerning the resources — that is, the assets or investments of Savings Banks — than concerning their statistics of growth, which are left to be reported by each institution in its own way. This "way" is, by some Savings Banks, very copious and minute, though not in a form to be tabulated without great labor, the report for each year being a summary for the whole period of the existence of the institution, from which the transactions of each year can be derived only by a mathematical calculation. This calculation was made by the writer in one instance, which sufficed to satisfy him that it was time poorly expended; as there were so few that reported in that way, that no general summary of the transactions of all upon that basis of calculation could be made.

The only thing that is uniformly reported by all, is the amount due to depositors, and even this will sometimes be found blank, indicating that no report was made in that year.

STATISTICS OF INDIVIDUAL SAVINGS BANKS.

WINDHAM PROVIDENT INSTITUTION FOR SAVINGS.

Commenced business January, 1847.

Name appears to have been changed to Vermont Savings Bank in 1872.

Statistics tabulated from Annual Reports.

YEAR.	Whole number acc'ts opened.	Amount due depositors.	Dividends.	YEAR.	Whole number acc'ts opened.	Amount due depositors.	Dividends.
1847..	.....	$139,249*		1862..	2,069	$444,635	‡ $30,689
		50,854†		1863..	2,417	557,782	23,115
to				1864..	2,666	629,452	27,607
1851..	848	$88,395	$10,020	1865..	2,509	545,042	27,438
1852..	.....	No rep'rt	......	1866..	2,443	550,448	24,966
1853..	1,378	172,877	......	1867..	2,706	664,420	‡ 69,200
1854..	1,650	220,224	31,902	1868..	3,312	751,551	33,231
1855..	1,918	234,855	42,435	1869..	.....	869,851	....
1856..	2,115	247,921	53,682	1870..	3,924	990,564	50,634
1857..	2,392	239,879	‡ 71,306	1871..	.....	1,064,335	55,177
1858..	1,184	235,111	11,184	1872..	.....	1,213,093	‡ 126,365
1859..	1,332	295,421	12,048	1873..	.....	1,299,802	84,314
1860..	1,729	365,798	15,253	1874..	.....	1,403,475	99,743
1861..	1,839	402,494	18,370				

* Deposits.
† Drafts.
‡ Include extra dividends.

The reports of the above institution were more full and complete, as well as more uniform, than many that are found in the published documents of the State. From this, some idea may be derived of the incongruous mass of items from which this and the following statistical tables are compiled.

From the above it will be seen that, down to 1857, the whole number of accounts opened from the date of organization, and the whole amount of dividends declared — and not those for each year — are given. After that time the accounts remaining open, and the dividends for each year respectively, are reported, except that in later years no mention whatever is made of the number of accounts.

Burlington Savings Bank.

Commenced business in 1847.
First report made in 1855.

Statistics tabulated from Reports.

YEAR.	Open accounts.	Due depositors.	Dividends.
1855	....	$26,949	....
1856	....	21,609	....
1857	....	23,991	....
1858	174	20,367	$890 32
1859	....	20,341	923 46
1860	256	25,260	1,044 63
1861	263	28,918	1,247 06
1862	299	34,883	1,297 87
1863	430	74,458	3,217 22
1864	610	104,294	4,025 92
1865	563	88,391	....
1866	....	72,888	....
1867	....	88,266	....
1868	749	146,512	....
1869	....	209,393	....
1870	1,378	434,267	17,522 94
1871	....	604,300	....
1872	....	834,804	....
1873	2,914	1,046,026	3 and 4 per cent
1874	3,395	1,297,104	3 and 4 per cent

The above fairly exhibits the irregularities in the form of reports made by the Savings Banks in Vermont. The number of accounts is given only about half the time; the dividends stated with great irregularity, and the last two years only the semi-annual rate is given.

Bellows Falls Savings Bank.

Commenced business January 1, 1848.

Statistics tabulated from Reports.

YEAR.	Open accounts.*	Amount deposited.	Amount withdrawn.	Due depositors.	Dividends.
1848 to 1850,	234	$40,072	$11,534	$28,538	$1,546
1851........	347	29,432	6,147	51,822	1,595
1852........	487	38,182	11,226	78,778	2,718
1853........	716	72,340	14,318	136,800	† 5,884
1854........	876	53,553	23,583	166,770	7,504
1855........	1,016	48,537	49,061	166,247	7,737
1856........	1,111	33,470	31,563	168,153	7,682
1857........	1,221	31,987	27,343	172,796	7,910
1858........	1,288	34,410	30,835	176,370	† 13,006
1859........	1,429	55,671	30,616	201,425	8,454
1860........	1,579	67,802	42,410	226,817	10,166
1861........	1,696	51,865	19,903	258,878	11,635
1862........	1,859	61,169	25,043	294,904	12,643
1863........	2,015	77,780	57,003	315,681	† 21,941
1864........	2,235	79,483	74,604	320,560	14,163
1865........	2,337	50,419	100,902	270,078	13,510
1866........	2,472	49,212	81,333	237,956	11,199
1867........	2,618	46,350	45,685	238,621	11,048
1868........	2,733	66,613	49,031	256,202	† 16,349
1869........	2,891	54,190	38,648	271,745	12,142
1870........	3,068	45,935	49,778	274,144	12,592
1871........	3,182	51,488	53,160	272,327	12,335
1872........	3,352	54,721	38,872	288,631	13,066
1873........	3,558	65,110	42,977	304,214	† 20,375
1874........	3,606	51,219	49,706	305,725	14,109
	......	$1,311,009	$1,005,296	....	$271,309

The amounts deposited and withdrawn are derived with much labor from the reports made, which give each year the sum of these from the organization of the bank. The amount due depositors is always given

* It does not quite clearly appear, from the form of the reports, whether the figures in this column represent open accounts or the whole number of accounts opened at the respective periods given, though the probabilities seem to favor the latter.

† Include extra dividends.

in the reports exclusive of the semi-annual dividend then due and declared, and which is included in the above table, which in this respect does not conform to the published statements, but to the *truth.*

WINDSOR SAVINGS BANK.

Commenced business February 3, 1848.

Statistics tabulated from Reports.

YEAR.	Open accounts.	Due depositors.	Dividends.
1852	317	$67,999	2½ per cent
1853	......	105,931	$5,432 21
1854	505	122,460	2½ per cent
1855	528	140,259	2½ per cent
1856	554	149,267	2½ per cent
1857	506	135,016	2½ per cent
1858	480	131,275	2½ per cent
1859	491	137,259	....
1860	527	151,172	....
1861	601	176,988	....
1862	662	190,950	....
1863	781	245,491	$15,618 08
1864	874	257,958	11,246 42
1865	828	230,104	12,768 34
1866	746	189,406	9,198 86
1867	786	204,227	9,792 89
1868	785	208,536	19,368 78
1869	828	218,614	10,597 71
1870	880	233,346	11,177 56
1871	909	243,613	....
1872	961	264,714	....
1873	1,011	279,515	2½ per cent
1874	997	273,912	2½ per cent

OTTAUQUECHEE SAVINGS BANK.

Commenced business March 15, 1848.

Statistics tabulated from Reports.

YEAR.	Accounts.*	Due depositors.	Dividends.
1848 to 1852	......	†$60,901 ‡23,165	
1852	326	$37,736	$1,577 44
1853	465	62,306	2,178 16
1854	570	73,777	3,728 65
1855	713	91,821	3,925 00
1856	803	90,084	4,169 24
1857	894	80,556	3,708 42
1858	950	69,611	3,439 08
1859	1,040	74,213	3,182 03
1860	1,152	85,189	3,762 17
1861	1,258	84,572	3,990 13
1862	1,360	78,153	3,759 45
1863	......	82,236	3,626 22
1864	......	93,056	4,880 21
1865	......	93,322	5,379 31
1866	524	86,055	4,665 26
1867	568	89,336	4,981 06
1868	......	96,825	5,316 80
1869	......	97,052	5,336 34
1870	......	103,030	5,686 40
1871	800	128,096	....
1872	......	140,370	7,661 42
1873	1,061	181,732	13,743 57
1874	1,200	203,050	10,689 17

* Until 1862 the whole number of accounts opened is given; thereafter, when any mention is made of them, the number remaining open is referred to.

† Deposits.

‡ Drafts.

Black River Savings Bank.

Incorporated 1847; commenced business April, 1848.

Statistics tabulated from Reports.

YEAR.	Accounts opened.	Due depositors.	Dividends.
1848 to 1850	360	$40,838	....
1851	......	No report	....
1852	673	79,776	$3,064 69
1853	867	114,860	5,635 97
1854	995	106,112	....

Failed and went into hands of receivers, December, 1854. It appears that the treasurer of the institution had "borrowed"—that is, used—the funds, without depositing security. No other officer was cognizant of the treasurer's transactions. Committees signed such papers as the treasurer prepared, without any knowledge of the facts or any examination to verify them. It was thought that the assets would net some seventy-five to eighty per cent of the liabilities, which, at the time the receiver was appointed, were $101,752.

RUTLAND SAVINGS BANK.

Commenced business February, 1851.

Statistics tabulated from Reports.

YEAR.	Accounts.*	Due depositors.	Dividends.*
1852	213	$32,900	$713 52
1853	454	78,321	2,076 11
1854	697	114,269	6,783 23
1855	896	111,121	11,530 65
1856	1,075	100,390	19,041 98
1857	1,307	116,610	24,040 10
1858	1,424	98,521	28,465 61
1859	1,623	116,133	33,894 64
1860	1,834	158,888	40,122 93
1861	2,025	156,555	51,545 03
1862	2,256	165,862	58,550 33
1863	2,555	183,359	65,930 65
1864	2,924	237,370	74,951 84
1865	3,257	219,655	84,924 92
1866	3,617	219,301	101,257 27
1867	4,078	264,770	112,227 05
1868	4,487	285,313	124,257 05
1869	4,878	293,184	137,477 46
1870	5,319	330,484	151,898 41
1871	5,837	381,389	181,276 93
1872	6,469	456,394	200,254 65
1873	6,985	491,400	221,926 71
1874	7,520	524,724	244,824 65

Amount deposited, including dividends $2, 349, 617
Amount withdrawn........................ 1, 824, 893

* The accounts given for each year are the whole number opened from the opening of the bank, and the dividends are stated in the same manner. The dividends each year are given for the later years; but our table was prepared for the other form, and the advantage is too slight to justify a change.

BRANDON SAVINGS BANK.

Commenced business August 8, 1853.

The first report, made July 22, 1854, shows the following: Accounts opened, 57; closed, 13; open, 44. Deposited, $5,832.19; withdrawn, $2,221.92; due, $3,610.57. Thereafter only the amount due depositors is reported each year, as follows: 1855, $2,835; 1856, $1,019; 1857, $671; 1858, $867; 1859, $880; 1860, $42.

Never attaining any considerable volume of business, it soon closed, without loss to depositors.

PASSUMSIC SAVINGS BANK, ST. JOHNSBURY.

Commenced business in 1853.

Statistics tabulated from Reports.

YEAR.	Open accounts.	Due depositors.	Dividends.
1853	158	$18,895	....
1854	301	37,482	$718 53
1855	307	42,966	....
1856	302	41,018	....
1857	293	36,859	....
1858	260	31,976	....
1859	245	30,832	1,539 93
1860	......	32,371	....
1861	300	43,133	....
1862	349	49,384	....
1863	......	87,462	....
1864	......	142,406	....
1865	......	108,558	....
1866	......	88,373	....
1867	......	89,063	....
1868	......	90,367	....
1869	......	96,236	....
1870	592	106,154	4,506 60
1871	890	118,803	5,203 29
1872	1,091	143,159	6,000 00
1873	1,114	174,876	* 14,556 04
1874	1,306	198,542	8,497 25

* Extra dividend included.

WINDHAM COUNTY SAVINGS BANK.

Commenced January, 1854.

Statistics tabulated from Reports.

YEAR.	Accounts.*	Due depositors.	Dividends.*
1854	55	$6,961	$68 00
1855	132	14,367	514 66
1856	182	19,463	1,378 79
1857	224	21,170	2,351 11
1858	241	21,750	3,360 42
1859	265	24,864	4,863 73
1860	294	28,092	6,091 53
1861	334	35,455	7,593 12
1862	269	41,147	....
1863	460	70,883	12,012 75
1864	588	89,737	15,229 06
1865	682	82,545	21,129 60
1866	750	77,997	24,731 81
1867	550	94,362	28,734 30
1868	613	111,214	33,682 52
1869	660	132,984	49,851 14
1870	732	149,267	7,940 53
1871	813	162,204	8,984 21
1872	845	163,360	9,352 17
1873	898	171,791	9,564 16
1874	932	174,004	15,391 14

BETHEL SAVINGS BANK.

Commenced business March 1, 1854.

Statistics tabulated from Reports.

YEAR.	Accounts.	Due depositors.	Dividends.
1854	30	$6,493	....
1855	39	2,491	$220 95
1856	37	1,151	29 40

Closed after this date on account of the small amount of business transacted, paying depositors in full.

* Until 1867 the whole number of accounts opened is given, except for 1862, when the open accounts only are stated, and the same appears to be the case from 1867 onward.

The whole amount of dividends also appears to be given until 1870, from which time the yearly amount only appears.

Wilmington Savings Bank.

Commenced business March, 1854.

Statistics tabulated from Reports.

YEAR.	Accounts.*	Due depositors.	Dividends.*
1854	26	$2,044	....
1855	63	5,607	$79 37
1856	95	6,028	341 90
1857	121	6,791	627 52
1858	105	5,301	940 16
1859	129	5,810	1,190 99
1860	144	6,972	1,507 89
1861	166	9,220	1,837 46
1862	183	8,221	2,263 75
1863	228	13,876	2,463 31
1864	305	24,484	3,480 45
1865	350	20,913	4,564 79
1866	395	19,824	5,546 46
1867	407	23,504	6,358 58
1868	427	25,930	7,414 92
1869	......	No report	....
1870	585	27,945	11,244 38
1871	......	32,026	....
1872	700	42,206	13,984 17
1873	340	59,125	2,722 47
1874	367	82,144	4,281 60

* Until 1873 the whole number of accounts opened is given; thereafter those open only. The like form of reporting dividends will be noticed.

Springfield Savings Bank.

Commenced business May 3, 1854.

Statistics tabulated from Reports.

YEAR.	Open accounts.	Due depositors.	Dividends.
1854	98	$8,509	None
1855	293	36,193	$1,056 83
1856	340	43,686	2,097 99
1857	304	33,982	4,070 06
1858	268	22,523	5,417 72
1859	274	26,044	6,619 13

SPRINGFIELD SAVINGS BANK—(Continued).

YEAR.	Open accounts.	Due depositors.	Dividends.
1860	310	$30,893	$8,081 40
1861	347	35,827	9,778 14
1862	408	40,694	11,723 58
1863	......	47,033	12,908 58
1864	485	53,183	15,282 88
1865	461	49,923	17,978 96
1866	461	47,106	20,692 74
1867	521	59,093	23,400 09
1868	613	73,871	27,859 21
1869	672	86,381	33,421 83
1870	738	94,415	39,815 73
1871	866	115,055	46,856 48
1872	1,006	130,826	55,333 04
1873	1,177	165,381	65,426 15
1874	1,345	203,238	72,160 46

The foregoing may be aggregated from the reports as follows:

Amount deposited	$467, 524 95
Dividends declared	72, 160 46
Deposits and dividends	$539, 685 41
Amount withdrawn	336, 446 98
Due depositors	$203, 238 43

CASTLETON SAVINGS BANK.

Incorporated 1852; first report made 1854.

The amount due depositors is given as follows: 1854, $13,078; 1855, $9,225; 1856, $7,643; 1857, $7,589; 1858, $5,978; 1859, $7,624; 1860, $38.

Dividends are reported only as follows: 1854, $780.27; 1855, $466.04; 1856, $411.20; 1857, $435.68.

No reports were made after 1860, and it was at that

time substantially closed from lack of encouragement to continue in business.

MIDDLEBURY SAVINGS BANK.

This institution never made a report, but went into the hands of a receiver, June, 1855, with assets stated $13,314.79, of which $10,600 were in railroad stocks and bonds of uncertain value. The balance of assets was said to be good. The amount due to depositors was $12,474.21. It is doubtful if they received fifty cents on a dollar.

NORTHFIELD SAVINGS BANK.

Commenced business July 27, 1869.

Reported due to depositors, 1870, $2,163; 1871, no report; 1872, $6,639; 1873, $20,438; 1874, $38,980.

A few other desultory items, relating to the number of accounts and to the amount deposited and withdrawn, are given at irregular intervals, rendering them worthless for compilation.

BRATTLEBORO SAVINGS BANK.

Commenced business January 2, 1871.

The following comprises its business as reported:

YEAR.	Accounts.	Due depositors.	YEAR.	Accounts.	Due depositors.
1871.....	350	$46,877	1873....	Not stated	$182,710
1872.....	691	114,360	1874....	1,248	239,701

WINOOSKI SAVINGS BANK.

Commenced business 1872.

Had in 1872, $37,668 in deposits; in 1873, $59,264, and in 1874, $67,232.

The accounts are given for 1873–74 only, and are respectively 284 and 305. The dividends for 1874 only are reported, and are for that year, $4,199.

The following table is a summary of the foregoing, in a form to show the only fact uniformly brought to view in the reports — the amount due depositors in each year. As no such summary is made by the auditor, in his report to the legislature, the computations had to be made by grouping the scattered returns made each year from 1850 to 1874. It was in the work of this compilation, and that of the preceding tables, that ample compensation was found for the limited development of the Savings Bank system in this State, as indicated by the number of institutions in operation!

To make the following as nearly complete as possible, rational estimates were made of the condition of institutions not reporting but known to be in operation in any year.

TABLE exhibiting a summary of the growth of Savings Banks in Vermont from 1850 *to* 1874.

YEAR.	No. of banks in operation.	No. of banks reporting.	Due Depositors.		Increase in Periods of Five Years.	
			Amount.	Gain or loss.	Amount.	Per cent.
1850	6	2	$199,376	....		
1851	7	2	282,217	$82,841		
1852	7	5	407,188	124,971		
1853	8	7	704,990	297,802		
1854	14	13	901,789	196,799	$702,413	352
1855	13	13	897,407	—4,382		
1856	13	13	897,432	25		
1857	12	12	875,909	—21,523		
1858	12	12	819,650	—56,259		
1859	12	12	940,846	121,196	39,057	4-10
1860	12	12	1,111,532	170,686		
1861	10	10	1,231,940	120,408		
1862	10	10	1,348,833	116,893		
1863	10	10	1,678,261	329,428		
1864	10	10	1,952,500	274,239	1,011,654	107
1865	10	10	1,708,531	—243,969		
1866	10	10	1,589,354	—119,177		
1867	10	10	1,815,662	226,308		
1868	10	10	2,046,321	230,659		
1869	10	9	2,301,940	255,619	349,440	18
1870	11	11	2,745,779	443,839		
1871	12	11	3,172,525	426,746		
1872	13	13	3,836,224	663,699		
1873	13	13	4,478,842	642,618		
1874	13	13	5,011,831	532,989	2,709,891	117

The fluctuations in the foregoing are quite exceptional in the history of Savings Banks in this country. There was a steady loss in deposits from 1854 to 1858, the gain in the following year barely sufficing to recover the ground lost with an increase for the semi-decade of less than one-half of one per cent. Though the increase during the first five years figures largely in the form of percentage, there is in fact very little significance in the aggregate result, and the large percentage derives its consequence rather from the smallness of the first term than from the largeness of the last term. Estimates and conclusions, derived from statements in the form of ratios, are not unfrequently deceptive, and in effect false. The practical lying that figures are made to do in this way, by pointing to false conclusions, perverting and falsifying the true relations of things, is a conspicuous feature in official statistics, especially where these can be wrought to support a pet theory.

Instituting, as we have done in respect to other States, a comparison between the investments at the earliest period at which they are reported and the latest period, we make the following table, which is as nearly correct as the defective material would admit.

INVESTMENTS, ETC.	Aggregate. 1854.	Aggregate, 1874.	Per cent. 1854.	Per cent, 1874.
Loans on mortgage..........	$445,494	$2,043,665	48	39.6
Loans on personal security..	294,528	1,773,662	32	34
Loans on collaterals.........	43,973	135,631	4.8	2.6
City, town and district bonds,	9,429	433,791	1	8.3
Stocks and bonds of private corp'ns (R. R. and bank) ..	47,910	86,882	5.2	1.6
United States and State b'ds,	....	381,732	0	7.3
Real estate owned...........	....	22,288	0	.4
Miscellaneous...............	2,735	61,667	.3	1.2
Cash on hand and in bank...	72,299	263,830	8	5
Surplus.....................	14,579	191,317	1.6	3.8

We have taken the year 1854 as our earliest period of comparison, as that is the first year in which reports were received from as many as thirteen institutions. Even in that year one Savings Bank in operation neglected to report, but we have, from the report made the following year, made a rational estimate of its condition and investments in 1854, and embodied the same in the foregoing.

In further explanation of the above, we may say that the collaterals upon which loans are made are quite commonly, though not uniformly, bank stock and railroad stocks or bonds, and that these also constitute the bulk of the securities of private corporations held for investment. The miscellaneous assets are chiefly interest accrued, or due and not collected.

EIGHTH SECTION;

SAVINGS BANKS IN THE STATE OF NEW YORK.

CHAPTER XXVII.

PRELIMINARY.

It is but natural that the writer should enjoy greater facilities for the preparation of a history of Savings Banks in this State than in any other. During an official residence of many years at the capital of the State, the public records were open to his inspection at such intervals of leisure as he could command from public duties. His official position brought him into such relations of confidence and trust — in very many instances, relations of personal friendship as well, with the trustees and officers of Savings Banks — that they rendered to him that cordial and essential assistance in supplementing defective records, which they would not so readily accord to a stranger. It will not be understood that in these suggestions any claim is asserted as against very great and very obvious defects in this section of our work. The writer can only affirm that here, as elsewhere, he has diligently improved his opportunities and these have been greater and more favorable concerning the Savings Banks of New York than concerning those of any other State, and he would thus disarm adverse criticism founded upon any appearance of favoritism in the more elaborate treatment of the subject in this section than was possible in other portions of the work.

It is proper to state here for the information of those outside of the State of New York, that this section of the work is based upon one originally prepared and published in 1870, in connection with the report of the superintendent of the bank department concerning Savings Banks in that year.

Indeed, the original conception of the present work was merely a revision of that history, with a somewhat more expanded reference to the subject-matter in other States than was compatible with that distinctively local record. It was under this view that the work was first announced to appear in a few weeks.

But very slight consideration sufficed to apprise the writer that he could not in justice to himself nor to the subject, nor to his readers, suffer a work to appear under his auspices, purporting to be a history of Savings Banks in the United States, which should in fact be a history of Savings Banks in one State, with merely incidental and very general allusion to their origin, and a statement of their present condition, in other States.

In short, the writer could not feel that he had dealt honorably with himself nor toward the subject selected for treatment, until he had made it as full and complete, as the resources which he could command would admit.

This not only expanded the area of his investigations, but rendered necessary a complete revision of the history of Savings Banks in New York; for access was obtained to sources of information upon many matters that had failed to reveal themselves when that history was prepared, so that the preparation of this section has been attended by no less labor, but rather by more, than attended its original compilation as an independent history. This truth will easily impress itself upon all who are familiar with the work in question, and care to make a comparison between it and the section upon which we have now entered, covering the same topics.

The greater fullness of detail which we are enabled to give concerning the origin and inception of Savings Banks in this State on the one hand, and concerning the growth and character of the business and dealings of each institution from year to year, on the other, seems to render expedient and desirable, if not altogether necessary, a more general subdivision of the entire record than into chapters simply, which have perhaps marked with sufficient accuracy the transitions from topic to topic hitherto.

The natural order in which the complete record of this State presents itself for our consideration, seems to be the following:

First, that which pertains wholly to the full and fair inception of Savings Banks in this State, as indicated by their public recognition through an act of the legislature, and the successful inauguration of the enterprise thus incorporated.

Second, that which notes the course and policy of

legislation and of official discussion concerning these institutions, both singly and collectively, whereby there was impressed upon them and disclosed concerning them a certain general character as a system of means having in view a common purpose or end.

Third, the more detailed statistical or financial history of each institution with such incidents in the career of any as we have been able to gain and as serve the further purpose of illustrating the development of this interest.

In other words, this section will embrace three distinct parts, as follows:

PART I.

Inception of the idea, and incorporation and successful establishment of the Bank for Savings.

PART II.

Policy of the Savings Bank system in this State as indicated in the course of legislation and of official discussion concerning these institutions.

PART III.

Details of the origin and growth of each Savings Bank in the State, comprising chiefly statistical tables of progress from year to year.

With this preliminary and explanatory matter disposed of, we are now prepared to proceed with our record in the order indicated.

PART I.

INCEPTION AND SUCCESSFUL INAUGURATION OF THE SAVINGS BANK IDEA.

CHAPTER XXVIII.

DAWN OF PHILANTHROPIC EFFORT.

Concerning the voluntary efforts of philanthropic citizens in New York which culminated in the incorporation of the first Savings Bank, and the inauguration of the system as a legally recognized institution in that State, I first transcribe from the memoranda of Mr. Warner, my indebtedness to whom I have already acknowledged in a previous chapter.

He says: "This institution (the Bank for Savings, incorporated 1819) owes its origin, undoubtedly, to Thomas Eddy, as is evident from extracts of correspondence published in his Life, by Samuel L. Knapp, 1834."

"Mr. Eddy had for many years been a correspondent of Patrick Colquhoun, one of the local magistrates of London, and connected with many of the benevolent institutions of that city. In a letter from Mr. Colquhoun to Mr. Eddy, dated London, 19th April, 1816, he says: 'Among other philanthropic establishments which are yearly rising in the great metropolis (of London), we are now anxiously engaged in forming a provident institution or Savings Bank, in the western district of the city, upon the principle suggested and explained in my Treatise on Indigence, published in 1806, but on a far more limited scale. The practical effect of these establishments was first manifested in Scotland, since which they have extended to several towns in England, and are likely to become *very general.* Their utility scarcely requires explanation. The object is, to assist the laboring poor to preserve a portion of their earnings for old age, and to give them provident habits. I send you under cover, the plan of our institution, which has just commenced, and which has been the result of much discussion and deliberation.'" [Knapp's Life of Eddy, p. 248.]

The following is an extract from the *Evening Post* of New York, of Monday, December 2, 1816, giving an account of a meeting, undoubtedly the first, for the purpose of establishing a Savings Bank in this city, and no doubt suggested by Mr. Eddy, after receiving the above letter from Mr. Colquhoun.

"At a meeting of a number of citizens convened in the assembly room of the City Hotel, on Friday evening, November 29, 1816, pursuant to public notice, for the purpose of establishing a Savings Bank, Thomas Eddy, Esq., was called to the chair, and J. H. Coggeshall, Esq., appointed secretary. The object of the meeting having been stated, and the principles of the proposed institution briefly and pertinently explained by Mr. James Eastburn, on motion of Mr. John Griscom, seconded by Dr. Watts, it was *resolved*, that it is expedient to establish a Savings Bank for the city of New York.

"A constitution was submitted by Mr. Zachariah Lewis, which, having been read, and its principles discussed, was unanimously adopted.

"The following gentlemen were appointed directors: Henry Rutgers, Thomas R. Smith, Thomas C. Taylor, De Witt Clinton, Archibald Gracie, Cadwallader D. Colden, William Few, John Griscom, Jeremiah Thompson, Francis B. Winthrop, Duncan P. Campbell, Jos. H. Coggeshall, James Eastburn, John Pintard, Jonas Mapes, Brockholst Livingston, William Bayard, Wm. H. Harrison, Rensselaer Havens, William Wilson, Richard Varick, Thomas Eddy, Peter A. Jay, John Murray, Jr., John Slidell, Andrew Morris, Gilbert Aspinwall, Zachariah Lewis, Thomas Buckley, Najah Taylor.

"A meeting of the directors was subsequently held, December 10, 1816, and several committees were appointed, one to obtain a place to commence its operations, another to apply to the legislature for an act of incorporation (Peter A. Jay, chairman), and one to draft an address to the public (De Witt Clinton, chairman).

"On the 17th of December, 1816, the following officers were elected: William Bayard, President; Noah Brown, 1st Vice-President; Thomas R. Smith, 2d Vice-President; Thomas C. Taylor, 3d Vice-President; Thomas Eddy, Jr., Cashier."

Meetings were held afterward, December 24 and 31, 1816. No entry of any other meeting appears on the minutes of the bank until April 5, 1819.

Mr. Eddy, in a letter to Mr. Colquhoun, dated New York, 4th mo. 9th, 1817, referring to this subject, said:

"Among the many philanthropic institutions with which your country abounds, there is none that appears to me more likely to be useful than Savings Banks. They are certainly most admirably calculated to be beneficial to the poor, by promoting among them a spirit of independence, economy and industry. Immediately on receiving from thee an account of the Provident Institution in your metropolis, I proposed to a number of my friends to establish a similar one in this city. A plan was formed, and a number of our most respectable citizens agreed to undertake the management of it; but we found that we could not go into operation without an act of incorporation, for which we made an application to the legislature, and the result is not yet known." [Knapp's Life of Eddy, pp. 265, 266.]

I regard it as fully established by the foregoing, that Savings Banks in this State had their inception in the active efforts of Thomas Eddy of New York, whose attention was directed to this means of relief from or protection against the evils of poverty, by his friend, Patrick Colquhoun of London.

The memoranda of Mr. Warner close with a statement of the effort, then undetermined, to procure for the Savings Bank an act of incorporation from the legislature. The result of this effort we are prepared to supply from the journals of that body.

SAVINGS BANKS IN THE LEGISLATURE.

ASSEMBLY, *February* 3, 1817.

The memorial of Robert Bowne and others, inhabitants of the city of New York, setting forth, that they have formed an establishment in said city, for the purpose of receiving, on deposit, such sums of money from persons belonging to the laboring classes of the community as they are able to save from their earnings, and to allow them an interest thereon, and praying that the legislature may grant an act of incorporation to said association, to be called "the Savings Bank of the city of New York," was read and referred to a select committee, consisting of Mr. Russell, Mr. Sharpe and Mr. Emmott.

ASSEMBLY, *March* 11, 1817.

Mr. Russell from the select committee to whom was referred the petition of Robert Bowne and others of the city of New York, praying for an act of incorporation, for a Saving Bank for said city, reported that the committee have had the same under consideration and have given it all that attention which the numbers and respectability of the petitioners, and the benevolence of their intentions may seem to require. The committee submit the following as the result of their investigations on this subject: That however desirable it may be to encourage the poorer class of community to save their hard earnings, and to produce habits of industry and economy by holding out motives of interest to them so to do, still the committee are not convinced, that, under the present state of society in this country, an institution like this, which may be beneficial under other circumstances, and in older countries, can be put into operation with advantage. The expense necessarily attendant in such an establishment will lessen, if not defeat, the benevolent views of the petitioners. And the committee have yet to learn, whether the object might not be accomplished, with a greater prospect of success, and at the same time avoid a new incorporation, by making an arrangement with one of the banks in New York, to allow one of their clerks to transact the business for a small extra allowance. But as the principle is a new one, the committee are unwilling to preclude, by any opinion of theirs, the subject from coming in the usual manner before the house, they therefore are induced to ask for leave to report by bill.

Ordered, That leave be given to bring in such bill.

Mr. Russell, according to leave, brought in the said bill, entitled "An Act *to incorporate the Saving Bank of the city of New York*," which was read the first time, and by unanimous consent was also read a second time and committed to a committee of the whole house.

Ordered, That the petitioners have leave to print the usual number of copies of the said bill, and the report thereon, for the use of the legislature.

ASSEMBLY, *March* 25, 1817.

Ordered, That the bill entitled "An Act *to incorporate the Saving Bank of the city of New York*," be the order of the day for Monday next.

ASSEMBLY, *March* 31, 1817.

The house then resolved itself into a committee of the whole on the bill entitled "An Act *to incorporate the Saving Bank of the city of New York*," and after some time spent thereon, Mr. Speaker resumed the chair, and Mr. Gale, from the said committee, reported progress, and asked for and obtained leave to sit again.

Ordered, That the committee of the whole house be discharged from the further consideration of the said bill, and that the same be referred to a select committee, consisting of Mr. Pendleton, Mr. Russell and Mr. Williams, to consider and report thereon.

ASSEMBLY, *April* 2, 1817.

Mr. Pendleton, from the select committee to whom was referred the bill entiled "An Act *to incorporate the Saving Bank of the city of New York*," to report thereon, reported, that they have had the said bill under consideration, made sundry amendments thereto, altered the title to "An Act *to incorporate an association by the name of the saving corporation of the city of New York*," and with those amendments recommend the same to be passed into a law.

Ordered, That the said bill be committed to a committee of the whole house.

This was its last appearance during the session.

The foregoing report of the special committee on this subject is deserving of special notice, as it brings to view one of the leading obstacles against which the projectors of Savings Banks in this State had to contend. This was the prejudice in the public sentiment and infused into the legislature, against the further incorporation of *banks*. The strife to secure charters for banking corporations was very great, and under the imperfect system relative to the security of their circulating notes, there was a prevalent apprehension that through the undue expansion and resulting debasement of the currency, disastrous consequences might ensue. Hence, the introduction of every bill to incorporate a "*bank*" was watched with jealousy, both by those opposed to extending banking privileges altogether, and by those who were intent only upon securing a charter for themselves. The principle of Savings Banks being but little understood, their dissimilarity to banks of discount and circulation not being comprehended, it was enough that the word "bank" appeared in the title to the act, to array against it the combined hostility of the foes of banks, and the friends of *a bank* for themselves. This condition is suggested in the facts concerning the origin of the Bank for Savings found in connection with the legislative history of that institution.

Hence, doubtless, the amendment suggested by the committee, changing the title to the act by substituting the name of "the saving corporation of the city of New York," for the "Saving Bank of the city of New York."

A SIDE ISSUE.

In this connection it is proper to notice an effort made at the same session to secure for a private corporation the patronage and favor of the sentiment which was being awakened in behalf of Savings Banks.

On the 10th of March, I find noted in the journal of the assembly the following: "Petition of M. Willet and many others, praying to be incorporated as the New York Interest Bank; referred to a select committee."

March 13, a bill to incorporate the New York Interest Bank was introduced by the committee and referred to the committee of the whole.

This is all that is recorded of the measure, the lateness in the session doubtless preventing the bill from being reached and considered. But it is evident, to my mind, that some sharp-eyed financier, cognizant of the movement in favor of a Savings Bank that should receive deposits and pay an interest on them, saw in the scheme plausible ground upon which to secure a private charter for a new banking corporation. I was unable to find the petition either printed in the journal or among the files of legislative papers, so that my convictions of the purpose of the petitioners is only inferential, but is strongly confirmed by a more elaborate and determined effort in the same direction subsequently, the particulars of which will appear in their proper place.

It will also be noticed, that the report of the first committee upon the subject looks somewhat in the same direction, by suggesting the expediency of reaching the proposed object through the agency of a regularly incorporated bank.

CHAPTER XXIX.

RE-ORGANIZATON AND RENEWED EFFORT.

The result of this first effort to secure legislative recognition was, as appears, a failure. But the record would seem to establish the fact that this first association was formed, primarily, to organize a Savings Bank. The call was for that purpose, it appears to have been explained as such in the statement of the objects of the meeting, and the motion of Mr. Griscom thereafter, was pertinent to such purpose and to no other, to wit: "That it is expedient to establish a Savings Bank for the city of New York." A constitution for *that* purpose was adopted, a board of directors appointed, and, subsequently, a committee to secure an act of incorporation, and, later still, officers were elected, one of whom "cashier," points clearly to the organization of a *bank*, and not of a general charitable association; and, finally, the memorial which they presented to the legislature in 1817, sets forth that they *had formed* an establishment for the purpose of receiving on deposit such sums of money, etc.

The evidence connecting the foregoing memorial and the action of the legislature thereon, with the association formed on Friday evening, November 29, 1816, is not such, perhaps, as would establish the fact in a court of law, but is such as to render it, in my judgment, historically conclusive. And this view is confirmed by the facts concerning the origin of the Bank for Savings hereafter given in connection with the statistics of that institution.

Though not successful in this first effort to secure a charter, Savings Banks had here their inception in this State.

In the records of organization furnished me, by Mr. Warner, there appears a hiatus from December 31, 1816, to April 5, 1819, which last date was shortly after the incorporation of the Bank for Savings, and the meeting was doubtless called in view of that event.

That hiatus I am fortunate in being able to supply from a statement furnished me by the Hon. P. W. Engs, of New York.

This gentleman was cognizant of some of the early efforts in the direction of the establishment of the Bank for Savings, and, at my request, not only refreshed his own memory concerning these efforts, but instituted inquiries in quarters where information was likely to be gained, and placed the results of his investigations at my disposal. It is my personal conviction that he took a more active part in the proceedings of the times narrated than his modest record reveals. Be this as it may, he has been from the first the zealous friend of these institutions, and has watched their growth and development with the keenest interest — an interest that abates not with advancing years. He is now, and has been, for several years, an officer in the Metropolitan, formerly Mariners' Savings Bank, incorporated in 1852, and whose deposits now exceed $6,500,000.

The foregoing passages were written in 1869. Mr. Engs died May 19, 1875, in the 85th year of his age. He continued till his decease to be an officer in the institution above mentioned, and notwithstanding his extreme age, no trustee was more faithful in his attendance, or more prompt in the discharge of duty, than he. Only three weeks before his death, though then sightless, he called at the bank to make inquiries concerning its welfare.

It will be seen that the record of Mr. Engs practically begins where that of Mr. Warner leaves off, and is erroneous in this only: that Mr. Engs infers that the proceedings of which he gives account, were the first at which the institution of a Savings Bank in New York was considered. This is disproved by the narrative of Mr. Warner already given. It is probable that the want of success attending the effort to secure the incorporation of a Savings Bank under the organization first formed, resulted in plans of a more general scope for the relief of the poor — plans that could be carried into some measure of effectiveness even though a Savings Bank were not incorporated as a part of the operations. Besides, it was perhaps thought, that under the auspices of a general society in the interest of the poor, a charter for a Savings Bank would be more likely to be favorably considered by the legislature, than when solicited by an association having only this distinctive purpose in view. The result justified the policy adopted, but detracts nothing from the merit of the earlier proceedings as being in fact the inception of the enterprise. The change in the form of organization was external only; it was still prosecuted in the same spirit by the same persons, with the addition of others whose philanthropy was incited by the zeal and labors of the original projectors of the scheme, and with the same ultimate object in view — the incorporation of a Savings Bank for the benefit of the poor classes.

With this explanation, the apparent contradictions between the statements of Mr. Warner and Mr. Engs are reconciled, and the narrative of the latter very consistently supplements that of the former.

STATEMENT OF HON. P. W. ENGS.

"Toward the close of the year 1817, a number of philanthropic gentlemen of this city, whose minds had been earnestly engaged in considering the condition of our poor, and seeking out plans for the welfare of the industrious and laboring classes, came to the conclusion that the condition of our population, and the best interest of the inhabitants at large, required that their views should be put in a shape that would awaken the public mind to its duty in regard to the condition and improvement of the humbler classes in many important respects; and it was agreed that a meeting should be called of persons who had given their thoughts to this labor of love; the result of this was an organization, as shown by the following extracts from their reports and other documents, confirmed by my own recollection and personal observation at the time.

"At a meeting of a very respectable number of citizens convened at the New York Hospital on Friday, 16th December, 1817, to take into consideration the subject of pauperism, General Matthew Clarkson was appointed chairman, and Divie Bethune secretary. On motion of Charles Wilkes, seconded by Wm. Johnson, Esq., it was unanimously '*Resolved*, That the citizens present, with those who may hereafter unite in the measure, be constituted *a society for the prevention of pauperism.*'

"*Resolved,* That a committee be appointed to prepare a constitution for the government of the society, and a statement of the prevailing causes of pauperism, with suggestions relative to the most suitable and efficient remedies. Whereupon the following gentlemen were appointed a committee for that purpose, viz.: John Griscom, Brockholst Livingston, Garrett N. Bleecker, Thomas Eddy, James Eastburn, Rev. Cave Jones, Zachariah Lewis and Divie Bethune, who were requested, when ready to report, to convene the society for that purpose.' 'At a meeting of the society on Friday, the 6th February, 1818, the report from the committee was read, and it was '*Resolved,* That one thousand copies of the report and constitution be published for distribution, under the direction of the same committee.'

"The committee named, directed their attention without delay to the objects of their appointment, and, as they proceeded in classing the cause of poverty, coming to the fourth head, '*Want of Economy,*' say, 'Prodigality is comparative among the poor, it prevails to a great extent in inattention to those small but frequent savings when labor is plentiful, which may go to meet privation in unfavorable seasons.' This is the first expression in their report which points to the Savings Bank principle. Subsequently, it is said, 'We therefore proceed to point out the means which we consider best calculated to ameliorate the condition of the poorer classes, and to strike at the root of those evils which go to the increase of poverty and its attendant miseries.' The first proposition *as a remedy* is to assist the laboring classes to make the most of their earnings by promoting the establishment of *Savings Banks,* or benefit societies, life insurance, etc., the good effects of such associations having been abundantly proved in Europe, and in America; Boston, Philadelphia and

Baltimore having each a savings bank.' Here, then, is the first germ of action upon the important duty of establishing a Savings Bank in New York. The same committee, in the second article of the proposed constitution, say that a leading effort shall be '*to hold out inducements to economy and saving from the fruits of their own industry in the seasons of great abundance.*'

"In a pencil note to my former friend John Griscom, on the title page of the report referred to, is the following: 'written by J. G.' 'This first report of the pauperism society was taken by me to Europe. A few months afterward this society germinated in my parlor in William street, though first established at the hospital.'

"Being a near neighbor," continues Mr. Engs, "I was present at this meeting, and remember to have seen Thomas Eddy, Joseph Curtis, John Pintard, and others whom I cannot name. 'Soon after the report was made and printed,' says a note from the son of Mr. Griscom to myself, 'a motion was made by my father that a Savings Bank be organized, which was immediately adopted, and the first Savings Bank in the State of New York was organized soon after in Chambers street, the same one now in Bleecker street, near Broadway, and of which you possess the record to the present time.'

"It is, therefore, a settled point that Savings Banks in this State owe their origin to the 'New York Society for the Prevention of Pauperism' and *John Griscom*, well known in this city during his life-time as devoted to philanthropic, educational and scientific objects, was the prime mover in forming that society, but made it his duty, after it was formed, to introduce as its most important feature the establishment of a Savings Bank. Surely, the city and the State owe to him and his associates a debt of gratitude, more especially as it is to be remembered that out of this Society came the establishment of the 'Society for the care of Juvenile Delinquents, or House of Refuge,' being the first establishment in the world on a similar plan, the great benefits of which have been known and appreciated wherever its example has been followed after. Succeeding the incipiency of these movements, public meetings were called by the parent society at the old City Hotel, in Broadway, which brought together leading public spirited men of our city, and there were heard the practical arguments and sound eloquence of that giant mind, the celebrated and reverend John M. Mason, and others of like reputation. I should fail to record *correctly* the names of most of these, and might misplace those whose public services I have been apt to treasure up as benefactors of the human race, were I to attempt a positive record, in this instance, from memory. They were, however, from the most energetic and useful portions of society, and have mostly gone to their account. These gentlemen and their co-workers, by placing the establishment of Savings Banks in the foreground of their efforts, were eminently successful in linking together minds and hearts from various grades of society, whose labors for the well-being of their fellow men have shed a lustre over our land."

It is probable that the claim made in the foregoing narrative, in favor of John Griscom as the mover of the resolution for the establishment of a Savings Bank as part of the plan, or as the leading feature of the society then organized, is well founded. It will be remembered that in the narrative of Mr. Warner, Mr. Griscom made the same motion at the meeting on the 29th of November, 1816, and it was natural and characteristic of the man that he should be the first to renew his motion under the auspices of the new movement, having still the same ultimate object in view.

Thus are the two narratives made consistent as a continuous history of the early efforts of philanthropy, resulting in the successful establishment of a Savings Bank for the poor, under the authority and protection of the law, and the correctness of both is confirmed by the brief narrative furnished by the treasurer of the Bank for Savings, of the origin of that institution, which will be found prefaced to the statistics of that institution.

In my researches among the legislative records of the State, I was for a time surprised to find nothing that presented evidence of a following up before that body in 1818, of the movement initiated in 1817, and could not be persuaded that I had not overlooked some evidence on the subject, through defective indices or imperfect files, until I had examined carefully every page of the journals of both houses, and every scrap of writing among the dusty and ill-arranged legislative records of that year. But the narrative of Mr. Engs, afterward received, explains the matter fully.

From this, it appears that the report of the committee upon a plan of action for the Society for the Prevention of Pauperism, was not presented until February 6th, 1818, a period quite too late in the session of the legislature, to hope for the successful introduction of the measure at a time in the history of legislation in our State, when important measures were commonly considered with great care and deliberation. Besides, the organization of the Society appears, even at this time, to have been quite informal, not being perfected until some months later, as stated in the memorandum of Mr. Griscom.

CHAPTER XXX.

MESSAGE OF GOVERNOR CLINTON, 1818,—ANOTHER SIDE ISSUE.

It will have been observed, that among the names of directors of the Savings Bank organized in 1816, was that of De Witt Clinton. That his far-seeing sagacity, afterward so conspicuously manifested in the administration of the affairs of State, should lead him to identify himself with this enterprise is not surprising. The conditions of pauperism demanding relief, and the agency of Savings Banks as a means to that desirable end, had doubtless been impressed upon his mind at the meetings of the society with which his name was identified, and by personal interviews with and appeals from the original and more active promoters of the enterprise. In the fall of 1817 he was elected governor, and brought to this elevated position a mind and heart deeply imbued with convictions derived from the associations referred to.

Accordingly, we find in his first annual message to the legislature, the following reference to the subject of pauperism, and to the various philanthropic agencies designed to mitigate its evils.

Extract from the Message of Governor Clinton, 1818.

"Our statutes relating to the poor are borrowed from the English system, and the experience of that country, as well as our own, shows that pauperism increases with the augmentation of the funds applied to its relief. This evil has proceeded to such an alarming extent in the city of New York, *that the burdens of heavy taxation which it has imposed, menace a diminution of the population of that city, and a depreciation of its real property.* The consequences will be very injurious to the whole State; for the decay of our great market will be felt in every department of productive labor. Under the present system, the fruits of industry are appropriated to the wants of idleness; a laborious poor man is taxed for the support of an idle beggar; and the vice of mendicity, no longer considered degrading, infects a considerable portion of our population in large towns. I am persuaded that the sooner a radical reform takes place, the better. The evil is contagious, and a prompt extirpation can alone prevent its pernicious extension. The inducements to pauperism may be destroyed, by rendering it a greater evil to live by charity than by industry; its mischiefs may be mitigated by diminishing the expenses of our charitable establishments, and by adopting a system of coercive labor; and its causes may be removed by preventing intemperance and extravagance, and by intellectual, moral and religious cultivation. It is the decree of heaven that our lives should be spent in useful or active employment. 'In the sweat of thy face shalt thou eat bread, till thou return unto the ground,' was the declaration of the Almighty to our first parent; and a course of blind, indiscriminating, prodigal benevolence defeats its own object by attempting to counteract the laws of our nature, and the designs of Providence. Charity is an exalted virtue, but it ought to be founded on reason and regulated by wisdom. While we must consider as worthy of all praise and patronage religious and moral societies, Sunday, free and charity schools, houses of industry, orphan asylums and SAVINGS BANKS, and all other establishments, which prevent or alleviate the evils of pauperism, by inspiring industry, dispensing employment, and inculcating economy; by improving the mind, cultivating the heart, and elevating the character, we are equally bound to discourage those institutions which furnish the aliment of mendicity, by removing the incentives to labor, and administering to the blandishments of sensuality."

To this we add the following extract from the reply made by the assembly:

"All such institutions as your excellency has enumerated, which are so obviously calculated to alleviate the evils of pauperism, by inspiring industry, dispensing employment, and inculcating economy, by improving the mind, cultivating and elevating the character, we shall consider as highly deserving the public patronage."

A joint committee of senate and assembly having been appointed, to whom was referred that part of the governor's speech (or message) relative to the relief and settlement of the poor, Mr. Crolius, from committee appointed on part of the assembly, reported (April 2, 1818):

"That they are impressed with a strong conviction, that the rapid increase of pauperism is an evil of an alarming nature, and that a speedy and radical reform of our pauper system is imperiously called for to remedy the growing evil; that, in consequence of the indisposition of the chairman of the joint committee, the calling of them together has been unavoidably omitted so long that there is not sufficient time, during the continuance of the present session, to mature a new and proper system." The committee were thereupon discharged.

A NEW SIDE ISSUE.

We noted in the history of legislative action upon the subject of Savings Banks in 1817, the memorial of M. Willett and others, praying for the incorporation of an interest bank.

The effort was renewed the following year by other parties, and seems to have been more favorably considered, or at least it occupies a far more conspicuous place in the journals of the legislature.

That this movement was stimulated by the effort to establish a Savings Bank upon purely philanthropic principles, is to my mind as clearly established as the relation of any two historical events well can be, though some of the names appended to the memorial would point to the conclusion, perhaps an erroneous one, however, that some of the parties, interested in the project of a Savings Bank, and despairing of success in securing the favorable consideration of the legislature, had lent their approval to this measure as the more hopeful scheme to win success, and as the best attainable good in the direction of a place of deposit for the earnings of the poor. But I am persuaded that the motive of its primary projectors was, by this device, to distract the attention of the legislature, and under the specious guise of the public good to be promoted, to make use of the growing sentiment in favor of Savings Banks, to secure to themselves a profitable franchise.

As this measure was more carefully prepared and more earnestly pressed than that of the previous year, I insert here the memorial of the applicants and the proceedings of the legislature thereon, as an interesting episode in the history of Savings Banks; for had the project been successful, and *interest paying banks* taken *this* form, they would have become merely commercial enterprises, with no distinctive history to record.

SENATE, *March* 11, 1818.

The petition of W. North and others, praying for the establishment of an interest and Savings Bank in the city of New York, was read and referred to a select committee consisting of Mr. J. I. Prendergast, Mr. Swart and Mr. ——.

PETITION.

To the Honorable the Legislature of the State of New York:

The petition of the subscribers, on behalf of themselves and their associates, for an act incorporating an interest and Savings Bank, respectfully showeth:

That your petitioners are well convinced that a bank giving an interest on money deposited in it would be a great public accommodation and benefit.

Your honorable body must be aware that there is a large amount of floating capital in all commercial cities, and that an institution which would concentrate this capital, and loan it to active, industrious and enterprising men, would be of infinite advantage, and greatly assist commerce, manufactures and trade. That such a bank, they firmly believe, would call forth an amount of deposits, equal to its capital, from a class of citizens who have never kept any bank account, and who have no interest in banking institutions; such, for instance, as the honest and fair tradesman, who pays his debts without a promissory note, but often acquires a property in money beyond his immediate demands, and who looks forward to the period when he may safely invest the savings of a series of years in real estate, or to the further extension of his business or calling.

That your petitioners are fully convinced that a bank can and ought to allow an interest on money deposited in it, and are willing to embark their funds in an institution on this principle, and take the chance of deriving from its discounts a compensation for the risk and trouble.

Your petitioners respectfully state it as their confident belief, that such an institution would have a happy tendency to check the unfortunate rage for speculation; to equalize, in some degree, the price of stocks and public funds; prevent those dangerous fluctuations in the value of merchandise; greatly assist and relieve persons whose property is at present locked up in courts of justice, trustees, administrators and others, who are not authorized to invest the property committed to their charge.

Your petitioners are convinced that an interest on a sum equal to the capital they ask for, is lost to widows, orphans, charitable and other institutions, as well as to many individuals who are compelled to keep considerable sums on hand, waiting for permanent objects of investment, or to meet emergencies.

That many such receive their incomes in sums greater than are required for immediate use, whereby they lose an interest which otherwise they will gain from an institution of this kind.

That it would beget habits of economy, of calculation, and of foresight in all classes of the community.

That it would attract to our State and city wealthy foreigners who would be glad to deposit their specie in the vaults of a bank giving a small interest, until time and experience should direct them to more profitable objects of investment.

It must also be well known to your honorable body, that, in all commercial countries except our own, there exists a means of obtaining an interest on floating capital. To the general objection, "That there are in the city of New York too many banks," your petitioners answer, that there is not *one* on the liberal principle of giving an interest on deposits, and your petitioners would not ask for privileges of banking which did not insure to the public greater advantages than of any similar institution yet established. A bank with the small capital asked for by your petitioners will not materially increase the paper circulation, especially as it must go into operation on a specie capital.

Your petitioners respectfully state, that an institution possessing public confidence, giving an interest to the depositor on the one hand, and regaining an interest from the borrower on the other, will rest on the only just principle of trade—reciprocal advantage.

It is here that the farmer may deposit the fruits of his agricultural labors, and wait a favorable opportunity to enlarge his patrimonial estate. It is in such an institution the mechanic may increase the profit of his former labors, until he finds himself able to build a tenement of his own. The widow and orphan may here see the interest of any principal left for their current maintenance accumulate in a ratio similar to compound interest. It is in such a bank the successful merchant may lay down the profits of a fruitful voyage, and contemplate its increase preparatory to a second adventure.

Such an institution will induce the hazardous speculator to pause before he ventures on the ocean of uncertainty, and give every man's reason time to check increasing avarice and overgrown cupidity. Such an institution will in short aid the administrator, the guardian and the trustee, by giving an interest favorable to the trust estate co-extensive with the right of the party to the principal.

Your petitioners assure your honorable body that their plan has obtained the general approbation and applause of the community. The advantages it holds out to men of small but increasing property; the equity and fairness of its principles; its general benefit and utility, will command the universal suffrage.

Such are the grounds on which your petitioners ask for a new banking institution from an enlightened legislature. They pretend to no patronage but reason and general utility. They offer no bonus but the public accommodation. They ask no privileges but such as will manifestly tend to the public good; and they will submit with deference to such decision as your honorable body shall be pleased to pronounce.

ALFRED S. PELL. W. NORTH.
CHAS. GRAHAM. WM. INMAN.
FRED. DE PEYSTER. DENNIS MCCARTHY.
C. WATTS.

NEW YORK, *February*, 1818.

SENATE, *March* 13, 1818.

Mr. J. I. Prendergast, to whom was referred the petition of William North and others, of the city of New York, praying for the establishment of an interest bank, reported as follows, to wit:

That they have had the same under consideration, and are of opinion that an institution that would become bounden to pay an interest on deposits would be of great utility, and merits the consideration of the legislature.

First. Because they are induced to believe that none of the present banking institutions pay an interest to private persons on deposits. *And, secondly*, in a large commercial city, where there are many mechanics, tradesmen and others, who would have a safe place to deposit their weekly savings, and receive an interest of five per cent thereon per annum, until it amounts to a sum sufficient to enable them to make a more profitable investment, would to such persons be of great advantage.

The committee are under the impression, that, in all commercial countries except our own, there exists the means of obtaining, through public institutions, interest on floating capital; and they believe that an institution giving a moderate interest to the depositor on the one hand, and regaining an interest from the borrower on the other, founds its claim to public patronage on the most equitable principles of trade and reciprocal advantage. They have, therefore, directed their chairman to prepare a bill, and ask leave to present the same. Thereupon,

Ordered, That leave be given to bring in such bill.

Mr. J. I. Prendergast, according to leave, brought in the said bill, entitled "An act *to incorporate the New York Interest Bank*," which was read the first time, and, by unanimous consent, was also read a second time, and committed to a committee of the whole.

Ordered, That the said report and bill be printed at the expense of the applicants.

The bill was considered in committee of the whole, April 6, and rejected by a vote of fifteen to seven, which was agreed to by the Senate.

On the 8th of April a motion was made to reconsider the vote agreeing to reject the bill, which was lost by fifteen to ten, and thus the bill failed.

CHAPTER XXXI.

INTRODUCTION, PROGRESS AND PASSAGE OF THE ACT INCORPORATING THE BANK FOR SAVINGS.

I propose herein to trace the proceedings of the legislature upon this subject, from the presentation of the memorial of the Society for the Prevention of Pauperism, until the approval of the bill for the incorporation of the Bank for Savings, by the council of revision. I regret that the memorial and report referred to have not been preserved in full among the legislative records.

We are thus brought to the year 1819, ever memorable in our history as that in which the Savings Bank principle was recognized by, and received the support, authority and protection of law.

None of those connected with the measure, as petitioners, corporators or legislators, dreamed of the magnitude and importance of the work thus inaugurated. Of the latter, some were consistently, and perhaps not unreasonably, opposed to the scheme from first to last, while others gave their assent doubtfully, and others indifferently. But among them there must have been some sagacious as well as zealous and persistent champions. I regret that I am unable to record the names of these, except as they appear in the reports of committees, for it would be a grateful service to transmit the names, not less of those who thus espoused the cause and gave to it legal and tangible form and embodiment, than of those who conceived the idea and labored to secure its acceptance and approval.

PROCEEDINGS OF THE LEGISLATURE UPON THE BILL TO INCORPORATE THE BANK FOR SAVINGS IN THE CITY OF NEW YORK.

ASSEMBLY, *Thursday, January* 19, 1819.

The memorial of M. Clarkson, president, on behalf of the Society for the Prevention of Pauperism in the city of New York, praying certain legal provisions in regard to tavern licenses, and also the incorporation of a Savings Bank in the said city, was read and referred to a select committee, consisting of the members attending this house from the city and county of New York.

ASSEMBLY, *Saturday, February* 13, 1819.

Mr. Ulshoeffer, from the select committee, consisting of the members attending this house from the city and county of New York, to whom was referred the memorial of the board of managers of the Society for the Prevention of Pauperism in the city of New York, reported in part:

That they have examined and duly considered the said memorial as it respects a *Bank for Savings*, to be established in the city of New York, and are of opinion that such an institution would be of the utmost utility. The efficacy and beneficial results of these institutions, affording a safe and profitable means of investing small sums of money, have been fully tested in Europe and the United States.

The memorial, and a report of a committee, from the before-named society, on the subject of such an incorporation, afford facts and arguments, which, in the opinion of the committee, will satisfy the most skeptical. It is to be wished that such institutions might become general throughout the land, and they ought to unite in their support every benevolent mind. The committee respectfully refer to the above-mentioned report, for the necessary information on this subject; they have approved of the draft of a bill submitted by the petitioners, which they now ask leave to bring in.

Ordered, That leave be given to bring in such bill.

Mr. Ulshoeffer, according to leave, brought in the said bill, entitled "An Act *to incorporate an association by the name of a 'Bank for Savings' in the city of New York*," which was read the first time, and by unanimous consent was also read a second time, and committed to a committee of the whole house.

Ordered, That the usual number of copies of the same be printed for the use of the legislature.

ASSEMBLY, *Saturday, February* 27, 1819.

The house then resolved itself into a committee of the whole on the bill entitled "An Act *to incorporate an association by the name of a 'Bank of Savings' in the city of New York*," and after some time spent thereon, Mr. Speaker resumed the chair, and Mr. Green from the said committee reported, that the committee had gone through the said bill, made an amendment thereto and agreed to the same; which he was directed to report to the house, and he read the report in his place, and delivered the same in at the table where it was again read.

Thereupon,

Ordered, That the further consideration of the report of the committee of the whole house be postponed until Monday next.

ASSEMBLY, *Monday, March* 1, 1819.

Mr. Adams, from the committee on engrossed bills, reported that the committee have examined the engrossed bill entitled "An act *to incorporate an association by the name of a 'Bank for Savings' in the city of New York*" (with others), and that the same is correctly engrossed.

Thereupon, the said engrossed bill entitled "An act *to incorporate an association by the name of a 'Bank for Savings' in the city of New York*" was read the third time.

Resolved, That the bill do pass.

SENATE, *Friday, March* 5, 1819.

The Senate then resolved itself into a committee of the whole on the engrossed bill from the honorable the assembly, entitled "An act *to incorporate an association by the name of a 'Bank for Savings' in the city of New York*," and after some time spent thereon, Mr. President resumed the chair, and Mr. Frey, from the said committee, reported that, in proceeding on the said bill and after the same had been read in the committee, the first enacting clause thereof, having been amended, was again read, and is in the words following, to wit:

Be it enacted by the people of the State of New York, represented in senate and assembly, That William Bayard, John Murray, Junior, Noah Brown, William Few, Brockholst Livingston, Cadwallader D. Colden, George Arcularius, Thomas Buckley, Duncan B. Campbell, Benjamin Clark, James Eastburn, Henry Eckford, Thomas Eddy, Philip Hone, John E. Hyde, Peter A. Jay, Zecheriah Lewis, Dennis McCarthy, Andrew Morris, James Palmer, John Pintard, Abraham Russell, Jacob Sherred, Joseph Smith, Najah Taylor, Jeremiah Thompson, William Wilson and Samuel Wood shall be and are hereby constituted a body corporate and politic by the name of "The Bank of Savings in the city of New York," and by that name they shall have perpetual succession, and shall be persons capable of suing and being sued, pleading and being impleaded, answering and being answered unto, defending and being defended, in all courts and places whatsoever;

and may have a common seal, with power to change and alter the same from time to time, and shall be capable of purchasing, taking, holding and enjoying, to them and their successors, any real estate, in fee simple or otherwise, and any goods, chattels and personal estate which shall be necessary for the purposes above recited, and of selling, leasing or otherwise disposing of the said real or personal estate, or any part thereof, at their will and pleasure: *Provided always*, That the clear annual value of such real and personal estate, exclusive of the profits that may arise from the interest accruing upon the stock, or from the sale of any stock in which the deposits made in the said bank may be invested;* and that the trustees or managers of said institution shall not directly or indirectly receive any pay or emolument for their services, nor shall they issue any notes, make any discounts or transact any business which belongs to or is transacted by incorporated banks other than is herein specified: *Provided also*, That the funds of the said corporation shall be used and appropriated to the promotion of the objects stated in the preamble to this act in the manner herein mentioned, and those only.

That debates were had thereon, and the question having been put whether the committee would agree to the said clause, it was carried in the affirmative.

That the yeas and nays being called for by Mr. Ogden, seconded by Mr. Bowne, were as follows, to wit:

For the affirmative — Messrs. Adams, Allen, Barnum, Barstow, Bowne, Childs, Dayton, Evans, Hammond, Hart, Knox, Livingston, Rosecrants, Seymour, Skinner, Swart, Van Vechten, Wilson, Yates and Young.

For the negative — Messrs. Austin, Ditmas, Lounsbery, Mallery, Noyes and Ogden.

Mr. Frey further reported that the committee had gone through the said bill, made amendments, and

* There is evidently an omission in the journal, probably of the words "shall not exceed the sum of five thousand dollars."

agreed to the same; which he was directed to report to the senate, and he read the report in his place, and delivered the same in at the table, where it was again read and agreed to by the senate.

Ordered, That the amendments be engrossed.

SENATE, *Saturday, March* 6, 1819.

The engrossed bill from the honorable the assembly, entitled "An act to incorporate an association by the name of a 'Bank for Savings' in the city of New York," was read the third time.

Resolved, That the bill and amendments do pass.

Ordered, That the clerk deliver the said bill and amendments to the honorable the assembly, and inform them that the senate have passed the same, with the amendments therewith delivered.

ASSEMBLY, *Saturday, March* 6, 1819.

Two several messages from the honorable the senate, delivered by their clerk with the bills therein mentioned, were read, informing that they have passed the bill entitled 'An act *to incorporate an association by the name of a 'Bank for Savings' in the city of New York*" (and another), severally with the amendments therewith delivered.

Thereupon the said bills and amendments were read, and the amendments having been again read,

The said bill and amendments first mentioned were laid upon the table.

ASSEMBLY, *Wednesday, March* 10, 1819.

The house then proceeded to the consideration of the amendments made by the honorable the senate to the bill entitled "An act *to incorporate* an association by the name of a 'Bank for Savings,' in the city of New York."

The same having been read, all of the said amendments, excepting the first, were agreed to by the house, and the first having been amended, was agreed to by the house.

Ordered, That the clerk deliver the said bill and amendments to the honorable the senate, and inform them that this house have concurred with them in their amendments to the said bill, with the amendment to their first amendment therewith delivered.

SENATE, *Friday, March* 12, 1819.

A message from the honorable the assembly, delivered by their clerk with the bill, amendments, and a copy of a resolution therein mentioned, was read, informing that they had concurred in all of the amendments of the senate to the bill entitled "An act to incorporate an association by the name of a 'Bank for Savings,' in the city of New York," except the first amendment which they had amended.

The said amendment having been read and considered.

Thereupon,

Resolved, That the senate do non-concur with the honorable the assembly in their said amendment to the first amendment of the senate to the said bill.

Ordered, That the clerk deliver the said bill, amendment, and a copy of the preceding resolution to the honorable the assembly.

ASSEMBLY, *Friday, March* 12, 1819.

A message from the honorable the senate, delivered by their clerk, with the bill, amendments, and a copy of the resolution therein mentioned, was read, informing that the senate do non-concur with this house in their amendment to the first amendment made by the honorable the senate to the bill entitled "An act *to incorporate an association by the name of a 'Bank for Savings,' in the city of New York.*"

Ordered, That the said bill, amendments and copy of a resolution be laid upon the table.

ASSEMBLY, *Monday, March* 15, 1819.

The house then proceeded to the consideration of so much of the first amendment made by the honorable the senate to the bill entitled "An act *to incorporate an association by the name of a 'Bank for Savings,' in the city of New York,*" which said amendment had been amended by this house, and in which said amendment so made by this house, the honorable the senate had non-concurred.

Thereupon, the said amendment being read,

Resolved, That this house do recede from their said amendment to the said first amendment by the honorable the senate to the said bill.

Ordered, That the bill be re-engrossed as amended by the honorable the senate.

Ordered, That the clerk deliver the said amended bill, amendments, and a copy of the preceding resolution, to the honorable the senate.

SENATE, *Monday, March* 22, 1819.

Six several messages from the honorable the assembly, delivered by their clerk, with the bills and amendments therein mentioned, were read, informing that they had concurred in the amendments of the senate to the bill entitled "An act *to incorporate an association by the name of a 'Bank for Savings,' in the city of New York*" (and others).

The amended bills having been examined,

Ordered, That the clerk return the same to the honorable the assembly.

ASSEMBLY, *Monday, March* 22, 1819.

Bill entitled "An act *to incorporate an association by the name of a 'Bank of Savings' in the city of New York,*" received from the honorable the senate, with a message that they had passed the same without amendment.

Ordered, That the clerk deliver the same to the honorable the council of revision.

Friday, March 26, 1819.

Message from the honorable the council of revision returning the bill APPROVED.*

* The foregoing proceedings of the legislature are as nearly a literal transcript from the journals of the two houses as it was practicable to make.

CHAPTER XXXII.

PRACTICAL RESULTS; FIRST REPORT OF BANK FOR SAVINGS; SUCCESS POPULAR AS WELL AS SUCCESSFUL! FIRST FRUITS.

It is proper briefly to note the practical success of this institution for a short period after its organization and the favorable effect of this success in disarming hostility to similar measures thereafter.

The first report of the institution was made to the legislature the following year, 1820, and was accompanied by an application for an amendment of its charter so as to authorize investments in loans upon real estate.

Concerning the subject generally, Governor Clinton, in his message to the legislature, says:

"The Bank for Savings in the city of New York, instituted at the last session, to cherish meritorious industry, to encourage frugality and retrenchment, and to promote the welfare of families, the cause of morality, and the good order of society, has already manifested its claims to your confidence by an accumulation of more than one hundred and fifty thousand dollars in small deposits, and by shedding a benign influence on society. The application of this institution to authorize loans on real estate, as well as any other provisions subservient to its salutary objects, will undoubtedly receive your sanction."

The following is the report of the Bank for Savings made to the legislature in 1820, covering the operations of only six months:

REPORT.

Conformably to the provisions of an act entitled "An act to incorporate an association by the name of a Bank for Savings, in the city of New York," the trustees now beg leave to present their first report to the honorable the legislature of the State, and the honorable common council of the city of New York, as follows:

First. That the Bank for Savings was opened for depositors in a room of the New York Institution, granted to the trustees by the Academy of Arts, and approved by the corporation, for the term of two years, gratis, on Saturday the 3d of July, 1819, when, from eighty depositors, the trustees had the satisfaction of receiving the sum of $2,807.

Second. That from the aforesaid 3d day of July, until the 27th of December inclusive, being a period of six entire months, there had been deposited in the Bank for Savings, by 1,527 depositors, the sum of $153,378.31.

Third. That the sum of $148,372.27, as will appear by the treasurer's account hereunto annexed, has been invested in the public funds, agreeable to law, and that the sum of $6,606 has been drawn out by the depositors. Of those who have drawn out, the number of forty-six have closed their accounts, and twenty-one have only taken out a part, and, therefore, their accounts remain open.

Fourth. The depositors having been classed under various heads, they stand in the books of the trustees as follows: [Here follows an enumeration of occupations of depositors, embracing mechanics, laborers, tradesmen and domestics, 840; minors, male, 287; minors, female, 276; widows, 98; orphans, 20; apprentices, 15; unclassified, 24; total, 1,527.] Having given those statements, which the act aforesaid and the sense of their own duty to the depositors required, the trustees hope that they shall stand excused in making such remarks as this interesting subject obviously suggests.

It was to be expected that an institution which, by inculcating economy among the middle and lower classes of society, and inducing them to spare their earnings for future exigencies, would necessarily withdraw them from places of public resort, and thus excite the enmity of those whose emolument was the fruit of prodigal expenditure. The trustees, however, are gratified in saying that few such instances have come to their knowledge. On the contrary, the classifications of depositors will furnish several instances, even of public tavern-keepers, who have brought their money to the bank for safety and increase. Nor are the trustees without hope that such examples will operate upon many of those whose conduct has heretofore been reprehensible. A reform at the sources of waste will soon spread its influences through a large portion of our population.

The board of trustees, previous to opening the books for the receipt of deposits, established a system of management and inspection for the bank which in its operation has proved highly beneficial. They appointed, in rotation, three of their number to attend at the bank as a committee for one month. It was made the duty of this committee to receive deposits, to see that the entries were duly made, to make inquiries as to the situation of the depositors, and ask such further questions as might promote the welfare either of the individual or of the institution. By this means the whole of the board of trustees have become familiar with the depositors, and while their confidence in those to whom they have committed the safeguard and improvement of their little funds has been confirmed, it has afforded an opportunity, readily embraced by the trustees, of giving such advice to many of the depositors as they believed would tend to promote careful habits and moral feeling. The gratification which they have received in numerous instances has amply repaid the attending committee this gratuitous labor.

The investment of the funds has been intrusted to a

special committee, consisting of Messrs. John Mason, Jacob Sherred and William Wilson, who report to the board at their monthly meeting the manner in which the funds have been disposed of. The treasurer also reports once a month the amount received from the deposits, and how it has been expended. By this mode every operation is at once known to each individual trustee; and such checks are furnished as to prevent the possibility of the smallest loss to depositors.

The different classes of depositors will furnish various reflections calculated to place Banks for Savings high in the esteem of the political economist, the practical philanthropist and the diligent promoter of sound morals.

In every part of an active population, and particularly in large cities, the difficulty of procuring the reward of labor is not so great as the power to preserve it. The man who attends to the regular discharge of his duties, and is enabled to lay up a weekly sum from his hard-earned income, is too often the dupe of the idle, the profligate, the designing, or the unfortunate. Incaution, and sometimes an excusable vanity, prompts the possessor of an increasing fund to reveal it to his less prosperous neighbor. The desire of accumulation, and the hope of bettering his condition, will induce the listener to try the means with which his friends can furnish him on some object of speculation. He tries, and both are ruined. There are others who live only to prey upon society; they insinuate themselves into the confidence of the unsuspecting; give the most plausible reasons for the small sums they ask, and the strongest assurances of a speedy repayment. The money is loaned; but the lender too soon finds that the fruit of his labor is gone forever.

Many cases have come before the trustees wherein the above was justified by ample details. The causes, as after stated by the sufferers themselves, arose alike from their want of some secure place of deposit, and their ignorance how to improve what they had laid up. The sums are generally too small to be received at any of the banks; and where this is not the case, it was found equally as difficult to retain it as if it had been actually in the owner's hands; the temptation to loan was the same. Though many depositors understood how to invest their money in public stocks, yet anticipating an early use for it, or fearing a loss from the fluctuation of the funds, they preferred letting it lie useless. In numerous instances sums from $100 to $300 had lain unimproved for many years, while others had loaned and lost the whole. The Banks for Savings provide almost the only remedy; they give security to the depositor, improve his little stock, and, at fixed periods, allow him to withdraw the whole, if his inclination or interest should prompt him.

The value of an institution is to be estimated by the evil which it prevents, or by the good which it produces. In some the effects are more remote, in others more immediate. Banks for Savings are among the latter; the attempt is no sooner made than the most salutary effects follow. It has formed the most pleasing and interesting part of the duty of the monthly committee to observe and note these effects.

The effect on the moral habits is not more certain than striking; he who has learned to be economical has first gotten rid of pernicious modes of spending money. Every time he adds to his amount he has an additional motive for perseverance. In the provision he is making for futurity is associated all which can gratify him as a father, a husband, a guardian or a friend. The talent which heaven has committed to his care he improves for the objects of his affections; this, again, endears them to him, and thus the sum of human happiness is increased and extended. It is impossible for men continuing to act on such principles to be immoral.

The trustees are glad to report, that the habit of saving among the depositors becomes very soon not only delightful, but permanent. Those who have brought their one dollar, are anxious to increase it to five, and so on. The number of re-deposits sufficiently confirms this fact; and such has been the effects on emigrants from Great Britain, that the very guineas which they received from the Banks for Savings at home, they have deposited in the one in this city immediately after landing.

There are several classes of depositors which the trustees cannot forbear to remark upon.

Seamen are proverbially improvident, not so much, perhaps, from a love of waste, as from a total ignorance how to dispose of their money. Having no one to direct them, the wages which they have earned, amidst storms and tempests, they scatter on shore without reflection. Of this useful class of men, a few have found their way to our bank, and the trustees will do all in their power to increase the number. One seaman in one of the regular traders for Liverpool, brought home with him, in silver, $360; his captain directed him to the Bank for Savings. He soon deposited his burden, and appeared heartily pleased that, under the guidance of his commander, he had at last found a harbor of safety for his small property.

The clergy are a body of gentlemen, perhaps, more entitled to our gratitude and care, than any other in the community. Their means in general are small, their families usually large, and, from the nature of their office, they are prevented by trade to increase their income. Many of them, however, can save a little, and they have availed themselves of the bank to deposit it for improvement. When the trustees look round on the number of destitute widows of once respectable and useful clergymen, they cannot but hail the institution as the means of affording, by the provident care of the living, comfort, and perhaps independence, for future widows and orphans.

The attention which has been paid by parents and guardians, since the opening of our bank, to the future comfort and security of minors, is not one of the least blessings which shall flow from this institution. The deposits for this class are very numerous; and while it is calculated to excite the gratitude of the young beings, for whose use these deposits have been made, it holds out to them, when arrived at maturity, the example and the means by which succeeding generations are to be benefited and improved.

As parents, as citizens, and as men, the trustees exult in the prospects which the Bank for Savings holds out to this growing city and State. The habits which a resort to it induce, hold out the best pledge for a reduction in the public burdens, as they are connected with indigence and want. They tend to inspire a spirit of independence, and in their moral operation lessen crime, poverty and disease. They teach man to depend upon his own exertions; encourage industry, frugality, cleanliness and self-respect; and effectually prevent those who are so fortunate as to be influenced by them, from applying either to public provisions or private bounty for support.

The trustees take this public opportunity of thanking the gentlemen connected as tellers, clerks and porters in the different banks, for the cheerful manner in which they have rendered their services on the evenings of deposit. Their kindness was both acceptable and useful.

In conclusion: The trustees are fully aware that they have undertaken an arduous task; but in the approbation of the public authorities, the countenance of their fellow-citizens, and the increasing comfort of the community, they will have a full reward.

WILLIAM BAYARD,
President.

JAMES EASTBURN,
Secretary.

Accompanying the foregoing report, and referred to therein, was the following financial statement of the operations of the Bank for the first six months. It is a noteworthy fact that this form of statement is preserved and used to this day in the financial exhibits of this Institution.

First Financial Statement of the Bank for Savings for 1819.

The Treasurer in account with the Bank for Savings.

1819.		Dr.
July.	To cash from depositors....	$40,262 52
Aug.	To cash from depositors....	26,783 69
Sept.	To cash from depositors....	25,720 78
Oct.	To cash from depositors....	21,108 75
	To interest................	1,217 38
Nov.	To cash from depositors	19,934 77
	To interest................	300 00
Dec.	To cash from depositors....	19,516 88
	To balance, due Treasurer ..	947 20
		$155,791 97

1819.			Stock.	Cr.
July 7.	By cash,	N. Y. long loan......	$4,331 80	$4,256 00
July 13.	"	N. Y. State sixes....	15,535 87	15,225 15
Aug. 5.	"	N. Y. State sixes....	20,781 37	20,781 37
Aug. 10.	"	N. Y. State sixes....	9,350 96	9,413 29
Aug. 16.	"	N. Y. long loan......	16,772 68	16,940 40
	"	withdr'n by deposit'r.	....	430 00
Sept. 8.	"	Canal stock.........	6,000 00	6,068 00
Sept. 14.	"	Canal stock.........	4,135 96	4,186 95
Sept. 16.	"	One million loan....	4,250 00	4,313 75
Oct. 6.	"	City loan............	20,000 00	20,250 00
	"	withdr'n by deposit's,	....	3,675 49
	"	for expenses	....	505 70
Nov. 1.	"	City loan............	30,000 00	30,184 56
	"	withdr'n by deposit's,	....	1,869 51
	"	for expenses	....	308 00
Dec.	"	Canal stock.........	16,752 80	16,752 80
	"	withdr'n by deposit's,	....	631 00
			$147,911 44	$155,791 97

NOTE.—On comparing this account with the books of the accountant. it appears that a loss of $50.92 has occurred, of which $27 was in counterfeit notes, and $23.92, losses in change.

The message of Governor Clinton from which we have quoted, refers to a petition from the Bank for Savings to the legislature, asking for an enlargement of its power in making investments, etc.

In this petition the trustees set forth that—

"They were restrained from vesting moneys except in government securities or in stock, created and issued under and in virtue of any law of the United States or of this State.

"That the price of such stock is fluctuating; that it produces but six per cent interest, and often a less profit, as the same cannot always be purchased at par.

"With a view to make their funds as productive as possible, the same being chiefly the property of the poor, they pray to be further authorized to loan their funds either on bond and mortgage on real estate in the city of New York, or to the corporation of that city.

"They also state the difficulties under which they labor, in consequence of small deposits being lodged by minors, who have not the power to withdraw such deposits, unless through the interposition of guardians, and pray that they may be authorized to pay such depositors without such interposition.

"They also pray that deposits of persons deceased, without leaving any representative, may, after sufficient time has elapsed, be applied to the objects of the institution."

The committee to whom the petition was referred, reported favorably concerning most of the provisions petitioned for, and introduced a bill, which was passed, to the following effect:

Authorizing the trustees to loan the moneys received to the corporation of the city of New York, at a rate of interest not less than six per cent per annum.

Also providing that minors depositing in said institution might withdraw the same to the amount of $250, though no guardian shall have been appointed, provided such deposit were made by the minor personally, and not by another, for his benefit.

Also providing that the books of the corporation should at all times be open to the comptroller or such other person or persons as the legislature might designate, for inspection and examination.

The notoriety given to the subject of Savings Banks by the proceedings and results that have been recited, was naturally followed by efforts to secure their benefits in other localities.

ALBANY SAVINGS BANK.

The petition of William James and others of the city of Albany, praying for the passage of an act authorizing the establishment of a Savings Bank in the city of Albany, was presented in the assembly January 28, 1820, and referred to a select committee consisting of Messrs. McKown, Irving and Sharpe.

On the 4th of February, the committee reported as follows:

"That they have considered the subject referred to them, and are of opinion, unanimously, that the experience which has been had in the establishment of Savings Banks, under proper regulations, has sufficiently tested their importance to public morals, and their great benefit to those classes of society who are usually the most improvident.

"The committee refer to the annual report of the Savings Bank in the city of New York, as the best comment on the practical utility of such an institution, and they have directed their chairman to ask for leave to bring in a bill conformable to the prayer of the petitioners."

The bill would appear from the journals of the legislature to have encountered no opposition. Even the ayes and noes do not appear to have been called for, in any stage of its passage.

It passed the assembly on the 18th of March, and the senate on the 23d, and was returned from the council of revision on the 24th, approved.

In 1821 a Savings Bank was incorporated for the *village* of Utica. In reporting favorably upon this bill, the committee take occasion to refer to the success of the Bank for Savings as evidence of the great utility of such institutions. This bank, however, never went into operation.

We have thus traced the origin of Savings Banks in the State of New York down to the period of their successful inauguration, under the sanction and regulation of law. To this point our record has been necessarily coincident with the History of the inception of the Bank for Savings in the city of New York. From this point the History of Savings Banks in this State naturally presents two phases: first, the course of legislation concerning them as a system of means in the promotion of industry and economy, in respect to the character impressed upon them through the provisions of their respective charters, and the general statutes regulating, restricting or enlarging their powers and privileges; and, second, the individual history of these institutions as indicated or revealed in their origin, growth and progress from year to year, from 1819 to the present time.

To pursue these separate branches of our theme

concurrently, is quite impracticable. We shall, therefore, as previously set forth, consider, first, the course of legislation and of official discussion concerning these institutions in respect to the various matters that affect their character and impart to them as a system, an individuality of its own. This will be followed by a detail of statistical growth and progress as revealed in their business transactions from year to year.

SAVINGS BANKS IN THE STATE OF NEW YORK.

PART II.

GENERAL LEGISLATION AND OFFICIAL DISCUSSION CONCERNING SAVINGS BANKS.

CHAPTER XXXIII.

POLICY AS ILLUSTRATED IN THE FORM OF ORGANIZATION.

OF THE CONSTITUENCY OF BOARDS OF TRUSTEES.

In this State the charters of Savings Banks have all been perpetual, subject, however, to modification or repeal by the legislature, and with two exceptions, to be hereafter noted, the original constituency of trustees has been named in the act of incorporation, and power delegated to these to fill vacancies in their number. There has never been any recognized principle of legislation concerning the number of trustees, nor would it be practicable to establish one. The largest number provided in any act of incorporation is forty-three, the smallest nine. Between these extremes the number varies, the larger proportion being between twenty and thirty. This diversity arises from the manner in which the incorporation of these institutions is promoted. As may be presumed, they never have their inception in the legislature. In the early history of these institutions, the presumption is and, I believe, the facts were, that one or more philanthropic individuals would conceive the idea of establishing a Savings Bank for the benefit of the poor in their neighborhood. These would confer with such others of like mind, as they could, or as they deemed it desirable to enlist in the enterprise, and they would draw an act of incorporation, usually copying the main features of one that had already received the favorable action of the legislature, and naming as corporators only themselves who felt an interest in the objects of the institution to be established. This they would present to the legislature, and receiving favorable consideration, the bill would become an act of incorporation. In this way, the number of trustees of the various institutions was determined by the judgment of the projectors of the enterprise as to the best number to secure harmony in their councils and efficiency in administration, or by extraneous conditions relating to the number of persons of the right spirit, character and influence, that could be induced to accept the responsibilities of the management. The question, as a practical one, seems never to have engaged the attention of the legislature, which accepted the proposed number as an incident concerning which it was unnecessary to inquire.

Later in the history of Savings Banks, other considerations than those mentioned, in some cases affected the question as to the number of trustees to be inserted in the charter to be submitted to the legislature. It was sometimes deemed desirable to enlarge the number of corporators in order to secure the benefit, for the experiment, of a wide range of personal character and influence. Still later came the practice, not yet gone wholly into disuse, of inserting names, not so much for their local influence in attracting patronage to the institution, and generally in giving to it character, and inspiring the public with confidence in its management, as for their real or supposed power to manipulate the legislature, and secure its favorable action upon the proposed enterprise. Whether preceding or following the last-named in the order of time, I am unable to say, but certainly, in these latter days, the number of corporators began to be affected by influences of this kind; after a bill was introduced, with the names of the projectors as corporators, the member from the district where the institution was to be located would see in it an opportunity to reward one or more political favorites, or — with a lively sense of favors to come — to gain political adherents, by causing their names to be inserted in the bill in committee — no very difficult feat in modern legislation — and thus the projectors of the enterprise, without having been consulted, would find their association enlarged, though, perhaps, not in their judgment improved. I have before me now, the private memorandum of a Savings Bank officer, who narrates such a proceeding as an incident in the organization of the institution with which he is connected; and I was made cognizant of an attempt, by an astute legislator, to change in this way the entire board of trustees named in a pending bill, by inserting in their place, favorites of his own. Whether it was the integrity and spirit of the committee in resenting the outrage, or the aroused jealousy of the local member in the other house, whose favorites were thus summarily thrust out, that defeated the attempt, is not material; the result was, if my memory serves me, a compromise between the honorable gentlemen, and the assignment to each, in the bill, of an equal number of their political and personal friends! The original number of corporators was probably not diminished by the operation.

It would be false to assert that Savings Banks no longer have their inception in motives of philanthropy—in a desire to promote the welfare of the humble poor. I could point to many institutions incorporated within the last ten years, whose organization has been characterized by a spirit as pure and self-sacrificing as that which marked the inception of the first Savings Bank.

But it is not the less true, that not every Savings Bank has its inception in those exalted motives, but rather in the hope of some personal advantage to be derived from it. A lawyer, desiring to extend his practice, sees in a connection with a Savings Bank, as its attorney, a large and profitable increase of his business. In the searches of titles for loans upon bond and mortgage he reads, with the eye of hope, his own clear title to a mansion on —— avenue, or to a villa on the Hudson. Or some one, ambitious for a secretaryship for himself or for some dependent friend, sees in the establishment of a Savings Bank, which his influence, or tact, or persistence, shall have promoted, the realization of his dream. These, combining together, or acting separately, prepare a charter after some model in the session laws, and display their knowledge of, and interest in, the subject-matter, by carefully copying all the grammatical blunders and logical incongruities of the original. For corporators, they insert the names of friends upon whom they can depend to concede to themselves the positions of which they are in quest, and whom they have consulted concerning, and committed to, their purpose, together with the names of a few gentlemen of high repute and commanding influence, to give character to the enterprise and produce a favorable impression upon the legislature, but whom they have carefully and delicately avoided consulting, and who, they very well know, will never accept the responsibilities thus gratuitously thrust upon them, but who will leave their places in the board vacant, to be filled by the friends and devotees of these embryo officers.

Of course the number of corporators will, in such cases, be determined wholly by considerations of its effect in promoting the original purpose of the projectors, to secure for themselves the emoluments of office. It would be a difficult problem to solve, which has precedence, at the present day, in the inception of Savings Banks; motives of direct personal advantage, like the foregoing, or considerations of political and partisan expediency, such as were previously suggested. They are not unfrequently united in the prosecution of the same measure.

But, without entering into any discussion of this point, enough has been said to illustrate and to establish the fact, that the legislature, as a body, has never concerned itself with the question of the number of trustees of which a Savings Bank corporation should be composed, in all cases leaving it to the control of extraneous influences, either within or without the body of original projectors, and acting upon it, when thus controlled, as an incident in itself of no considerable importance.

The practical result has been, as might have been predicted, the great diversity already noted, and this diversity being a practical fact, governed by no established or recognized principle of action, it marks no feature of historical growth and progress, but characterizes the system in the whole course of its development. The first Savings Bank had twenty-eight corporators; the next two had each nineteen; in 1834 one was incorporated with forty-three trustees; some later ones with but nine; and a recent one with twenty-eight, the same as the first. In 1871, it was made lawful for the trustees of any Savings Bank by resolution, to be incorporated in their by-laws, to reduce the number of trustees named in the charter to not less than fifteen, by omitting to fill vacancies that might occur.

QUORUM.

In this connection it may be proper to note that the question of the number or proportion of trustees constituting a quorum, for the transaction of business has, equally with that last considered, been governed by no principle in legislation, but apparently has been left to the judgment, wishes or caprice of those who prepared the charter for submission to the legislature. In most charters the number is fixed, but the proportion which this number bears to the whole number of trustees is extremely various. In some it constitutes a majority, but in most a much smaller proportion. The smallest fixed number is five, which is found in several charters; and the smallest proportional number is six, in a board of forty-three. Neither does this feature possess any historical interest as marking the growth or development of a principle embodied in or applied to these institutions, but is a mere independent fact pervading the system, and no more marked at one period of time than at another. Nor, except as connected with the causes producing the diversity, is there any considerable significance or importance to be attached to either the question of the number of trustees or the number constituting a quorum. Institutions with the larger and with the smaller number of trustees, and with a greater or less actual or proportional quorum, have alike flourished or languished, seemingly little affected by this element in their organization.

In the same act of 1871, above referred to, it was further made lawful for the trustees of any Savings Bank to designate the number constituting a quorum. But such number was not to be less than seven, except when the charter authorized a smaller number. When less than a majority was thus designated, the presence of the president or a vice-president, and of the secretary, was required.

GROUNDS OF EXCLUSION FROM TRUSTEESHIP.

While the number thus forming the constituency in the management of Savings Banks have never been regulated by any governing principle, the elements of which that constituency should be composed, or rather the consideration of excluding from the constituency certain elements deemed hostile to the interests of Savings Banks, has engaged the attention of the legislature.

But it was not until 1853 that any policy upon this subject was declared. In that year, the legislature, by an act made applicable to New York and Kings counties only, among other things, provided that it should not be lawful for any trustee of a Savings Bank to be a trustee of more than one Savings Bank at the same time, nor for the trustees of any Savings Bank thereafter to be incorporated to be directors at the same time in any bank wherein any part of the moneys of such Savings Bank should be deposited.

The object of the last of the above provisions was, obviously, to exclude from the control of Savings Banks such persons as would have an interest of their own adverse to that of the institution. The admission into the councils of the board, of directors of banks of discount and deposit, it was thought might result injuriously in the direction of a policy of keeping too large a proportion of the moneys of the institution on deposit uninvested, or of keeping too large a proportion of the necessary deposits in one bank, the selection of which might be determined by the personal interests of members, rather than by a consideration of the safety or security afforded by the standing and resources of the deposit bank.

But the policy thus sought to be impressed upon the

Savings Bank system of this State never became, in fact, a vital feature of it. The provision, as before stated, was operative only in New York and Kings counties, and there only prospectively, and herein was subject to practical nullification by each succeeding legislature, which, in naming as corporators in a Savings Bank those who were at the time directors in banks of discount, would, by such later enactment, substantially, so far as such new institution was concerned, repeal the restrictive provision, or at least render it inapplicable to the persons whom it had, by act of law, named as corporators. Besides this, the legislature subsequently, within two years, from 1855 to 1857, incorporated no less than eight Savings Banks, whose trustees were nearly, if not quite, identical with the boards of directors in banks of discount, and gave to the Savings Banks thus organized the names of the banks whose directors were thus constituted their guardians. Hence, it will be seen, that upon this feature of Savings Bank policy, the legislature of this State has been contradictory rather than uniform, and that no settled policy or principle of action has been adhered to.

Of the impolicy of so organizing or constituting a Savings Bank Board of Trustees that its affairs may fall wholly under the control of a bank of discount, the writer expressed his views quite fully in a special report on Savings Banks, presented to the Legislature of the State of New York in 1868, and as pertinent to the subject-matter of this chapter, that article is here reproduced substantially as originally written.

It may further not be out of place here to remark that I shall find frequent occasion to quote extracts from that report, not as expressive of the highest wisdom, nor of convictions that have not been more or less modified by a longer period and more extended range of observation, but as marking a phase in the public discussion and legislative consideration of the topics treated of, which, in fact, constitutes a part of the History of Savings Banks in this State.

Besides, the arguments, conclusions and recommendations of that report have come to be so widely accepted as a standard of authority in Savings Bank policy, and have so considerably moulded and given form and direction to public opinion and legislative action in this and other States, that the omission of them altogether from these pages, which profess to reveal the growth of public sentiment and the character of official exposition concerning this interest, would indicate a mere affectation of modesty.

Extracts from a Special Report on Savings Banks, New York, 1868, *pp.* 97–107.

RELATION OF SAVINGS BANKS TO BANKS OF DISCOUNT.

The specific office of each of these two classes of institutions is clearly defined. They are so wholly distinct and unlike, that there is, or should be, no antagonism between them. For the same reason there should be no intimate connection between them.

It is the business of the bank of discount to make money for its stockholders, for those who have contributed to its capital, by the commissions, discounts, interest or whatever the gains may be called, which it receives for the accommodation afforded by it to the public. They are a public benefit as a great many other private enterprises are a public benefit. But they are still private enterprises, instituted by their projectors for their own advantage and emolument. Their capital and resources are largely invested in what is called business paper, that is, the notes of business men, having as their basis of security, the products in various forms, and liable to various contingencies, in which they deal.

Of course such a business is more or less hazardous, especially when we reflect that the resources thus invested are not alone the capital which is paid in, and which, in the form of bank notes issued to the public, is payable on demand, but their deposits, which often greatly exceed the capital, and which are likewise payable on demand. In the ordinary course of business, therefore, every bank has outstanding liabilities payable on demand, which it has resources to meet, payable usually in from one to ninety days.

Such is the general character of the business, and though the salutary provisions of law for the enforcement of contracts and the prevailing commercial integrity of business men, and the course and laws of trade and commerce, enable those long practiced in watching financial movements to steer clear of the more imminent dangers to which such business is necessarily exposed, still it is more or less hazardous, and can attract capital to it as an investment only by the prospect of larger gains than ordinary investments in bond and mortgage, or other securities at six and seven per cent will yield.

The bank of discount receives deposits not primarily for the benefit of the depositor, though it is a fact that his convenience is promoted by the operation, but the bank uses them as a means to increase its own profits. In short, all the operations of a bank of discount in issuing notes, receiving deposits and discounting paper, are for the purpose of making money for the stockholders. The public so understand it, and expect to pay and *do pay* accordingly, for the accommodation which they receive. The business of such banks is perfectly legitimate, honorable and important to the interests of the community, but that does not make Savings Banks of them, nor entitle them to be invested with Savings Bank powers.

Saving Banks, on the contrary, are instituted, not for the promotion of the interests of their projectors, but for that of the depositors. SECURITY is their *first* consideration, *profit* for the depositors the second and subordinate consideration.

The purpose of their institution will admit of *no hazards;* they must be SAFE. Hence the profit to be realized from them, when conducted upon this basis of absolute security, can never exceed, can rarely equal the lawful rate of interest at which safe investments may be made, for into these same investments the deposits must be transformed, and the expenses of conducting the business will take something from the legitimate and moderate profit thus earned.

A Savings Bank, therefore, is not merely a bank that pays interest on deposits, but is an institution in the hands of disinterested persons, receiving deposits for the purpose of investment in those securities which experience has demonstrated to be the most reliable and safe. The profits of such an institution are the interest it receives, the occasional premium on securities sold, or the discount on securities purchased, rents from apartments in its banking house not required for its own use, and a few other incidental sources. These, after deducting the necessary expenses of conducting the business, inure to the benefit of the depositor, in dividends, or in a reserve for surplus for his greater security, or both.

Such is the character of the business of a Savings Bank. Whenever it departs from this, and engages in discounting paper, or in buying or selling exchange, or doing any of the various kinds of business which banks of discount do, in so far it abandons its real character, and any tendency in this direction should be discountenanced and corrected. And so, too, banks of discount should be restrained from assuming the title or the character of Savings Banks, by the offer of interest upon individual deposits. The hazards of banks of discount, from the causes already noted of being liable to respond to their depositors on demand, from resources not yet due, are quite enough, without the weakening of their resources by the payment of interest upon those deposits which they hold by so precarious a tenure.

The only feature in common between a Savings Bank and a bank of discount is this: They *both receive deposits.* But from this common point, in all their theory, purpose and mode of operation they diverge. A law of this State prohibits any bank from holding itself out to the public as a Savings bank.

The principle recognized in this prohibition is a salutary one and might with great propriety be extended further and prohibit banks of discount from accomplishing the same purpose without sign or notice, by allowing interest upon individual deposits. The only object of such practice is, of course, to attract deposits, but where there is no competition, deposits will come in the legitimate course of business without offering a bonus for them, and where there is competition, the result is that all advantage to either is effectually destroyed, by both or all engaging in a practice which all would be better off to abandon.

So, too, there is no good reason why private bankers should not be subjected to the same prohibition, for in some localities the practice of these in paying interest on deposits, is the most serious obstacle to success against which Savings Banks have to contend. The ignorant and unwary only know that a *bank* is a *bank*, and have no idea of the essential difference between a Savings and any other Bank. They fall into the office of the private banker, and are impressed with the advantage of a certificate of deposit bearing interest and transferable by indorsement, over a deposit book not thus transferable. They know the banker, and suppose him to be responsible; they know the chief officer of the Savings Bank, and judge of the safety of the institution in the same way, from a knowledge of his personal responsibility. Supposing both, therefore, to be equally responsible, he chooses between the respective forms of deposit on the score of *convenience.* Not unfrequently, too, his ear is poisoned by the suggestion of the non-liability of the trustees of Savings Banks, and the greater safety, in consequence, of the deposit with the private banker, whose whole estate is a pledge to the depositor!

Such practices are a fraud upon the public, and a serious hindrance, oftentimes, to the progress of Savings Banks that have to compete with them. The distinction between Savings Banks and banks of discount, whether private or incorporated, in regard to their practices, should be as clearly defined by law as are their objects in the theory of the institution of each respectively. If the law should make that distinction to consist in withholding from the latter the right to pay interest on individual deposits under $5,000, the public would soon come to a realizing sense of the difference between them in this respect, and might in time learn the essential difference in the character of their security.

If the duty of the State to foster Savings Banks, by protecting them from this embarrassing competition, were not enough to justify such a prohibition, the duty it owes to the public at large, in protecting them from the perils to which they are exposed by these practices, is not only a *sufficient justification*, but, indeed, calls loudly for such action in the name of justice. The air has hardly yet ceased to vibrate with the wails of widows and orphans who trusted their little inheritance to a discount bank that promised six and even seven per cent interest to the depositors, and of course *failed* in the effort to make a profitable use of such deposits, except in hazardous speculations that proved ruinous to all concerned.

But whatever the State may do for the further protection of Savings Banks from such competition, and of the public from fraud and imposition, by amending the provisions of the act of 1858 in the manner indicated, its salutary purpose will, to a great extent, be defeated under the new dispensation of banks not amenable to the authority of the State. I have before me the advertisement of a NATIONAL BANK in this State, proclaiming itself a SAVINGS BANK, and offering in that capacity six per cent interest upon deposits! What margin, I ask, is there for a safe and profitable employment of these deposits, in legitimate business, after paying the internal revenue tax upon them of one-half per cent? The Comptroller of the Currency has turned his attention to very many petty and inconsequential details in the administration of his pet banks. Would he not do well to turn to the weightier matters that affect the safe and successful operation of this gigantic monopoly?

But these are instances of the assumption of the functions of Savings Banks by banks of discount upon their own responsibility and in their own name.

There is danger of another sort, against which it may be important to provide, and that is, the taking possession, wholly or in part, of a duly incorporated Savings Bank by a bank of discount, and using it for its own special interest and advantage. There are three forms in which this appropriation may be made.

First. If a sufficient number of the trustees of a Savings Bank, to form a majority of a quorum, are at the same time directors in banks of discount, they may combine in the interest of their several institutions, and appropriate a larger proportion of deposits than is necessary or desirable to keep in that form.

Second. Where trustees are indisposed to tax themselves with the labor of overseeing the operations of their trust, they may contract with the directors of a bank of discount to receive deposits, and generally to transact the business of the Savings Bank through their machinery, and thus the conduct, and to a great extent, the interests of the Savings Bank be made subordinate to the interests of the bank of discount.

Third. The trustees of a Savings Bank may be constituted chiefly or wholly from the directors of a bank of discount, and thus the institution become only a tender to the latter.

The first of these provisions is guarded against in the cities of New York and Kings by prohibiting any trustee from being at the same time a director in a bank of discount where the Savings Bank deposits are kept.

The design of this provision is salutary, though it doubtless operates disadvantageously at times, in preventing an institution from securing the services of a competent financial adviser as a member of the board of trustees.

The question of extending the provision so as to apply to all Savings Banks in the State has engaged my attention not a little. In the towns and cities of the interior it would often be found difficult to secure the right class of men for trustees of a Savings Bank, without including some who were directors in a bank of discount. Whether the difficulty is an insuperable one may admit of doubt, but that it would often times prove extremely embarrassing is quite evident to my mind.

Besides, to get the full benefit of such a provision, it should have effect immediately, which would break up the existing organization of some institutions entirely, and perhaps in that way inflict greater evils than those from which we seek to escape.

The object being to prevent any bank, or combination of banks, from getting control of the deposits of the Savings Bank in their own interest, this might be effected by limiting the proportion of deposits that might be kept in any one bank to some rate per cent, and the proportion in all banks to not exceeding twenty per cent, and placing all under watchful supervision, to see that there is no violation or evasion of the law, and all opportunity to abuse of the power confided to trustees would, I believe, be effectually removed.

The delegation to a bank of discount of the powers and duties of the trustees of a Savings Bank, is a reprehensible practice. Though the trustees have possession of the securities, and direct the investments, the relation between two institutions so diverse in their character and objects, is too intimate to be of mutual advantage, and if either is to suffer from the connection, we may rest assured that it will not be the institution whose *business is to make money.* No bank is going to undertake the labor of conducting the working operations of a Savings Bank, unless there is something *to be made out of it.* The guarantee to pay expenses, means that they will employ some of their clerks, or a special clerk for the purpose, to receive and pay money and keep the accounts, and charge for the service — usually all the difference between the income and the dividends to depositors. In short, no such relation can exist between these institutions, without the strength or usefulness of the Savings Bank being impaired by the connection.

And as a rule, the discount bank takes the business as a speculation, making the most it can from the investments and deposits, paying the smallest practicable dividends, and taking the difference for its trouble and expense. But as more can be made from discounts than from permanent investments at six or seven per cent, of course it is the policy of the discount bank to have a large portion of the Savings deposits uninvested, for its own greater convenience and profit. In illustration of this tendency, note the large per cent of deposits in those banks which are conducted by banks of discount under contract with the trustees.

It is this tendency to expose the deposits of Savings

Banks to the hazards of the successful management of a bank of discount, that renders this close intimacy of association between these institutions dangerous and improper.

I would not close my eyes to the fact that there are instances in which the business of Savings Banks is conducted by banks of discount, where this tendency is overcome by the wise and considerate control of trustees, where these make a convenience of the bank of discount, and do not allow it to sacrifice the safety of their trust to its own pecuniary advantage. But even here is the danger ever lurking, that in the progress of events, through changes in the constituency of the boards of trustees, a more lax policy may sometime prevail, from which peril may impend and disaster befall.

The third form of appropriation of a Savings Bank, by and in the interest of a bank of discount, has the same tendency and the same dangers as the last mentioned, besides, from its more intimate connection and identity of interest, added dangers peculiar to itself.

Exemplifications of this intimacy of relation, where the trustees of the Savings Bank are largely composed of the directors of a bank of discount that transacts the business of the institution, are too frequently found. Of this class, one, under the requirements of its charter, keeps its deposits quite closely invested. Of the remainder, all have much the larger portion of their deposits in bank, two have all in that form, and but one has any surplus worth mentioning.

Could the impolicy of this intimate connection between Savings Banks and banks of discount have stronger confirmation than is afforded by such disclosures?

But besides these, there are other dangers to which the prosperity, if not the security of Savings Banks thus controlled, is exposed. If the discount bank finds upon its hands depreciated stocks, as New York State 5s, that will command but 93 to 95 in the market, they have, to say the least, a strong *temptation* to sell the same to the trustees of the Savings Bank (themselves in that relation), at par! I do not *know* that this has ever been done, but if not, it has not been from lack of motive and opportunity. The exposure to such *chances* of mal-administration is enough to mark the combination of rival interests, in the same individuals, under which it may be effected, with emphatic condemnation.

But the rival interests of Savings Banks and banks of discount assume, at times, another form of development to the prejudice of the former.

The Manufacturers' Savings Bank of Troy has exhibited a gradually diminishing line of deposits, from $129,569 in 1861 to $22,714 in 1867. Presuming that this indicated a voluntary winding up of the affairs of the institution, this Savings Bank was marked "closing" in the last annual report from this Department. On inquiry, however, I find that the trustees have no intention of relinquishing their franchise, but true to their instincts as directors of the Manufacturers' National Bank, which all of them are, depositors are advised to make their deposits directly in the National Bank, and take a certificate bearing interest. In this way one of the half per cents of government tax is saved that would have to be paid if the deposit was first made in the Savings Bank, and by the Savings Bank made in the National. If only this financial acuteness could be secured in the interest of the Savings Bank, it could not fail to be a most prosperous institution!

The depositors knowing no distinction between what should be the security of a Savings Bank and the security of a deposit bank, which indeed in this, as in some other instances, is a distinction quite without a difference, and being assured, besides, that in this way they get the added security of the liability of the stockholders of the National Bank, are easily persuaded to make their deposit in the form proposed.

Other banks in that city do the same thing, but not to the same demoralizing extent. Can the impolicy of a relation that admits of such results, as even a remote possibility, require further illustration or enforcement?

The system that permits such practices is wrong, because it destroys the essential and vital distinction between Savings Banks and other banks, which consists in the secure and reliable investments of the former, removed from all the hazards of business misfortunes that attend the latter.

It is wrong, in that it makes the prosperity of the Savings Bank subordinate to the prosperity of the bank of deposit.

It is wrong, in that it gives countenance and support to the error, too prevalent in the community, that savings and other banks are necessarily exposed to the same hazards, and that the commercial or financial crisis that destroys the integrity of the latter must, in the same degree, impair the security of the former, whereby such crises *do* reach and affect, with frenzied apprehensions, the depositors in Savings Banks, to their own detriment and that of the institutions which they patronize.

And, to state a paradox, *it is wrong* because *if it is right*, then the whole theory of Savings Banks, as a peculiar institution, is false and unfounded, and banks of discount can be made to serve every purpose equally well.

It is no answer to these objections to point to the high character of the deposit banks that thus direct the operations and control the destinies of Savings Banks. Other banks of standing equally high, and having the confidence of the community in full as great a degree, have come to grief within our recollection. There was nothing in their history, condition or circumstances, prior to their failure, that would not have justified their connection with the affairs of a Savings Bank as intimate and responsible as that enjoyed by any deposit bank to-day.

The boasted additional security derived from the personal liability of stockholders is purely visionary. Are A, B and C more responsible than the government of the United States, or of the State of New York, or even than the city, county or town of which their wealth is but an insignificant fraction? Their possessions in houses and lands may pass from their grasp, and creditors receive no benefit from them under their new proprietorship, but these properties will continue to pay taxes, and in this way maintain the credit of the State or municipality to which they belong.

And as a final consideration, if more can be needed, these banks of discount are now for the most part foreign corporations, over whose operations the State can exercise no control. They have possession of the books and records of the Savings Banks whose agents they are; they receive and disburse the deposits; they incur and pay expenses; and the State is powerless but by their grace and favor to exercise any scrutiny over their proceedings. I have in my intercourse received only courtesy from the officers of these institutions; but contrast the meagreness of the details which they report under the statement of Cash Transactions, hereafter given, with the fullness of the same from institutions that are free from these "entangling alliances," for confirmation of this view, that the more intimate the connection between Savings Banks and banks of discount, the further removed are the former from the protection, supervision and care of State authority.

That Savings Banks can be conducted with safety and success upon an absolutely free and independent basis, using banks of discount only in their legitimate sphere, as the public use them, as depositories for funds which they may require in the daily operations of business, is demonstrated by the sound and prosperous condition of these institutions in Newburgh, Poughkeepsie, Hudson, Oswego, Yonkers, Southold and other localities that might be named; not to mention those in Utica, Syracuse, Rochester and Buffalo, that still more perfectly exemplify this position. Most of these were organized prior to 1857, and successfully passed the ordeal of that trying year. If in these towns of limited population, Savings Banks can be made strong, successful and prosperous, without leaning upon a bank of discount for support, surely they require no such adventitious aid elsewhere. And not only *do* they survive and prosper, but, judged by any true and proper standard applicable to Savings Banks, they are *stronger* and *more successful* than any of the institutions which subsist under the *vulturous protection* of National Banks!

EXCEPTIONS NOTED.

The two exceptions noted as to the constituency of the boards of trustees, are the Institution for Savings of Merchants' Clerks, incorporated in 1848, and the People's Safe Deposit and Savings Institution at Syracuse, incorporated in 1868. The special features that distinguish the organization of the former will be found in connection with the history and statistics of that institution; and a full exposition of the character of the latter organization will be found in Senate Document No. 39, vol. 3, 1869, and some further account of it will also be found in the chapter on Savings Bank failures. Suffice it to say here, that this latter was the first charter that *ostensibly* combined a moneyed corporation, having capital stock, and a Savings Bank. Such form of organization is not uncommon in other States, but in New York is exceptional, being limited to this institution.

CHAPTER XXXIV.

OF INVESTMENTS: 1819 TO 1846.

We come now to a consideration of how the discretion of trustees, in regard to the disposition of the funds committed to their keeping, has been controlled by legislative action. This subject embraces the whole theory and policy of investments.

The policy contemplated in the institution of Savings Banks in this State was that of absolute and unquestioned security to depositors, with such profits only as should be compatible with that primary condition. Doubtless, the necessities or exigencies to which Savings Banks might be exposed, were not and could not, at that time, be anticipated and provided for. The first act of incorporation, therefore, whose history we have already given in detail, authorized investments to be made in "stock created and issued under and by virtue of any law of the United States or of this State, and in no other way." The following year, however, 1820, the charter was amended by authorizing the trustees to loan moneys to the corporation of the city of New York; but the Albany Savings Bank, incorporated that year, was restricted in its investments to stocks of the United States and of this State, and the same limitation was applied to the Troy Savings Bank, incorporated in 1823.

In 1827 the powers of the trustees of the Bank for

Savings, in regard to investments, were still further enlarged, by authorizing them to invest in the public stock of the State of Ohio, or in the stock of the city of New York. The latter was hardly an enlargement of the power previously conceded, which authorized loans to be made to the corporation of New York. So far as the character of the investment is concerned, in the matter of security, there was no change, but the form in which the investment might be made was adapted to give greater freedom of action to the trustees, and to enable them to secure advantages from the state of the money market, denied to them under the original form of investment. But the admission of the stock of another State, as an authorized investment, was a new feature, and why the stock of the State of Ohio was selected as the exceptional investment does not appear from the record. Probably the action was taken upon petition or application in some form of the trustees of the Bank for Savings, who were incited thereto by negotiations for the sale to them of Ohio stocks on advantageous terms. But, whatever may have been the incitement, the legislature by this act first opened the door to investments outside of our own State.

At the same session, however, the charter of the Albany Savings Bank was amended so as to authorize the trustees to invest moneys "in the *stock* of any or either of the BANKS in the cities of Albany or Troy," or to loan moneys to the corporation of Albany. The latter provision does not differ in principle from that already recognized in authorizing loans to be made to the corporation of New York; it merely applied the principle to another institution, and extended the range of its operation so as to embrace the city in which that institution was established, thus increasing its power of local usefulness.

But the authority to invest in the stock of banks was an entirely new feature, and was not only exceptional then, but, most fortunately, continues so to this day. Whether the trustees ever availed themselves of this extension of their powers, does not appear; but they might have done so with most disastrous consequences to their trust, as the subsequent career of some banks in the city of Albany sufficiently attests.

It is noteworthy, however, that the charter of the Brooklyn Savings Bank, incorporated the same year, 1827, embraces none of these more liberal provisions concerning investments that were then finding favor, but restricted the trustees to investing in stocks of this State, or of the United States.

In 1829, however, the Brooklyn Savings Bank secured an amendment to the charter, authorizing investments in "Brooklyn *village* stock!" and also in stocks of the city of New York, and loans to be made directly to the corporation of either New York or Brooklyn.

In the same year the Seamen's Bank for Savings was incorporated, with authority to invest in the stocks of the United States, or of this State, or of the States of Pennsylvania and Ohio, as also in the stocks of the city of New York. These provisions only enlarged those already existing, by admitting for investment stocks of the State of Pennsylvania.

In 1830, "An act for the relief of the Bank for Savings, in the city of New York," was passed, by which their powers in regard to investments were enlarged, so as to embrace the stock or securities of any State in the Union, and loans "to the Public School Society of New York on satisfactory real security;" and they were also authorized to make temporary deposits in any of the incorporated banks in the said city, and to receive interest thereon at such rates, not exceeding that allowed by law, as should be agreed upon.

This, as will be seen, was a very considerable departure from the policy that had hitherto prevailed, and the action appears to have been influenced by two considerations. First, the unexpected success of the Bank for Savings, resulting in an accumulation of more than two millions of dollars, made it difficult in those times to make profitable investments within the narrow range to which they had been confined by law. At the same time, this success, and the annual reports of the condition of their funds and investments, had demonstrated that the trustees had most worthily secured the confidence of the community for prudence and fidelity in the discharge of their trust, and hence it was inferred that they might with safety be invested with a wider discretion than, at the outset, it would have been deemed prudent to confer. In the legislative documents of that year, 1830, I find the report of the committee on banking, to whom was referred the application of this bank for an enlargement of its powers in regard to investments, which fully confirms my conjecture as to the considerations influencing this favorable action. Among other things was the fact, that United States stocks had matured and been paid off, leaving the bank with a large accumulation of funds on hand, seeking investment within a very narrow range. The committee note particularly the success of the institution, its benevolent objects, and the fidelity and skill that had characterized its management. The power to make loans upon "satisfactory real security," thus leaving the discretion as to the ratio of the loan to the value of the security, wholly with the board of trustees, doubtless was a dangerous precedent to establish, and one which, as we shall see hereafter, was not incorporated into the general policy of the State concerning Savings Banks. But from this time forth, the security of bond and mortgage became, under established restrictions only exceptionally departed from, a permanent feature of Savings Bank investments.

It is noticeable that we find in the foregoing amendment the first authority for using banks of discount as depositories for the moneys of Savings Banks awaiting investment, or held in reserve for the current business of the institution. What they had done previously to this authorization, whether they had kept their moneys in safes or vaults of their own, or deposited them in banks of discount merely for safe-keeping, does not appear, but it is probable that the latter was the more common practice. But this salutary provision enabled them to make the deposit under the sanction of law, and to derive some profit, however small, from what must at times have been an embarrassing accumulation of idle capital.

In the charter of the Poughkeepsie Savings Bank, incorporated in 1831, investments were authorized in the stock of the United States, of the State of New York, or of any of the States, or in loans on "bond and mortgage on real estate of double the value of the sum loaned." This last provision, which has now become a distinguishing feature in Savings Bank charters, appears for the first time in this act. Later charters, as we shall find, sometimes imposed other and further limitations, as to the amount to be thus loaned to any one individual, and, in respect to the locality, as to the county where the Savings Bank was located or to one adjoining, but the limitation of the ratio of the loan to the value of the security, here declared, became an established feature in the policy of legislation.

But even this had its erratic exceptions, as, at the same session, there was incorporated the "Rochester Savings Bank, in the village of Rochester," which was authorized to loan moneys "upon bond and mortgage as the board of managers may deem amply sufficient."

The charter of the Poughkeepsie Savings Bank further recognized the new feature in the charter of the Bank for Savings, of allowing deposits in incorporated banks with interest, but by the terms of the charter they were restricted to banks in Poughkeepsie. In 1832 this privilege was still further extended to this institution by an amendment of the charter authorizing these deposits to be made with the New York Life Insurance and Trust Company, or with any incorporated bank in the city of New York.

In 1832, the Brooklyn Savings Bank received authority from the legislature to loan moneys upon bond and mortgage on real estate worth double the amount loaned, and the Seamen's Bank for Savings was authorized to invest in the stocks of any State in the Union, and to make temporary deposits in any incorporated banks of the city. From this time the authority to make such deposits may be regarded as an established feature of the Savings Bank system, and only the modifications or limitations of this general power will be noted.

The Greenwich Savings Bank, incorporated in 1833, had conceded to it authority to invest in the public stocks of Pennsylvania and Ohio, and to loan money to the Public School Society of New York, on satisfactory real security, herein copying from the amended charter of the Bank for Savings.

The Schenectady Savings Bank, incorporated in 1834, was also authorized to invest in the stocks of any State, or to make loans on bond and mortgage, but the real estate was required to be of double the value of the loan, exclusive of buildings, a feature that characterized many subsequent charters, but not with any degree of uniformity. It seems to have been introduced or excluded entirely according to the caprice of the projectors of the institution seeking incorporation.

As a further illustration of the capricious character

of legislation in regard to loans upon bond and mortgage, it may be noted here, that the Bowery Savings Bank, incorporated in this year, 1834, like others preceding it, was authorized to loan moneys to the Public School Society of New York on satisfactory real security "*worth thirty per cent more than the amount loaned thereon!*" The following year it received authority, generally, to make loans on bond and mortgage in New York and Brooklyn, to half the value of the property given as security, herein copying from an amendment, made the previous year, to the charter of the Seamen's Bank for Savings.

In 1836 the powers of the Greenwich Savings Bank were enlarged so as to authorize loans upon bond and mortgage on real estate in the city of New York, worth double the amount loaned, exclusive of buildings, and at the same session, the Bank for Savings was authorized to make similar loans upon real estate worth at least fifty per cent more than the sum loaned, that is, to an amount equal to two-thirds the value of the security. The capricious character of special legislation is herein conspicuously illustrated.

In 1839, the Savings Bank of Utica was incorporated, with powers of investment similar to those already granted to other institutions, including that to invest in the stocks of the city of Utica, and to make temporary deposits in the incorporated banks of that city, and the powers of the Troy Savings Bank were enlarged so as to embrace investments in the stocks of the city of Troy.

In 1840, the Albany Savings Bank was authorized

to invest in the stocks of the cities of Albany or New York, and to make loans secured by bond and mortgage on real estate in the city worth fifty per cent more than the amount loaned, or in the State, outside the city, worth double the amount, exclusive of buildings.

In 1841, an amendment was made to the charter of the Greenwich Savings Bank, extending its powers of investment, but not to a degree equal to that already enjoyed by other institutions. Besides other powers conferred, it was authorized to make loans upon bond and mortgage secured by real estate in the city of New York worth double the amount loaned, provided the improvements thereon should be insured, and the policy duly assigned to the bank. This feature is noticeable, from the fact of its being the first recognition of a form of collateral security which became thereafter very common, though not uniform in its application to loans upon bond and mortgage. Doubtless, the practice to require the assignment of a policy of insurance, where the property mortgaged as security consisted in part of buildings, was very general, though I have no assurance of it beyond my own convictions, founded upon the evident prudence with which the affairs of these institutions were conducted; but this was the first instance, I believe, in which the obligation to take such security was imposed by the legislature, and it prepared the way for similar requisitions in subsequent charters and amendments.

A common feature of Savings Bank charters, down to 1842, prohibited the trustees from investing in any securities, or from making any loans other than those specifically named. These, we have seen, in their application to the several institutions then incorporated, embraced the stocks of this State and of the United States, and in a few cases the stocks of any of the States, the stocks of the cities of New York, Brooklyn, Albany, Troy and Utica, loans upon bond and mortgage under various forms of limitation, and deposits in incorporated banks, drawing interest.

In 1842, the Utica Savings Bank was authorized, by an amendment of its charter, to make loans upon personal securities, provided the aggregate of such loans should not exceed five thousand dollars, and provided further, that any such loan should receive the consent of a majority of the whole board of trustees.

Thus limited, the provision was not a dangerous one in itself, but it was the inception of a new and dangerous principle, a departure from the policy hitherto rigidly enforced of accepting no securities which did not rest upon the broad foundations of public credit and public faith.

And this brings us directly to the inception of a feature of Savings Bank policy which has grown with the growth and strengthened with the strength of that system, until it bids fair to be one of its most conspicuous, as I believe it to be one of its most dangerous, characteristics.

Thus far the course of legislation concerning investments has been illustrated by reference to the charters of Savings Banks, and the amendments thereto from time to time. This method has been pursued for purposes of convenience only, and not with a view to present the special features of each particular charter, any further than these would most easily serve the general purpose of illustrating the course of legislation in the matter referred to. The features of each particular charter, as they existed in January, 1868, will be found, by those interested in noting them, in the appendix to the Special Report already referred to, pages 238 to 338.

The further development of legislative policy concerning investments will be indicated generally without citation to the particular institution to which the legislation illustrating it was applied, and, of course, with no purpose to disparage those institutions whose charters are amenable to the charge of looseness of construction, or of dangerous license in respect to the powers conferred. The very first instance which we shall have to record is a standing protest against imputing to the management of the institution any participation in the imprudence which characterized the legislation concerning it. As before stated, we are not now considering these institutions upon their individual merits, as disclosed in the prudence or imprudence of their management; these must be sought in the statement of their assets, and in their general condition as found in the annual reports from the Bank Department. We are now concerned with them only as their charters illustrate the spirit and tone of legislation in providing safeguards for the depositors by the restrictions imposed upon investments.

CHAPTER XXXV.

INVESTMENTS; A NEW POINT OF DEPARTURE.

The year 1846 may, in this regard, be said to have marked a new era in legislation in this direction. We have noted how guarded in the main had been the provisions concerning investments hitherto. In this year, however, a Savings Bank was incorporated whose charter, after authorizing investments in the stocks of this State and of the United States, "or in such other manner as is authorized by this act," and after some other provisions common and essential to all charters, proceeds as follows:

"No moneys deposited in the said institution shall be invested, except in the securities or stocks mentioned in this section, in opposition to the vote of any trustee; but by the consent and approbation of all the trustees present, at a regular meeting, amounts, not exceeding one thousand dollars to any one individual, may be loaned on unincumbered real estate, worth, exclusive of buildings thereon, at least double the amount to be secured thereby." And it is further provided, that "it shall be the duty of the trustees of said corporation to invest, as soon as practicable, in public stocks, or public securities, or in bonds and mortgages, as provided for in this act, all sums received by them beyond an available fund of not exceeding fifty thousand dollars, which they may keep to meet the current payments of said corporation, and which may by them be kept in deposit, on interest or otherwise, in such available form as the trustees may direct."

Let us examine the bearing and effect of these provisions separately. At first view, the former *appears* to be no more than an awkward form of conferring upon the trustees the power to make loans upon real estate, which had not been provided for in the previous part of the act, relating to investments. I have no doubt that this was the sole *intent* of the committee that considered, and of the legislature that enacted the measure, and perhaps also of the corporators who drafted the bill. Certainly, nothing in the policy of the trustees would indicate that they conceived it to have any wider scope, for a more solid and substantial class of investments is nowhere to be found than that of this same institution to-day. But we are considering legislation, not management; powers, not their exercise; precedents, and the dangers to which a system is exposed by those of a doubtful character. In this view let us analyze this provision.

Under the fictitious guise of abridging the powers of the board of trustees, it in fact enlarges them. As the trustees derive their powers wholly from the charter, it follows that without this clause they would have no authority, not even *with a unanimous vote*, to invest the moneys deposited with them in any other securities than those mentioned. The absence of power is in itself a negative upon the exercise of power. To superadd to this a further conditional negative, that they shall exercise this power which they have not, only when such exercise is unanimously approved, is to incorporate a double negative into the provisions concerning powers, and with the well-known grammatical effect in such cases, to establish an affirmative. True, it is a conditional affirmative; but it not the less affirms the right to invest in *any* securities whatever, provided only these have the approval of the entire board acting upon the question. It establishes, as a precedent, the delegation of full discretion to the board of trustees, instead, as heretofore, of controlling that discretion by clear and well defined if not always wise and consistent limitations. It substitutes the judgment of a quorum of the board, when unanimously expressed, for that of the legislature. And the danger is, that the precedent once established, the restrictions by which it is guarded will in time be relaxed, and the dissent of two or three be made the condition upon which the investment in miscellaneous securities shall be denied. How fully these apprehensions are realized in subsequent legislation we will leave for that future legislation to reveal.

But let us note, more particularly than we have done, the insidious form of this provision. After thus declaring a practical affirmative in the exercise of a power to which no opposition shall be expressed, it proceeds in the use of a direct affirmative to point out a special investment other than those named in the first part of the section, which investment it authorizes to be made with the consent of all the trustees present at a regular meeting.

The impression conveyed by this connection of the two clauses is, upon the first hasty glance at the language, that the latter is designed, exclusively, to limit and define the application of the former. I do not doubt that such was the conviction of committees that examined and recommended, and of the members of the legislature that supported, the bill. But while such, doubtless, was the intent of the legislature, in so far as the attention of that body was directed to the language of the act, I am free to say that to my mind it clearly will not bear that restricted though salutary construction. The first clause is marked by no limitations except the lack of opposition to the free exercise of the power which it confers; the second clause, besides requiring this unanimity of concurrence, imposes other limitations upon the character of the investment therein authorized. This clause does, therefore, limit and define the action of the former, but only concerning the single matter of loans upon bond and mortgage. Concerning these, the provision is surely quite guarded enough; so guarded, indeed, that no Savings Bank could possibly derive any advantage from its exercise. And this is one of the insidious features of this provision. Attention being attracted to the extreme safeguards against an abuse of discretion in the matter of loans upon bond and mortgage, it is by this device diverted from observing the very wide range of discretion in regard to other investments by which this carefully guarded exercise of power is introduced.

I am not by any means certain that whoever drafted this bill had in view this construction of its powers. If it was prepared under the direction of the trustees, as I have said already, nothing certainly in the history of its management would justify the assumption that unusual powers were sought by them to be secured. But the precedent was established in this charter, and we shall see how, in the future, it was accepted and followed.

We pass on to consider the second new feature of this bill, by which the trustees are authorized to keep an

AVAILABLE FUND

of fifty thousand dollars in deposit, on interest or otherwise, in such available form as they may direct.

This is the first appearance in the legislation concerning Savings Banks of the term "available fund." The term is an appropriate one when appropriately applied, nor can it be said that it is otherwise than appropriate in the present instance. Fifty thousand dollars for a Savings Bank with $500,000 or more of deposits is not a large sum to keep in reserve for current payments and for the exigencies of unusual drafts.

But the provision, in the form in which it is here found, is objectionable on two grounds. First, the limitation is to a fixed sum. It may be too much or not enough, according to circumstances, a principal element in which would be the total amount of deposits held by the institution. For a deposit of $100,000 it would be too great a proportion; for a deposit of $1,000,000 it might be quite too small a proportion. But for either, there it remains, arbitrary, fixed, inflexible. A more rational way of determining the amount which might thus be held uninvested for the daily business of the bank, and to meet unusual demands, would be to make it a percentage of the whole amount of deposits, provided, of course, the percentage were not fixed too high. This provision was found to be inadequate in this very instance, and when the deposits had accumulated to nearly $1,000,000, finding this arbitrary limit irksome and embarrassing, an amendment to the charter was secured, making this reserve or available fund fifteen per cent of the total amount of its deposits, a provision far more rational and consistent than the previous one.

But the more objectionable feature of the provision, and the one which, as a precedent, was too generally accepted and acted upon, is that which gives to the trustees full discretion to keep it in such available form as the trustees may direct. Hitherto the authority to keep funds temporarily on deposit in banks had served all the purposes of Savings Banks in regard to the reserve necessary for the exigencies of their business. I believe it was an evil day for these institutions when, for this security for such reserve, there was substituted the "discretion of the trustees," and "such available form as they should direct." At least one failure of a Savings Bank, and heavy losses sustained by another,* are directly traceable to this pernicious "discretion," here for the first time recognized and authorized by law.

And yet this bill, which marked the point of departure from some of the most conservative and salutary restraints upon these institutions, was the subject of an elaborate report by the committee to whom it was

* Which losses sustained by that "other" have culminated in disastrous failure since these pages were written.

referred, in which they deprecate the extreme laxity *then* prevailing in the laws relating to these institutions, and take occasion to say "that the bill which they have the honor to submit for the consideration of the house is much more acceptable than the existing charters of this class of corporations, and contains many additional guards against the fraud or misconduct of its officers, which might be profitably applied to other institutions."

These "guards against fraud, etc.," consisted in requiring the consent of the county judge or treasurer or city recorder, in addition to a vote of eight trustees in a quorum of ten, for the "sale, pledge or transfer of any securities belonging to the institution;" also, in requiring the approval of the county treasurer of the election of a trustee; subjecting trustees to removal by a majority of the common council of the city, and the institution to examination annually by a committee appointed by the board of supervisors for that purpose.

These restrictions were, doubtless, all very well meant, but some of them must be very embarrassing, or else have degenerated into such mere formality as to have lost all value as a safeguard against fraud.

The report, however, contains many valuable suggestions, and is an interesting feature in the history of legislation concerning Savings Banks, if in no other view than that of revealing the fact that the subject was at times thoughtfully and earnestly, if not always wisely considered, and hence as a feature or incident affecting the development of a legislative policy, its insertion here is deemed desirable and appropriate.

Report of the committee on banks and insurance companies, on the applications for Savings Banks at Buffalo and Rochester; also on the general bill on the subject of Savings Banks.

IN ASSEMBLY,
February 5, 1846.

Mr. S. Lawrence, from the committee on banks and insurance companies, to whom were referred numerous petitions of citizens of Buffalo, for an act to incorporate the Buffalo Savings Institute; also, the petition of the citizens of Rochester for an act incorporating a Savings Bank of that city; also the bill entitled, "An act to authorize the establisment of Savings Banks," reported to the house, in 1845, by Mr. Crosby, and referred to the committee, by resolution, on the 16th of January last, reports,

That, on examining the documents of both branches of the legislature for the last year, the committee find reports from banks of this description, showing the amount of deposits held in the month of January, 1845, to be $8,603,538.*

The amount now held by these banks has probably risen to more than ten millions of dollars.

The reports of these banks show that a very large proportion of this large amount of funds is owned by mechanics, laborers, widows and orphans, who have resorted to them as safe depositories for the small sums which they have been enabled, from time to time, to lay by from their wages.

These institutions appear to have been well conducted and successful in their operations, and, as yet, have faithfully discharged the duties imposed upon them by their several charters. They have been found useful in our large commercial cities, by affording these

*It will be seen that this differs from the amount given by me in a subsequent table, which difference may be explained by supposing that the committee included as deposits the total reported assets. The Poughkeepsie Savings Bank, with $15,000, is omitted by them, and the Schenectady is estimated $35,000 too high. The figures in our table, $8,577,207, may, therefore, be accepted as more nearly correct than the above.

different clasess a safe depository for their earnings, and at the same time securing to them a reasonable and fair income on such deposits.

The committee, on examining the charters of these incorporations, were surprised to find that great want of care was manifested on the part of the legislature which granted them.

Some of them do not even contain any provision or authority to enable the managers or trustees to require security from the officers of the bank for the faithful performance of their several duties; and all are without any provision requiring the trustees or managers to give any security whatever to the public, or to the depositors.

The only guarantee the public now have against loss by fraud and defalcation is the high character and standing of these several boards of trustees.

This, it is true, thus far, has as yet been found sufficient, so far as all the banks of this kind now existing are concerned; but it does not follow that this guarantee will always be found a sufficient protection.

The history of banking incorporations has demonstrated that human nature is not proof against the powerful temptations which are presented in the management of these institutions.

It will not be denied that more men of high standing and unimpeachable character have been corrupted and led astray by the temptation presented through banking corporations than any other branch of business of the same extent in our country; and the consequences have been more disastrous, accompanied with more suffering and distress, than in any other department of the business operations of the country of the like extent.

When a commercial house happens to fail or become bankrupt, the creditors are generally, to a great extent at least, persons who are not materially injured by the operation; but when a bank explodes, it spreads ruin and distress in every direction; a large proportion of the creditors are those who are least able to bear the loss.

It may be said that there is no analogy between the cases of failure alluded to and the banks before us; that the managers or trustees cannot dispose of or control the funds of the depositors.

A moment's examination will show that this is an erroneous view of the subject; all these banks are authorized to invest in stocks, and bonds and mortgages upon real estate, either of which are convertible at all times into cash.

In some of these charters one-third of the trustees, with the president or vice-president, constitute a quorum for the transaction of business. In others less than half the number of trustees, with the president, constitute a quorum.

The committee have not been able to find any barriers in the way of those having the control of these banks from following in the footsteps of defaulters and swindlers in other moneyed corporations; certainly there is nothing to prevent these few persons from converting every dollar's worth of property belonging to the bank into funds that can be divided among themselves; and they could easily manage to be in Europe or Asia before they would even be suspected.

When the fact is announced, that in a single bank of this class in the city of New York near five millions of dollars are held by so frail a tenure, the committee think the public will be surprised, and will call for some additional securities from those having these banks in charge. If nothing more is required, they should be subjected to a more rigid accountability; the trustees and officers should be required to take and subscribe an oath, to be filed with the Comptroller, faithfully and honestly to discharge the duties imposed by their charter. They should be prohibited from making any transfer of stock, or of bonds and mortgages, without the concurrence at least of two-thirds of all the trustees. They should be subjected to the visitation and inspection of the Comptroller, or some officer to be designated by him, whenever he shall think proper. In these views the committee all concur, and some of them believe that the managers ought to be required to execute to the people a joint and several bond for the faithful performance of all the requisitions of the charter; said bond to be filed in the Comptroller's office. It may be said that these managers get nothing for their services, and therefore they ought not to be liable.

This fact can never change in the slightest degree the moral obligation resting upon the corporation, and upon every member of it, to discharge to the utmost extent the liability incurred.

This circumstance, the committee believe, instead of sustaining the argument of non-accountability, proves the reverse. It is well known that where men get nothing for their services, they are sure to become careless in their supervision of such matters, and the inevitable consequence must be, to leave the control of the bank in the hands of the few, who can easily arrange its affairs to suit their own purposes.

As yet the public have not suffered from any mismanagement on the part of these corporations; but it is not because there is not abundant means within the reach of those several boards of managers to defraud the depositors of every dollar invested.

This enormous sum, in the aggregate, held by these several banks may now be perfectly safe. The committee indulge the hope that it is so, but the question is, will it remain so?

The duty of the Legislature is to protect the public against any possible loss by means of these ideal creatures of the law, called corporations.

Take the application before us for illustration. The board of managers named in the bill for the Savings Bank of Buffalo are all men of high standing and unimpeachable character, and would probably discharge the duties intrusted to them with fidelity; but it must be recollected that they cannot long control its affairs. The corporation lives forever, and contains within its charter the power of perpetuating its own existence.

Suppose, in the lapse of time, a generation should arise like the celebrated Benjamin Rathbun and his cotemporaries, and get the control of the bank asked for, would they hesitate to pocket the funds? Certainly not.

Men who could defraud the people, as was done in that city but a few years since, through the agency of corporations, would not hesitate to rob the widow and the orphan through one of these charters, had they control of it.

The exhibition we have had in that city and elsewhere, by means of bank corporations, the committee think should prove a warning to the Legislature on the subject of creating these creatures of the law which, in so many instances, have proved recreant to their duty, and inflicted such extensive injuries upon the country.

These remarks are not prompted by any hostility to moneyed incorporations. The committee freely admit, to a certain extent, their utility and usefulness, and they are not disposed to recommend any measures which will embarrass the proper action of those now in existence; but they do not entertain a doubt that the great latitude heretofore given to corporations has tended to lead them astray, which, to a certain extent, has turned public opinion against them. Had they, from the commencement, been surrounded with proper restrictions and guards, we should not have had the failures which have occurred and corporations would have been in much better repute than they now are.

In granting these charters, the Legislature should have been quite as cautious and careful as they would have been had they known the applicants were, what too many have proved themselves to have been, without the requisite integrity to shield the public from harm.*

The committee believe that some additional restrictions are called for in relation to the existing banks of this kind, and have directed their chairman to ask leave to introduce a bill entitled "An act for the better regulation of Savings Banks."

The committee are disposed to favor the application of the petitioners from Buffalo, for a Savings Bank in that city. The population and business, present and prospective, of that flourishing and important commercial city, would seem to justify the location of such an institution at that point, and the committee have instructed their chairman to report by bill on this application. The committee take this occasion to say, that the bill which they have the honor to submit for the consideration of the house is much more acceptable than the existing charters of this class of corporations, and contains many additional guards against the fraud or misconduct of its officers, which might be profitably applied to other institutions.

The committee are not satisfied that a second bank of this character is necessary at Rochester. This conclusion is drawn from the fact that the one now doing business there is not a very large concern, as appears by their last reports.

These banks should not be unnecessarily multiplied.

The committee have examined the bill introduced at the last session of the legislature, by Mr. Crosby, entitled "An act to authorize the establishment of Savings Banks," which was referred to this committee by resolution of the house, on the 16th of January

*This assumes that by surrounding a charter with prohibitions, designed as safeguards, its administration may with safety and propriety be committed to men destitute of integrity! The reader will not fail to note other logical inconsistencies in the course of the report, nor its general careless and slovenly style. We do not insert it as agreeing with all its conclusions, but in part as an historical exhibit of the status of legislative intelligence at that period.

last, and are of the opinion that such a law ought not to pass at this time.*

From the digression into which we have been led by the introduction of the foregoing report, let us return to the precedent in legislation established by the act under consideration, of allowing an available fund to be kept, at the discretion of the trustees, in such available form as they should direct. The reports of the Bank Department, particularly of late years, are full of protests against this unwise and dangerous power, and to these the reader is referred for a more full exposition of the abuses to which the provision is liable.

We are now prepared to observe the progress of legislation under the guidance of the precedents above considered.

*This allusion is to an effort to enact a general law for the incorporation of Savings Banks to which reference will be made hereafter.

CHAPTER XXXVI.

INVESTMENTS; LEGISLATION UNDER THE FOREGOING PRECEDENTS.

The legislation of 1847 was confined to an amendment of the charter mentioned in the last chapter, enlarging the discretion in the matter of loans upon bond and mortgage, as it ought to have been known would have to be done to make the power available at all, practically; renewing the unlimited discretion as to the disposition to be made of the available fund, excepting that it should *not* be employed in discounting commercial or business paper, and increasing the amount to $100,000, whenever the deposits with the institution should exceed $400,000. A general act was also passed, rendered necessary by the change in the banking system of the State, whereby deposits were authorized to be made with any banking association as well as with incorporated banks.

The legislation of 1848 was characterized by the incorporation of three Savings Banks in the city of New York, to no one of which was granted any of the extraordinary discretionary powers already commented upon. The securities in which investments were authorized were of the same class as had already been sanctioned by precedent and experience, and deposits were authorized to be made in the banks of the city, though in two of the charters the amount of these was limited, in the one to $40,000 and in the other to $20,000, while in the third, there was no limitation, a fact which in itself illustrates the capriciousness of legislation upon this subject.

In 1849 we find the "available fund" in "available form" again moving the legislation in regard to Savings Banks, limited, however, in one case to the modest sum of $25,000, and in another extended to "one-third of the total amount of deposits with said institution." By this it will be seen that one-third of the entire deposits was made subject to the absolute discretion of the trustees, and from this time forth this became a characteristic provision in Savings Bank charters; a recognized feature of the Savings Bank system of this State. It did not appear in every charter, being sometimes limited to one-fourth, sometimes to one-fifth, and sometimes to a definite sum, but the prevailing proportion was one-third, and in all cases where found, the form in which it should be kept was subject to the absolute discretion of the trustees. That "form" has commonly assumed the shape of call loans, secured by collaterals. The character of these has varied with the supposed exigencies of the institution in respect to its income, or with the prudence and sagacity of the trustees. The trustees of many institutions set their faces inflexibly against the acceptance of any thing as a collateral, in which they are not authorized to invest permanently, and where this is done, of course, the dangers arising from this "form" of the use of the funds are almost, if not quite, wholly overcome;

though I have not yet been brought to look upon call loans, even with *gold* as a collateral, except as a mere temporary expedient, with any considerable degree of satisfaction. Solid investments, which the bank can call its own, subject to no monetary fluctuations as regards the income to be derived from them, giving rise to no questions concerning the legality of their conversion into money when the occasion requires, are the characteristics of all well managed and, under every emergency, unquestionably *safe* institutions.

In this same year, 1849, the legislature for the first time discarded favoritism, or the claims of locality in the matter of investments in city stocks, by granting, in one of its acts of incorporation, power to invest in the stocks of any city in this State; and in the same charter was the "double negative" provision previously considered, whereby any investment could be made that had the approval of *all* the trustees present at any meeting.

The authority to invest in the stocks or bonds of any city in this State became thereafter so common, though not altogether uniform a feature in Savings Bank charters, as to require no further special mention, and the same may be said of the "one-third" "available fund" clause, and of the provision justifying any investments having the unanimous approval of any meeting. The modification by enlargement, of the latter power, by making it available against the opposition of as many as two trustees, will be noted presently.

In 1850 several acts of incorporation were passed by the legislature, one of which was modeled after the earlier forms, and contained none of the modern loopholes for miscellaneous investments, but this was amended the following year by the introduction of the one-third available clause; and the others embraced more or less of these unguarded features. In one, besides the direct authority to invest in the stocks of any city in the State now so common a feature in charters, the discretion was enlarged by permitting the trustees to invest in the stocks of any village in this State.

The legislature of 1851 was distinguished by the incorporation of a larger number of Savings Banks than in any preceding year, in all of which the liberal features which we have characterized prevailed. In this year the provision concerning investments that might be made, by the unanimous action of the board at any meeting, was modified in several charters, so as to require the opposition of three trustees instead of but one, to defeat otherwise unauthorized investments, though with singular inconsistency some of these still required unanimous consent to authorize loans upon bond and mortgage.

The legislation of 1852 was characterized by no distinguishing features. Three Savings Banks were incorporated, with the provisions concerning investments then applicable to most of these institutions.

It will be remembered that those now specifically named and recognized were the stocks of this State, of the United States, sometimes of other States, and of any city in this State, and in bond and mortgage, with varying limitations.

So far as these indicate the intent and purpose of the legislature, they were conservative and salutary. The provisions upon which we have commented, under which a wider discretion concerning investments and loans is claimed, and in many instances exercised, are so far exceptional in their character, and are commonly expressed in such terms, and are found in such connection with more restricted requirements, that we may well believe the legislature was ignorant of their real purport and of the construction to which they were liable.

In 1853, besides the incorporation of several Savings Banks, generally with the usual powers conferred upon such institutions, we find the first general act regulating the investment of their funds. I denominate this a general act, though restricted in its operation to the Savings Banks of New York and Kings counties, because these were then, as they are now, so large a representation in the Savings Bank system of the State and because the provisions were applicable generally to so large a number of institutions, and not specifically by direct amendment of the charter of each.

The language of the first clause of this act is not only ungrammatical, but is so obscure as to leave a doubt as to its real intent. It is as follows:

"It shall be lawful for the several Savings Banks and Institutions for Savings in the city and county of New York and county of Kings, now chartered or which may be hereafter chartered, in addition to the powers granted by their respective acts of incorporation, to loan the moneys which they have received or shall hereafter receive on deposit, or the accumulations thereof, *on or purchase of* any stock or securities for the redemption or payment of which the faith of any State in the Union shall be pledged, or in the public debt or stock of any incorporated city, county or town in this State which shall have been authorized by the Legislature of this State to issue such stock; provided that the cash value of such stock or securities shall, at the time of making such investments, be at or above its par value; and such loans, so made, shall not exceed in amount ninety per cent of the par value of such stock or securities."

I have indicated by italics the ambiguous phraseology of this section. The banks are authorized to "*loan moneys on or purchase of*" any of the securities mentioned. It would seem that it was the intention to authorize these securities both for investment and as collateral for loans. But the requirement that for the former purposes they should be at par in the market, which was plainly intended, rendered the act of little service in extending the powers of Savings Banks, and deprived them of any advantage resulting from a temporary depression in the market for even the best securities. They might thus purchase United States fives at 110, but could not purchase them at 90. This would seem to have been enacted in the interest of the borrower rather than of the Savings Banks.

But that to which it is our purpose more especially to direct attention is not the terms upon which these investments were authorized, but the new class of securities hereby admitted for investment upon any terms. These are the bonds of counties and of towns in this State, which here for the first time receive recognition in that relation from the Legislature.

In several acts of incorporation passed this year, a new feature was also introduced, which thereafter became quite common in Savings Bank charters, and was, not unlikely, suggested by, or gave suggestion to, the provision in the general act already noted.

Hitherto Savings Bank charters had never specifically authorized loans to be made upon any other security than real estate, this being naturally and properly regarded in the light of an investment, having permanence, and investing the bank with absolute ownership and power of disposition of the collateral (bonds and mortgages) given to secure the loan. We have seen, however, that under the wide discretion conferred by the available fund clause, first introduced in 1846, loans on call became permissible. But the specific language of Savings Bank charters continued still to limit the use of moneys to "investing," etc.

In this year, however, the clause which hitherto defined the object of the corporation to be to receive and to *invest* moneys, etc., was in several charters modified so as to read to *invest in or to loan upon*, etc., thus giving to the corporation the choice between permanent investments and temporary loans. Whatever may be thought of the wisdom and expediency of this authorized departure from the original policy of investment, it was not without some compensating advantages. It defined the class of securities which should be accepted for loans, instead of leaving these to the discretion of the trustees under the guise of an "available fund," kept in "available form," and it rendered superfluous the provision for an available fund, which was accordingly omitted from charters which thus provided in general terms for loans upon the securities authorized for investment.

SUBSEQUENT LEGISLATION.

From this time there was no material change in the policy of legislation concerning the investments of Savings Banks.

Though county and town bonds had been recognized by the act of 1853, its operation was limited, as we have seen, to the Savings Banks in New York and Kings counties. The first specific authorization to a Savings Bank, in its charter, to invest in the bonds of a county, was granted in 1857, but this was confined to the bonds of the county in which the institution was located. This precedent was followed in many cases thereafter, in one or two the privilege being extended so as to embrace the bonds of one or more neighboring counties. Town bonds were first specially authorized by charter in 1863, but were limited to the bonds of the town in which the bank was located.

In this year also (1863) a general act was passed, authorizing Savings Banks to *loan their funds* on the bonds of counties and cities in this State, provided that provision was made in the act authorizing the issue, for the payment of such bonds by tax. This was, however, only extending the provisions of the act of 1853, in this respect, to Savings Banks outside of New York and Kings counties. In 1864 Savings Banks were authorized to make loans to counties, to be secured by their bonds, issued in pursuance of law, which was but the extension of another feature of the act of 1853, to banks heretofore excluded from it.

Both these acts received their incitement from the large amount of bonds then being issued by counties for the purpose of raising money to pay bounties to volunteers for the war.

Since this time, bonds of counties have become a marked feature of the authorized investments for Savings Banks, and still more recently, town bonds have in some instances been authorized. The latter, however, have not been admitted without very considerable opposition in the legislature, and specific charter authority to invest in them must still be regarded as exceptional. But in 1869, a general act for the bonding of towns in aid of the construction of railroads, provided that Savings Banks might invest in them.

Since that period there has been no material change in the policy of the State concerning Savings Bank investments, until the enactment of the General Savings Bank law in 1875.

DEPOSITS IN BANKS.

In order not to break the connection of events concerning investments, and loans as a substitute for investments, we did not stop to consider the action of the legislature concerning the deposits that might be made by Savings Banks after the general authority conferred by chapter 478, Laws of 1847, to deposit in any of the banking associations of this State, as well as in incorporated banks.

The act of 1853, which we have already cited, in

section 2, limited the amount that any Savings Bank should deposit in any bank or association, to ten per cent of the capital stock paid in of such bank, provided further, that such amount should not exceed twenty per cent of all the deposits held by such Savings Bank. The principle recognized in this provision is wise and salutary; whether the best proportions of capital and deposits are selected for its exemplification we will not stop to discuss. This section was in 1858 amended, most unwisely, in my judgment, by limiting the amount that might be kept in any one bank to $100,000. I should remark, however, that by the act of 1853 the amount of deposits authorized by section 2 might be exceeded, by requiring and receiving from the depository such securities, in amount equal to the excess, as the law required to be deposited as security for circulating notes. I presume this provision never became operative, however, in practice.

Another provision of the act of 1853, worthy of notice as illustrating the disposition of the legislature to carefully guard the depositors of Savings Banks against loss, was one making the deposits of Savings Banks in banks of circulation a first lien upon the assets, in the event of failure, after making up any deficiency in the sale of the securities to redeem their circulating notes. This provision is now, however, of little practical value, since so few of the banks in this State are organized under its laws, or are subject to its authority in the matter of their liquidation; and besides, it has been adjudicated, that a State bank, upon being thrown into bankruptcy, is to have its assets distributed according to the provisions of the bankrupt act, and which does not recognize this statutory preference. And this brings us to the act of legislation concerning deposits in bank, which, in 1865, authorized deposits to be made in national banks, a measure rendered necessary by the very general conversion of State into national banks, under the new financial and monetary regime precipitated by the war.

The act of 1871, already cited under other topics, provided, also, that any part of the available fund of any Savings Bank might be deposited in any duly organized bank or trust company, but further provided that the bank or trust company, in which the deposits were made, should be designated by a vote of a majority of all the trustees, exclusive of such as were directors in any bank or trust company in which it would be lawful to make such deposits — a restriction more severe, we believe, than was contemplated — and which, if regarded, must have been very annoying in some institutions. The amount of deposits in any one bank or trust company was limited to twenty per cent of its capital; also to ten per cent of the deposits of the Savings Bank making the same.

DEPOSITS IN TRUST COMPANIES.

It only remains in this connection to consider the action of the legislature in 1854, in the enactment of the following: "It shall be lawful for any Savings Bank or Institution for Savings to make temporary deposits in any trust company incorporated under the laws of this State, and authorized by the supreme court to receive and hold trust funds, and subject to examination by said court."

It will be observed that this provision contains none of the restrictions imposed by the act of 1853, concerning deposits in banks of circulation. The reason for this is set forth in the following report of the committee on banks in the Assembly, upon the bill in question, which appears to have first passed the Senate with these restrictive clauses inserted. The report says:

"Your committee deem it unnecessary that the section making the deposit of moneys in trust companies conformable to the act of 1853, relative to Savings Banks, be inserted in the bill, as the amount of capital, namely, one million of dollars, of the trust companies actually paid in and invested, would, in the judgment of your committee, be a sufficient safeguard for the security of the deposits made with them. But in addition to this, all moneys deposited with the trust companies are, by their charters, required to be invested *in the same manner* as are the funds deposited in the Savings Banks, and would therefore be equally safe *if* invested *through* the trust companies, as if they were invested by the Savings Banks in which they are first deposited. Your committee could, therefore, see no good reason why the restriction inserted in the Senate bill should be permitted to remain therein, more especially, as the effect of it would be to defeat the object of the bill, which your committee deem a good one, and would therefore recommend the passage of the bill as amended."

The first portion of the argument of the committee I regard as fallacious, and the latter as conclusive and unanswerable. The fact that trust companies are now *even more* restricted in the range of their investments than Savings Banks, would seem to mark them as peculiarly safe as depositories for the moneys which Savings Banks must keep in reserve for the exigencies of their business, and, as a rule, the interest allowed by them on balances is fully equal to that allowed by banks of discount. When added to this, is the fact that they are subject to the laws of our own State, and amenable to its authority, subject to the supervision of its officers, and have a deposit of $100,000 with the Superintendent of the Bank Department, as an additional protection to depositors, it would seem that the selection of these as depositories by Savings Banks, in preference to foreign corporations, with no local responsibility, would become general if not universal. The strongest claim which, in my judgment, they present to public favor is, the restriction imposed by their respective charters upon the investment of their funds, whereby the hazards attending the discounting of business paper are never encountered. If there were superadded to this, the provision in the act of 1853, making the deposit of Savings Banks a first lien upon their assets in case of failure, and a mandatory requirement that the Superintendent of the Banking Department should annually examine their affairs and report thereon, I should regard their security as depositories as nearly perfect as it is possible to make any merely human institution; and without these latter safeguards, they still possess certain decided advantages over others that are authorized.

Since the foregoing passages were written, the restrictions upon trust companies in respect to their loans and investments have been very considerably relaxed; and the suggestions herein made of preferring Savings Bank deposits made in trust companies, and of subjecting trust companies to examination by the Superintendent of the Bank Department, have been incorporated into the legislation affecting these institutions.

CHAPTER XXXVII.

OF DIVIDENDS TO DEPOSITORS.

The original theory of the Legislature concerning dividends to be paid to depositors was, that the entire profits of the institution should be divided ratably among them, and a provision to this effect was inserted in the first charter, and has been inserted in nearly the same terms in every charter since that time, down to the very latest.

But this general provision was first modified in 1831, by an amendment, probably at the solicitation of the bank securing it, authorizing a difference of one per cent in the rate to be paid to depositors of $500 and under, and to those of over $500; the smaller deposits receiving the higher rate. In subsequent years this authority was conceded to other institutions, and by the act of 1853, section 5, was made imperative upon the Savings Banks in New York and Kings counties, though it is not certain, from the language, that this provision was not confined to Savings Banks that should thereafter be incorporated. It was commonly so construed by the institutions in operation at the time of the passage of the act, and only such institutions conformed to the requirement as were favorable to the policy indicated by it; and institutions "incorporated thereafter" regarded the later provisions of their respective charters as of higher authority to them than this general act. So that this provision in the act of 1853 has ever been practically inoperative. In fact, the whole subject of the regulation of dividends to depositors, except the general one of assuring to them the profits after payment of expenses, has been controlled, in the main, by the views and wishes of the trustees of each institution, who have secured from the Legislature such provisions in this respect as they desired.

Our views of the proper designation of the profits of Savings Banks allowed to depositors, have been expressed *ante*, p. 134. Still, so commonly is the term interest employed that we unconsciously, at times, fall into that form of expression, and the terms interest and dividends are also found interchangeably in the statutes. The use of the term interest in this relation was probably derived from the practice of many institutions, in late years, of agreeing to pay a certain rate without reference to the earnings or profits, which practice savors more of the characteristics of interest than of dividends. But in our judgment the *practice* is wrong, being in derogation of the fundamental principle upon which Savings Banks are instituted. There is nothing in the theory of Savings Banks to justify it; on the contrary, every thing in their theory and constitution is opposed to it.

During a discussion in the New York Legislature, the question arose as to the proper term by which to designate the profits declared to depositors. Some advocated "interest," others "dividends," as the proper term to employ, the former being the prevailing notion.

The entire discussion threw very little light upon the subject, but did serve to reveal the prevailing ignorance amongst the members concerning the nature and characteristics of Savings Banks. One senator, who, from his connection with a leading Savings Bank in the State as an officer therein for many years, might naturally lay claim to a better understanding of the subject than his associates, proposed to make a distinction between the profits regularly distributed, semi-annually, and the extra allowance made at irregular and longer intervals. The former he would call interest, the latter, dividends. But his distinction was founded upon the same erroneous conception of the character of the regular division of profits which we have already characterized, and was derived, as above explained, from the custom in his own bank, of agreeing in advance to pay a certain defined rate per cent.

There is no difference in the essential character of a regular and of an extra division of the profits or earnings of a Savings Bank, that should justify the application to one of the term interest, and to the other the term dividend. They are produced in precisely the same way, and have precisely the same relation to the deposits and to the depositor. Where it is true that the one has been agreed upon and promised in advance, it has been in violation of true Savings Bank principles, and it may be in violation, as it is certainly in excess, of the authority conferred by law. It is an agreement that could not be enforced against the corporation, if by any means it were to turn out that the agreed rate could not be paid without trenching upon the deposits. The liability in such case would be individual, falling upon the trustees personally, and not upon the deposits of which they are only the guardians, and which they have no authority whatever to pledge to the payment of dividends *declared* but not *earned!*

In short, we repeat what we said before, that the division of Savings Bank profits, whether regular or extra, partakes of all the characteristics of dividends, and none of the characteristics of interest.

The whole question of dividends was quite fully considered in the Special Report on Savings Banks, and as showing the phases of the subject, as the same has been presented to and considered by the Legislature of New York, we will here insert the views of the dividend question there presented.

Extract from Special Report on Savings Banks, 1868, *pp.* 118–128.

OF DIVIDENDS.

As upon almost every other subject of importance connected with Savings Banks, so in regard to this, it will be seen that the law is various.

The more common provision is expressed in the various charters with a great degree of uniformity in the following words:

"It shall be the duty of trustees to regulate the rate of interest (dividends) to be allowed to depositors, so that they shall receive, as nearly as may be, a ratable proportion of all the profits of the corporation, after deducting all necessary expenses."

A few charters authorize a rate of interest one per cent greater on deposits of $500 and under, than on those above that amount; a less number makes such a classification of rates imperative.

Two authorize a classification of rates, having regard to the time the principal sum has been on deposit; while a few leave the whole question to the discretion of trustees.

The act of 1853, to which reference has so frequently been made, and which applies to Savings Banks in New York and Kings counties only, in the sixth section provides, concerning all Savings Banks thereafter to be incorporated, "that the rate of interest on all deposits of $500 and under, shall be one per cent per annum greater than shall be allowed on any sum exceeding $500."

But the institutions incorporated since the passage of the act have very generally disregarded this requirement, either by authority of special provisions in their charters, inconsistent with the requirement, or because the inconvenience of submission has more terrors for them than the possible consequences of a violation of the law.

Others, and generally the older institutions in New York and Brooklyn (the only part of Kings county in which there are any Savings Banks), make this classification in the rates of dividends paid, on their own motion, as a matter of policy, tending to the encouragement of the poor and humble, whose accumulations must be small, and to discourage large deposits, from those who are able to seek other investments, and for whose benefit Savings Banks were not instituted. These are uniformly quite emphatic in their expression of opinion that the provision is a salutary one, and should be enforced.

Nothing is clearer than that as a mandatory provision it should be uniform. If any institution is to be required to classify its rate of dividends upon the basis under consideration, then all should be. The real question is whether such a provision should be mandatory or only permissive, or whether, indeed, such a classification of rates should not be prohibited, and a uniformity of rate upon all sums be absolutely required.

Few I think would go to this length in the enforcement of uniformity, those favoring uniformity being content that the question should be left to the discretion of the trustees.

But the distinction between making such a provision mandatory, and leaving it permissive, is radical, and one concerning which a very earnest sentiment is entertained and expressed on either side.

The grounds upon which such a provision is favored, have been stated above. To repeat, they are in brief:

1. To encourage small depositors whom Savings Banks were instituted exclusively to assist and benefit.

2. To discourage the accumulation of large deposits from those who are presumed to be competent to make their own investments.

The high regard which I entertain for the character and worth of those gentlemen who earnestly advocate the enforcement of this provision, their sincerity, their disinterestedness, the careful thought which I know they have given to the subject, and the experience in the practical workings of Savings Banks which they have enjoyed, all combine to entitle their opinions to a careful and candid consideration. In such a spirit, and with the sole purpose in view of arriving at a conclusion the nearest *right*, just, safe and salutary, let us examine this question from their standpoint.

First, as to the encouragement of small depositors.

I think a fallacy has unconsciously wrought itself into this proposition. It seems to be assumed that the encouragement is found in the distinction between rates, and not in the rates themselves. Put in form, it would involve an absurdity like the following: "The Savings Bank that pays five per cent to depositors of $500, and but four per cent to depositors of larger amounts, thereby encourages the smaller depositors more than the Savings Bank that pays six per cent to all depositors." Unquestionably this is not the form that it was intended the proposition should take, but the facts before us and which must be made a part of the argument upon this question, compel the proposition to assume that form. What are the facts? That with a single exception the highest rate of dividends paid last year by any Savings Bank that had classified rates, was six per cent, while the Savings Banks that had a uniform rate for all depositors generally paid six per cent. Thus, under either policy, the smaller depositors received six per cent. Wherein then were they the more "encouraged" by the one than by the other? Obviously, the policy of different rates possesses no peculiar features of encouragement to any class, unless this be found in the selfish gratification of having received more than somebody else, which is our repudiated proposition over again. If, therefore, there is in reality no superior attraction to the small depositors, in the policy of classified rates, as the facts of the case seem conclusively to establish, then the argument for a compulsory enforcement of such classification, upon this ground, is deprived of all force.

The argument to have weight must be predicated upon conditions like this; out of an ascertained amount of profits to be divided, a uniform rate of but so much per cent to each depositor can be allowed, while with a classified rate, confining that per cent to depositors of over $500, one per cent more can be allowed to depositors of $500 or under. The argument is good if these conditions exist, and not otherwise. The practical action of these institutions as detailed above would seem to show that these conditions are, to say the least, unusual. I have, besides, an illustration directly in point in the case of the South Brooklyn Savings Bank, which for sixteen years had, under a by-law, enforced classified rates of dividends, upon the basis which we are now considering. During the present year they have adopted the policy of uniform dividends, on the ground in the first place, that an arbitary limitation of $500 was too easily evaded by the depositor, who would open different accounts in the same institution, in trust for wife, children or friends; and secondly, that the institution could as well pay six per cent on all, as five per cent on those of over $500, and six per cent on those of but $500 or less, and they exhibit this calculation in support of that view. The dividends credited to depositors for the year 1866, at five and six per cent, amounted to $84,522.99. It would have required but $4,769.14 more, to have made them uniformly six per cent.

It seems to me that this single instance sufficiently illustrates the impolicy of an enforced regulation of this kind. Here, such a law would compel the institution to withold from depositors what it had, and could afford to give, in order simply to note a class distinction between the *poor* labeled $500, and those of *affluence* labeled $501, or upwards! Nothing is thereby added to the gains of the poor, but something material is taken from the earnings of the others. And among the latter may be a widow, whose only support, besides her own labors, is $1,000 in the Savings Bank. The ten dollars which her deposit has *earned*, and of which she is thus deprived, would go far to furnish her winter's coal or bread.

I by no means contend for an enforced uniformity; I would in this matter leave each institution free to act according to the conditions by which it shall find itself surrounded.

The second consideration of the undue encouragement given to depositors of large sums to make use of Savings Banks for other than their original purpose, I regard as being fully answered in the discussion of the limitation of the amount of deposits to be received from one individual.* The Savings Bank cannot, as a rule, become attractive to depositors of independent

*See discussion of the topics, LIMITATION OF DEPOSITS, *post*.

means, so long as the ordinary dividends are less than the legal rate of interest. The insecurity attending deposits of considerable amounts, I would provide against, by proper safeguards, as indicated in that discussion, and having done that, the more free for *all classes* the access is made to Savings Banks, the greater will be their prosperity, and the greater will be the benefits they confer upon those in whose special interest they were primarily instituted.

But it by no means follows that the trustees of Savings Banks should be left to the exercise of an unlimited discretion in the matter of dividends. Whatever policy or practice in regard to dividends, as in regard to any thing else, is calculated to impair the perfect security of depositors, or to operate injuriously to the system, or to work injustice to any individual or class of depositors, should be prohibited. Thus it seems to me the dictate of the commonest prudence, that no dividends should be declared in advance of ascertained profits.

It is customary for many Savings Banks to advertise that they will pay a given rate of interest. How do they know that they will be able to pay such a rate? They may have been able to pay that amount in previous years, and they *may* be able to pay it again, or they *may not.* Let them refer to their past record as an earnest of future probabilities, but give no pledges upon the contingency of future profits.

Doubtless, as a rule, the older institutions, with large surplus, might do this and not forfeit their pledge, but even these would do better to adhere to the principle of not *dividing* what they have not earned. But it is commonly the newer institutions that make the greatest parade of promises, and, of course, for the purpose of attracting deposits.

Even upon the organization of banks their trustees not unfrequently advertise that they will pay the highest rate of interest. Of course they will struggle to do this, but what are the probabilities that they can do this out of *fairly earned profits?*

Let them do their best, and when their profits are assured, declare their dividend.

Doubtless the impulse is strong with a new Savings Bank to hold out inducements equal to those of older institutions. But how *can* they do it with no resources? The older Savings Banks have a surplus, the profits on which enable them to make greater dividends to depositors than they could do otherwise. Take, for instance, the Bowery Savings Bank; the interest on its surplus, at seven per cent, is nearly one per cent on the whole amount due its depositors; and as there is always a large amount of deposits that are not entitled to dividends, it is doubtless fully one per cent on the deposits that are so entitled. If, therefore, the Bowery can only declare an average dividend of six per cent, one per cent of which is earned from a surplus that receives no dividend, how can the bank that organized, say on the first of May, and on the first of January has $200,000 deposits, declare dividends of six per cent, all of which must be on the profits of the $200,000? True, they do not have to declare dividends on the whole $200,000, but only on such portion of it as has been in the bank for not less than three or four months. But it is equally true that they have not profits from the whole $200,000. Some has been kept on hand for daily transactions, some in the bank at four per cent to meet immediate demands; and for the balance we cannot assume certainly a larger per cent of profit than is enjoyed by older institutions. With these disadvantages it does not seem possible that any Savings Bank can, during the first year, nor, indeed, during the first five years of its existence, pay dividends equal to older institutions, without, first, anticipating profits; or second, investing in doubtful securities at larger than average profit; or third, leaving no reserve for surplus. I anticipate an answer to these suggestions, that if new banks in the immediate neighborhood of old institutions do not declare as high dividends, they cannot secure the deposits. They cannot, of course, expect, by the mere fact of proximity, to withdraw depositors from the old institutions; and if they cannot, it is because no new Savings Bank was needed for the accommodation of the public. If a community or neighborhood have no Savings Bank facilities sufficiently attractive to induce deposits, the offer of such facilities will stimulate deposits. If it has such already they do not require any thing further.

The organization of new institutions should proceed wholly upon the theory of the wants of a community. These wants should be such as a moderate suggestion of profits at first will stimulate to action. All proper inducements should be employed to stimulate the habit of saving, but safety, with small profits, must be the leading idea of Savings Banks, and especially in their early history. If this will not secure deposits, it is because the facilities of older organizations are more attractive, or because *that* community is not ripe for the experiment. But this aspect of our subject has been elsewhere fully discussed.

A sound principle of finance, allied to the last discussed, but far more vital, is that no dividend shall be paid or credited except out of profits actually earned. It might seem that a principle so obvious could require no enforcement from argument or from the law. But the fact that three Savings Banks did last year report dividends in excess of their profits from interest received, making no allowance for expenses, is conclusive that the obviousness of the principle has not prevented its being disregarded.

The State has not found it beneath its dignity to enforce this principle by salutary provisions of law concerning banks of issue, whose directors are prohibited from declaring dividends except from profits; are not the depositors in Savings Banks entitled to equal consideration with those who have capital to invest in banking enterprises?

Such a prohibition concerning Savings Banks would not only be salutary in its restraint upon practices dangerous to their integrity, but would tend to check the disposition to establish new institutions in localities where Savings Bank facilities are already sufficiently provided. Indeed such a provision alone, rigidly enforced, would effectually remove all dangers that threaten our system from the reckless multiplication of these institutions.

There is considerable diversity in the practice of Savings Banks concerning dividends, in other respects than those named. They are generally supposed to declare dividends semi-annually, and most of them on the first of January and July in each year, a few at other periods.

Most institutions declare dividends only on moneys that have been on deposit for three months prior to the dividend; thus moneys deposited on the first of July and withdrawn on the 30th of December would be entitled to no dividend; while a deposit made on the 1st of October, and remaining until the 1st of January, would be so entitled.

Dividends are estimated by these institutions only for full periods of three months, that is, a deposit made in August and remaining until January 1st would be entitled to a dividend for only three months, the time from August to 1st of October not being estimated. Some only declare dividends on sums deposited for full six months.

Other institutions allow deposits to become entitled to dividends from the first of the calendar month after the same are made, and to the first of the calendar month in which the same are withdrawn, while others allow the dividend to commence from the first of the month subsequent to the deposit, but declare it on none that have been withdrawn prior to the day for which the dividend is declared. The practical operation of these two methods would be, that under the first, a sum on deposit during any entire calendar month would receive its proportionate rate of dividend for that time, while under the second, a sum to be entitled to a dividend from the first of the month subsequent to its being deposited, must remain on deposit until the next dividend is declared.

These are matters which the Legislature has heretofore left to the discretion of trustees, and I do not know that any interference or control of this discretion is desirable. Some of these practices seem liable to the charge of discriminating unjustly against short term deposits; but it is the long term deposits that earn the interest, and the security afforded is quite sufficient repayment for a deposit of only one or two months. Besides, it is a part of the policy to encourage not simply *deposits* of savings but their *accumulation;* and this cannot be affected without some extra inducement to keep the deposit undisturbed.

I should be apprehensive, too, that to allow dividends on deposits for a month, when it is well known that for such period they can earn little or nothing for the institution, was undertaking more than could be done with due regard to safety, to say nothing of the injustice to depositors for a longer term, whose money alone really earns the interest that is thus divided. Still, if the trustees are restricted to making dividends out of earnings, and required to reserve something for surplus, the danger from *over doing* will be substantially averted.

There is, however, a practice now becoming quite common in the cities of New York and Brooklyn, which I regard as unsafe for the institution, and unjust to the larger portion of the depositors.

This is to offer, at the beginning of each quarter, to allow dividends from the first of the month on the deposits made on or before the twentieth.

If the suggestion should be made that no Savings Bank will do this unless it can *afford* to do so, and that it is the best judge of what it can afford to do, I reply:

First. That we have evidence that under pressure Savings Banks *will do* that which they cannot afford to do, as where they pay more in dividends than they receive from investments; and,

Second. If a Savings Bank can *afford* to pay more than six per cent on a deposit for two months and ten days, then it can afford to pay more than six per cent on deposits that have remained for at least three months, and helped to earn the higher rate. It is unjust to the depositors for the longer time, that *their* earnings should be taken to enhance the profits of the short term depositors.

But aside from the injustice wrought by this practice, it is opposed to sound policy. Let us illustrate its natural effects.

Seeing the offer, A, on the 20th of April, withdraws from his usual balance of $7,000 or $10,000, in a bank of issue, $5,000, which he deposits in the Savings Bank. On the 1st of July he withdraws it, together with $75 dividend, earned in 72 days, while B, who deposited $5,000 on the 1st of April, gets no more. That is, A realizes on his investment at the rate of over seven and a half per cent per annum, while B, whose deposit has earned more for the institution than A's, realizes but six per cent. If the Savings Bank can thus *afford* to pay A seven and a half per cent, it is only because it *does afford* to deprive B of his just due.

But A is worldly wise, and withdraws his deposit to use in Wall street, or to loan on call, until the next quarter preceding dividend day shall offer him a further opportunity to make seven and a half per cent out of B's earnings.

The deposits which are secured by this system of bonuses are of little value to the institutions that offer them; they are short lived, and cannot, in my opinion, as a rule, earn nearly as much as they receive.

The tendency of this practice must indeed be to destroy the real character and purpose of Savings Banks as incentives to industry and economy, and to convert them into financial drawing-rooms, where scheming men of the world, rapacious birds of prey, may repose for a time, while resting their pinions for some higher flight into the realms of stock fancy.

It is true that about the first of January and July, in each year, it is customary for Savings Banks to allow a few days of grace for depositors. Receipts, from various sources, fall due about this time, but do not come to hand until after the first of the month; and to lose a quarter's interest for one or two days of unavoidable delay, seems a hardship. I would provide for say five days' grace at such periods, and believe that this is the best that can be done consistently with justice to all, and safety to the institutions themselves.

CHAPTER XXXVIII.

OF SURPLUS.

Allied to this question of interest to depositors, is that of surplus, which has now become a marked feature of general as well as of special legislation.

We have seen that the original idea of a Savings Bank was the accumulation of small sums, the scant savings of the poor, securely invested in the stocks of this State or of the general government, yielding to the Savings Bank, an income, it was presumed, not exceeding six per cent, which income, after deducting the necessary expenses of clerk hire, rents, etc., would leave certain net profits, all of which were to be divided ratably among the depositors. This theory, of course, excluded all idea of any accumulation of profits for any purpose. But a few years served to demonstrate the expediency of allowing a surplus to accumulate, with which to provide against a loss to depositors, resulting from a forced conversion of securities into cash at a time when the market value of stocks might be depreciated below par or cost. Of course, such accumulation could only be made by refraining from dividing the whole amount of net profits each year, as interest to be credited to depositors, retaining some small percentage as a reserve to meet the contingencies in business above referred to. This policy first received legislative recognition in

1831, through an amendment to the charter of the Bank for Savings, in the following terms: "The board of trustees of the Bank for Savings, in the city of New York, are hereby authorized to accumulate gradually, and hold invested, a surplus fund not exceeding *three per cent* on the amount of deposits, to the end that in case of a reduction in the market price of the public stocks and securities, held or to be held by the said bank, below the par value thereof, any loss to the depositors by reason of such reduction may be prevented or made good by means of the said fund."

Amendments in similar terms were made to the charters of other Savings Banks the following year, and in 1836, the charter of the Bank for Savings was further amended by enlarging the surplus that might thus be accumulated to ten per cent, and in 1839 the provision for accumulating a surplus fund of ten per cent was applied to all Savings Banks by a general act.

The charters of many Savings Banks, thereafter incorporated, made provision for the accumulation of a specific amount, commonly twenty-five thousand dollars, by requiring all the profits above that amount to be divided among the depositors. But ten per cent may be regarded as practically authorized to all, under the general act of 1839, though in a few special charters, as high as twenty per cent is allowed.

The aspects of this question of surplus, as presented for the consideration of the legislature in the Special Report, to which we have had and shall have such frequent occasion to refer, were as follows:

Extract from Special Report on Savings Banks, 1868. pp. 58–60.

Surplus as an Element of Safety.

In previous pages of this report, the surplus of Savings Banks has been considered as a sign of their prosperity. It is proper in this connection to consider this surplus as an indispensable element of strength and safety.

If a Savings Bank were subject to no contingencies in its business, if it were possible to protect every institution from any possible loss, no surplus would be required. But this we have shown and know to be impracticable. The profoundest wisdom, the most penetrating sagacity, the most consummate financial skill, is vain to place any one of these institutions upon a basis of absolute exemption from loss. These qualities, with strict integrity and conscientious care, may greatly diminish the chances of misfortune, but cannot eliminate them altogether. It must needs be that, sooner or later, slight or heavy losses will come. A bank of issue in which savings deposits are kept may fail, a claim for insurance may be successfully resisted, skillful burglars may get access to the cash, investments must sometimes be made at a premium that only return par on the day of redemption, or securities must sometimes be converted at a discount to meet unexpected emergencies. In these and many other ways, which we need not enumerate, Savings Banks are exposed to perils which all cannot be so fortunate as to escape. We can only guard against needless exposure to these perils, and provide a means whereby the severity of the misfortune, when it comes, shall be greatly mitigated; means that will enable the institution to sustain its losses without impairing its ability to meet in full the demands of every depositor. But this can only be done by the accumulation of a surplus of assets over all liabilities for the purpose of meeting such contingencies. In no other way can perfect security against loss be assured to the depositor. In this way it can be assured; and yet, strangely enough, the provisions of the statutes in regard to this surplus, upon which the security of the depositor so greatly depends, are only permissive. If any thing connected with the management of Savings Banks should be obligatory, this should be. If in any thing the discretion of trustees should be controlled by law, this upon which so much depends should surely be thus controlled.

No Savings Bank should be permitted to declare more than five per cent dividends until it has accumulated a surplus of at least five per cent of its assets.

With regard to Savings Banks to be organized hereafter, such a provision is practicable, and would have the salutary effect of checking the mania for organizing these institutions in localities already sufficiently accommodated. To make such a requirement of Savings Banks already organized might lead to consequences not only perilous to their own integrity, but embarrassing to kindred institutions. Concerning these it will be better to leave them at liberty to declare such dividends as they can, from actual earnings, after paying necessary expenses, and putting aside one-half per cent per annum to account of surplus.

The amount of gross surplus which Savings Banks should be authorized to accumulate presents a question upon which honest opinions may differ. The weight of opinion so far as it has been expressed by Savings Bank officers, in answer to my inquiries, favors from fifteen to twenty per cent. With five per cent as a minimum, I regard fifteen per cent as a safe and sufficient maximum on a basis of the par value of securities. If the market price of securities is to be taken as the measure of value, twenty per cent of surplus would not be excessive.

There is no possible danger to be apprehended from the accumulation of surplus. Every thing in that direction, even to excess, favors safety. Practically no injustice is wrought by such an accumulation. The primary idea of a Savings Bank is a place of safety for the deposit of savings. Whatever promotes safety promotes the first and chief object of those who resort to these institutions.

There is no injustice wrought toward any one of them, then, if each year a portion of the profits realized, is reserved for security, instead of being divided and added to the personal deposit of each. True, we may assume, that if he shall withdraw his deposit, he will have less if such reserve is made than if it shall have been allotted to him as a dividend, and hence the reserve will inure to the advantage of depositors who remain, and of future depositors, rather than to his own. That is a condition which he himself precipitates, by withdrawing his deposit, and for which the policy of reserving a surplus is not responsible, that policy being designed as much to benefit him as others. Without such a policy, the security of his whole deposit is impaired. The incidental fact that this wise provision for his security may, by his own act, inure to the benefit of others more than to his own, cannot change the essential wisdom or beneficence of the policy in question.

Nor is this aspect of the question changed by the fact that the withdrawal of a deposit may be the result of necessity rather than choice. That is always a misfortune. But it is a misfortune against which it is simply impossible to provide. To say that he should receive special consideration where his deposit is withdrawn from necessity and not from choice, is, if the logic of this doctrine be pushed to its utmost limits, to say, that he should still participate in the benefits of the institution, because of his misfortune. Every one will repudiate the principle expressed in this bold form.

If we have then established the doctrine, that the accumulation of surplus works no injustice to any one, that it promotes security, without which Savings Banks are no longer what they profess to be, that all danger to these institutions comes from the policy of no surplus, or small surplus, and no danger attends the largest possible accumulation, then we might safely leave to managers the largest liberty concerning the largest possible surplus.

In 1870 the legislature was seized with one of its periodical spasms concerning the peril ultimately to befall the State, if not the whole country, from the accumulations in the Savings Banks, and was moved to an effort to prevent the absorption of all the capital of the State in these institutions, by taking possession of this surplus on behalf of the State! In view of this menace against the property of the Savings Banks system, the subject received consideration in the report of the superintendent, concerning Savings Banks, in that year, being the first report made by the Hon. D. C. Howell, who had recently been appointed to that position. The following is the text of so much of his report as relates to this subject:

Extract from Savings Bank Report, 1870.

SURPLUS MONEYS OF SAVINGS BANKS.

Concerning these, as also concerning what are called "unclaimed deposits," of which we shall treat presently, there exists a very general popular misapprehension, which, in the interest of those vitally concerned, I deem it most desirable to correct. To this end I solicit the attention of your honorable body to the following facts:

1. The first charter—1819—and all subsequent charters of Savings Banks in this State, contain substantially the following provision, to wit: "That it shall be the duty of the trustees to regulate the rate of interest to depositors, so that they shall receive a ratable proportion of all the profits, after deducting therefrom all necessary expenses authorized by this act to be incurred."

It is evident that under this provision, standing alone and unqualified, no Savings Bank could accumulate any surplus, as all the profits or earnings, after paying expenses, are required to be paid or credited to depositors.

2. A few years of experience in conducting these institutions demonstrated the propriety, and indeed the necessity, of making some provision to secure depositors against loss arising from a depreciation in the value of the securities, in which, under the law, their moneys had been invested; accordingly, in 1831, the first act was passed, authorizing a Savings Bank to accumulate a small surplus to meet any loss thus occasioned, or rather to prevent any loss to depositors from this cause; and in 1839, a general act was passed authorizing all Savings Banks to accumulate a surplus for this purpose, of not exceeding ten per cent of their deposits. Thus, a Savings Bank whose accounts with its depositors showed a liability amounting to one million of dollars, might have assets

amounting to one million one hundred thousand dollars. By this means an average depreciation of eleven per cent in the value of all the assets held by such Savings Bank, would still enable it to pay its depositors in full.

3. The wisdom of this salutary provision has never, to my knowledge, been seriously questioned; not only has no depositor — the party chiefly interested — ever raised his voice against it, but, on the contrary, the assurance of perfect security thus imparted has perhaps done more than any one thing to inspire confidence in these institutions, and has contributed to their wonderful success.

4. Besides the strength to the institutions and the security to depositors which the possession of a surplus of assets in excess of its liabilities imparts, it is obvious, further, that an institution thus provided can pay a higher rate of interest to its depositors than another having no such endowment. Thus, if the average earnings or profits of a Savings Bank derived from its investment or assets are, in the two cases above supposed, six per cent respectively, the Savings Bank which has the surplus will receive $6,000 more of income to divide as interest to depositors than the one with no surplus.

5. It is obvious, upon inspection, that the original provision requiring *all* the profits, after deducting expenses, to be divided among the depositors is still in full force, except as modified by the authority subsequently conferred, to accumulate gradually and hold for the purposes mentioned this surplus of ten per cent. It follows, therefore, that whenever this limit of ten per cent of surplus is reached, this accumulation must cease; and thereafter, all the net profits of the institution will, under the operation of that original provision, have to be divided among the depositors. Instances could be cited of Savings Banks that have increased their rate of interest to depositors upon reaching the limit of surplus authorized.

6. The whole question may be summed up as follows :

1st. The authorization of a surplus to secure depositors against loss is a wise and salutary provision, with which the parties most concerned are well satisfied; and as this surplus is an accumulation from *their* moneys, and inures exclusively to *their* benefit, the legislature and the outside public generally ought to be satisfied.

2d. Concerning the ratio of such surplus to deposits, ten per cent has been found, after an experience of thirty years, to be as nearly just, safe and equitable as any that could be named.

3d. Apprehensions suggested in some quarters lest this surplus should some time exceed the deposits, and eventually absorb the entire personal property of the State, may be allayed by considering that there is no authority—except in one or two special charters which fix a higher limit—under which a sum exceeding ten per cent of the deposit can be accumulated.

And, finally, any action of the legislature interfering with or reducing the amount of this surplus is directly opposed to the interests of depositors, by impairing their security and lessening the amount from which their profits are derived, and cannot fail to operate most unfavorably upon these institutions themselves, whose depositors, becoming restless or alarmed by legislative interference, will withdraw their deposits.

Whether in deference to the views of Superintendent Howell, as above expressed, or to other influences, we are unable to say, but the proposed assault upon the integrity of the Savings Bank system of the State, failed to be consummated.

The subject of surplus in this aspect of its incitement to the rapacity of legislators, will be further considered in connection with the topic of unclaimed deposits.

INDEX TO VOLUME I.

EXPLANATORY NOTE.

The following comprises a series of Indexes within a general Index, in which latter the topics are introduced generally, and in alphabetical order,—and in the former or Sub-Indexes, specially and more fully under the respective States to which they relate—these being found in the regular alphabetical arrangement of the General Topics. Thus, CONNECTICUT will be found under "C," VERMONT under "V," etc.

The topics pertaining to each State follow in alphabetical order after the name of the State is introduced. The names of particular Savings Banks will be found only under the States in which they are located, alphabetically arranged, under the sub-title SAVINGS BANKS, etc., for each State treated of in the volume. The names of Savings Banks are abbreviated herein so far as compatible with their perfect identification.

A.

B.

C.

56

D.

E.

I.

L.

M.

N.

58

O.

P.

R.

S.

U.

V.

HISTORY OF SAVINGS BANKS.

SYNOPSIS OF CONTENTS OF VOL. II.

The second volume of this work will resume the consideration of topics interrupted by the close of Vol. I, opening with a continuation of the eighth section—"Savings Banks in the State of New York."

PART II.—"COURSE OF LEGISLATION AND OF OFFICIAL DISCUSSION."

The topics considered in this part of the work are the following:

Limitation of deposits: 1. In the Aggregate; 2. Of Individuals.

Compensation of Trustees.

Borrowing Savings Bank Funds by Trustees or Officers.

Concerning Reports.

Supervision, Examination, etc.

Dormant, Inactive (or Unclaimed) Deposits.

This topic, which has come to be a source of constant agitation, and of menace to the integrity of the Savings Bank system in some of the States, particularly in New York, is quite exhaustively treated.

Savings Bank General Law:

Herein the course of effort to enact a General Law for the incorporation, regulation, management and supervision of Savings Banks in the State of New York is traced from its inception, in 1846, until its final consummation under constitutional requirement in 1875.

Taxation of Savings Banks.

Miscellaneous Topics, viz.: Banks of Discount with Savings Bank Functions; Multiplication of Savings Banks; Deposits of Minors and Married Women; Conclusion.

PART III. — STATISTICS OF SAVINGS BANK PROGRESS.

This comprises three series of tables, as follows:

FIRST SERIES:

Carries the statistics of each Savings Bank in the State of New York, concerning generally, the number of accounts opened, closed and remaining open, and concerning the amounts deposited, withdrawn, remaining on deposit and interest or dividends credited, in each from its organization to 1868. Sketches of Savings Banks are introduced.

SECOND SERIES:

Commences with the totals of the foregoing for each Savings Bank and carries the items forward for each year to 1874. Thus the two series cover the first fifty and five years of the operations of Savings Banks in this State.

THIRD SERIES:

Sums up the totals of each Savings Bank into a grand aggregate of the work accomplished during the above period. Another table gives the like aggregates chronologically from 1819 to 1874. Other explanatory and comparative tables complete the series and conclude the eighth section.

Thereafter follow in their order other sections, giving in such detail as the resources at command will permit, accounts of Savings Banks in New Jersey, in Pennsylvania — where they had their inception in this country; in Maryland, where they were early introduced; in Virginia, of which there is very little to be said; in California, where they have had a wonderful development; and in other States from which any record or reliable information could be procured.

The disastrous experiment of the National Government in introducing, fostering and regulating a Savings Bank business receives appropriate consideration.

GENERAL TOPICS.

A general review and summary of the development and condition of the Savings Bank interest in the country at large as derived from the preceding account of the same in the several States, is presented.

GENERAL TOPICS—(*Continued.*)

A chapter is devoted to a consideration of the proportion in numbers and amounts, respectively of the deposits of less than $500, less than $1,000, and of larger amounts, embracing a table which presents some unique and interesting features.

Savings Banks in time of Panic.

Savings Bank Book-keeping.

Savings Banks in the Future, with the problems to which their development therein gives rise.

Savings Bank Investments—considered with reference, not only to the question of security, but also in their relation to conditions of the public welfare.

Savings Banks as an Element in our Social, Industrial and Financial Economy.

Savings Bank Failures:

Incidents, Conditions, Causes.
Prevention, Responsibility of the State concerning, etc., etc.

Savings Bank Incidents, in Illustration of their Benefits.

Other Subjects of vital interest to Savings Banks follow in due course.

In the Appendix are the charters of the early Savings Banks, with other documents, records and matters of interest.

www.ingramcontent.com/pod-product-compliance
Lightning Source LLC
LaVergne TN
LVHW020917110826
845150LV00004B/699

* 9 7 8 1 4 2 5 5 5 6 0 0 6 *